CONVERSATIONS BY THE SEA

Reflections on Discipleship, Ministry and Mission

Andrew R. Rollinson

British Library Cataloguing in Publication Data:
a catalogue record for this publication
is available from the British Library

ISBN 978-1-912052-78-3

Typeset in 11.5pt Minion Pro at Haddington, Scotland

Published with the assistance of a grant from
the Drummond Trust, 3 Pitt Terrace, Stirling

Printing and cover design by
West Port Print and Design, St Andrews

Contents

Acknowledgements

This writing project has proved to have had many happy parallels with the very setting of the book, namely a long beach walk. It has been, at turns, enjoyable, stretching and invigorating. But like any good walk it has been the companionship of others that has made it stimulating and worthwhile. I am grateful to Dr David Smith who first urged me on as I shared the idea of this book and to Dr Nigel Wright for reading an early draft and encouraging me to publish. A good number of friends and colleagues have read individual chapters and offered comments: Iain Harris, Fiona Barnard, Marion Carson, Terry Griffith and Suk Yu Chan. I am grateful to Kathryn Oldfield, Euan Johnstone and Paulus de Jong for each reading the final manuscript and offering critical comments.

Particularly memorable was a two day retreat with pastoral colleagues Brian More and David Lazenby. In the very congenial setting of Brian's holiday flat on Lossiemouth's harbour front on the Moray Coast (exactly where Brian's father had moored his fishing vessel) the content of the book was debated. Those conversations by the sea were so very helpful. I am especially grateful to Dr Jock Stein, editor of the Handsel Press for his careful reading of the manuscript, for his belief in its value and for guiding it through to publication. Janet, my wife, has been my chief supporter in this whole project. Far more, over all the years of ministry, she has prayerfully and sacrificially shared with me so much of what has been written here.

I am very grateful to the Drummond Trust for their generous grant towards publication.

I dedicate the book to the three congregations I have been privileged to serve and whose partnership in the gospel has so shaped and energised me:

- Westgate Baptist Church, Newcastle-Upon-Tyne
- Morningside Baptist Church (now Central) Edinburgh
- St Andrews Baptist Church, St Andrews, Fife

November 2022

Preface

The majority of this book was crafted during the global coronavirus pandemic of 2020-22. This time has now thankfully passed but we still bear its marks. The more I wrote the more I became acutely conscious of the reality that, along with so much else in the world, Christian ministry and mission will never be quite the same again. Disruption and despair began to shape our human existence in ways none of us could have imagined. New levels of stress and uncertainty upended us personally, nationally and globally. Yet alongside such pressures welcome signs of hope also emerged. Fresh manifestations of communal goodwill, environmental awareness and family responsibilities were witnessed. Creativity in communication and online resources exploded. In Christian terms, meeting online for worship, discipleship and leadership has cast new light on the nature of the church and approaches to mission. All this and more, heightened attentiveness as to the relevance of what I was writing.

In the severity and kindness of God the pandemic has been a warning shot across humanity's hubris and yet at the same time a demonstration that 'God's favour can be found in the desert.'[1] It is a grace that has helped free us from old paradigms and imagine a new future. In the early months of lockdown I found myself listening on Zoom to a pastor from downtown Chennai, India, expressing his near disbelief that there was absolutely no sound outside his front door! The familiar background cacophony of taxi horns, auto-rickshaw's 'tuk-tuk-ing', shouting tradesmen and chattering crowds had suddenly become an eerie silence.

A few weeks later I spoke to my niece and her husband in Astana, Kazakhstan, where normally winter air pollution levels are dangerously high. But in lockdown the skies were bluer and the surrounding spacious steppe landscape clearer than for years. Such silence and clarity have been two gifts of lockdown spiritually as well as physically. In the silence we have heard God in fresh ways and seen his purposes with fresh clarity.

---

1 Jeremiah 31:2 quoted by Walter Brueggemann, *Virus as a Summons to Faith. Biblical Reflections in a time of Loss, Grief and Uncertainty* (Paternoster 2020), 32.

Yet care needs to be taken not to over-state the rhetoric of a new era and a new normal. Post-pandemic, the world, though very different, still has many of the same defining cultural, social and spiritual contours. The powerful shaping narratives of our time – secularism, consumerism, pluralism and religious scepticism – have hardly been deconstructed by a virus. The narcotics of possessions, power and pleasure still retain their addictive grip. Like a tsunami that devastates a landscape yet leaves the underlying geology untouched, the pandemic has changed much of our social topography but not the underlying values. So too, the Gospel of Jesus Christ is still as life changing as ever, the call of Jesus to follow is still as urgent as ever, the ministries which the ascended Christ has given us are still as needed as ever. Approaches to leadership and Christian service are in major transition but the underlying shaping principles remain. It is with this dual conviction of the need for a re-imagination of ministry combined with a rootedness in the never-changing foundational ministry of Christ that I have approached this project.

All the reflections that are to be offered in this book flow from just one chapter of the Gospels, John Chapter 21. There is risk in this venture but also the potential of richness. I take the risk because of my conviction that what ultimately renews, re-energises and reimagines all discipleship, ministry and mission is exactly the equivalent of the encounter experienced by seven disciples on the Galilean shore. To meet the Risen Christ is what matters. To hear his call, to experience his power, to enjoy his fellowship, to be shaped by his words and receive his grace is the only way to lasting fruitfulness.

The Text (NIV): John Chapter 21

1 Afterward Jesus appeared again to his disciples, by the Sea of Galilee. It happened this way:

2 Simon Peter, Thomas (also known as Didymus), Nathanael from Cana in Galilee, the sons of Zebedee, and two other disciples were together. 3 "I'm going out to fish," Simon Peter told them, and they said, "We'll go with you." So they went out and got into the boat, but that night they caught nothing.

4 Early in the morning, Jesus stood on the shore, but the disciples did not realize that it was Jesus.

5 He called out to them, "Friends, haven't you any fish?"

"No," they answered.

6 He said, "Throw your net on the right side of the boat and you will find some." When they did, they were unable to haul the net in because of the large number of fish.

7 Then the disciple whom Jesus loved said to Peter, "It is the Lord!" As soon as Simon Peter heard him say, "It is the Lord," he wrapped his outer garment around him (for he had taken it off) and jumped into the water. 8 The other disciples followed in the boat, towing the net full of fish, for they were not far from shore, about a hundred yards. 9 When they landed, they saw a fire of burning coals there with fish on it, and some bread.

10 Jesus said to them, "Bring some of the fish you have just caught." 11 So Simon Peter climbed back into the boat and dragged the net ashore. It was full of large fish, 153, but even with so many the net was not torn. 12 Jesus said to them, "Come and have breakfast." None of the disciples dared ask him, "Who are you?" They knew it was the Lord. 13 Jesus came, took the bread and gave it to them, and did the same with the fish. 14 This was now the third time Jesus appeared to his disciples after he was raised from the dead.

15 When they had finished eating, Jesus said to Simon Peter, "Simon son of John, do you love me more than these?"

"Yes, Lord," he said, "you know that I love you."

Jesus said, "Feed my lambs."

16 Again Jesus said, "Simon son of John, do you love me?"

He answered, "Yes, Lord, you know that I love you."

Jesus said, "Take care of my sheep."

17 The third time he said to him, "Simon son of John, do you love me?"

Peter was hurt because Jesus asked him the third time, "Do you love me?" He said, "Lord, you know all things; you know that I love you."

Jesus said, "Feed my sheep. 18 Very truly I tell you, when you were younger you dressed yourself and went where you wanted; but when you are old you will stretch out your hands, and someone else will dress you and lead you where you do not want to go." 19 Jesus said this to indicate the kind of death by which Peter would glorify God. Then he said to him, "Follow me!"

20 Peter turned and saw that the disciple whom Jesus loved was following them. (This was the one who had leaned back against Jesus at the supper and had said, "Lord, who is going to betray you?") 21 When Peter saw him, he asked, "Lord, what about him?"

22 Jesus answered, "If I want him to remain alive until I return, what is that to you? You must follow me." 23 Because of this, the rumour spread among the believers that this disciple would not die. But Jesus did not say that he would not die; he only said, "If I want him to remain alive until I return, what is that to you?"

24 This is the disciple who testifies to these things and who wrote them down. We know that his testimony is true.

25 Jesus did many other things as well. If every one of them were written down, I suppose that even the whole world would not have room for the books that would be written.

Introduction

On retiring from the pastorate of St Andrews Baptist Church in Scotland my wife and I were presented with a beautiful oil painting of the iconic West Sands in St Andrews. It had been especially commissioned by a local artist known to us. One striking feature of the painting was that there were just two figures leisurely strolling down the beach, no doubt representing ourselves! It was a far more fitting gift than either the artist or the church knew. Conversations by the sea have been a significant part of my life.

Christian ministry began for me on the east coast of Yorkshire, engaged in rural evangelism among local Methodists and living in a coastal village near Hull. Many a day I would wander the beach, a bleak and inhospitable stretch studded with half-eroded concrete pillars from the Second World War, and I would talk to God and seek to listen to Him. In some ways it was a lonely time in my life after all the buzz and stimulus of university life but it proved foundational, and that beach became and has remained a sacred place.

I now reflect, nearly fifty years later, on those early 'conversations by the sea' and realise how formative they were. Ten years earlier, just thirty miles up the coast in an equally unspectacular coastal hamlet called Ulrome, I had first given my life to Christ at a Christian camp. The first two churches I eventually came to pastor were in Newcastle-on-Tyne and Edinburgh and again, for both, there were stretches of coast in Northumberland and East Lothian where, on days off and days of retreat, the Risen Christ graciously met me, spoke to me, encouraged me and re-energised me. Later I became Ministry Advisor for the Baptist Union of Scotland and had the privilege of travelling to many of the Scottish Islands where, yet again, times alone on some spectacularly unspoilt beaches became precious. And now this painting as I left St Andrews, so fitting for all I have been privileged to enjoy.

John Chapter 21

All the reflections of this book are rooted in the narrative of just one chapter of the New Testament, John 21. This is an unusual approach[1] and to structure the book in this way runs a serious double risk. On the one hand it could easily lead to the straining of the text well beyond its proper limits. On the other hand it holds the danger of straight-jacketing the themes to be explored. But the appeal of John 21 has been overwhelming. Topographical connections are only a small part of the attraction. The narrative centres on conversations by the sea between the Risen Christ and two of the most fascinating characters of the Gospels. Sensing their excitement, observing their reactions, overhearing their dialogue, seeing hope re-born has been hugely stimulating. I have felt myself drawn in to their conversations and found myself, like those first disciples, in discovery mode. What I offer as a result is a series of reflective essays, arising out of the 'depth' of the text and aimed at exploring some of the fundamental dynamics, challenges, paradoxes and ironies of Christian living and ministry.

It is, if you like, an attempt at a 'midrashic' reading of the text. Jewish 'midrash' is an interpretation of Scripture where, though there is serious engagement with the text, space is also created for interpretation, imagination and application. In so doing, it seeks to catch the true heart-beat of the narrative. I write with the aspiration of David Ford when he comments, 'The midrashic imagination is constantly improvising new meaning at the cutting edge of the drama. It is the jazz of text, being wise in the Spirit.'[2] Changing the metaphor, my aim is to use the narrative of John 21 as a 'biblical scaffolding'[3] on which to construct, shape and explore an understanding of discipleship in general and the pastoral vocation in particular.

---

1   The idea came to me after reading David W. Smith's book, *Moving Towards Emmaus. Hope in a time of uncertainty* (SPCK 2007), a stimulating exploration of world mission issues all based around just one chapter, Luke 24.

2   David F. Ford, *The Drama of Living. Becoming Wise in the Spirit* (Norwich: Canterbury Press 2014), 180.

3   Alan Ecclestone, the radical social activist and Anglican priest (1904-1992), has written a fascinating reflection on John's Gospel with the title, *The Scaffolding of the Spirit: Reflections on the Gospel of John* (D.L.T. 1987).

This final chapter of John's Gospel appears in many ways to stand apart from the rest of the Gospel, with the natural conclusion to the Gospel seeming to be at 20:31, 'But these things are written that you may believe that Jesus is the Christ, the Son of God, and that by believing you may have life in his name.' Yet, for myself, I am persuaded by a number of recent scholars who, rather than viewing John 21 as a separate appendix, see greater evidence for it being integral to the Gospel and a fitting epilogue.[4] It is not, as it were, a sort of extra disc of 'special features' after the main film! Indeed there seems to be an intentional balance between John's Prologue which reaches right back to creation and this epilogue describing the advent of not just a new resurrection day but a whole new creation.[5] My conviction is that the post-resurrection encounters and dialogues of this chapter hold the potential to deeply shape our life in Christ and excite us as we look forward in discipleship, ministry and mission to the dawn of a new day.

The drama and characters of John 21

Given that John's Gospel begins with a deeply theological and philosophical Prologue we could be forgiven for thinking that what would naturally follow would be a learned treatise with grand concepts and sweeping conclusions. But what actually follows is *a story*; an accessible, utterly engaging and dramatic story. Indeed, the very Prologue itself is the heart of the drama, the world-shattering cosmic drama of the Word that became flesh and dwelt among us. Then, in three great Acts, (the early public ministry of Jesus, his passion and his resurrection) what unfolds is a carefully constructed narrative of moving scenes. The stage becomes occupied by key witnesses, miraculous signs, symbolic gestures, tension and struggle, profound teaching and redemptive action.

---

4   See my appendix for the arguments that John 21 is not an appendix!
5   R. Bauckham 'The Prologue sketches the pre-history of the Gospel story, whilst the Epilogue foresees its post-history.' He goes on to point out, somewhat intriguingly, if not very convincingly, that the Prologue consists of 496 syllables (a triangular number and perfect number) and the Epilogue 496 words! 'The Fourth Gospel as the Testimony of the Beloved Disciple' in *The Gospel of John and Christian Theology*, eds. Richard Bauckham and Carl Mosser (Grand Rapids, Michigan, Cambridge, UK: Eerdmans 2008), 127.

Key themes serve to heighten this drama; the importance of 'the hour', the constant reference to the Jewish festivals and the 'I am' sayings. John 21 fits into this drama and is as dramatic as the rest of the Gospel. In a series of vivid scenes recorded nowhere else in the New Testament the resurrected Lord reveals himself and restores, equips and commissions his disciples.

The central character of the whole Johannine drama, the Word made flesh, Jesus the Messiah, is the focus of John 21 too. The writer deliberately repeats that the Risen Lord 'reveals himself' (21:1, 14).[6] David Ford has recently proposed that the author of John's Gospel, already in possession of all three earlier Gospels, wrote his Gospel as tensions arose in the early church over how to apply the ethical teaching of Jesus in Matthew, Mark and Luke. Ford proposes John wrote his account to highlight above all else the centrality of the person of Jesus and belief in him and thus to encourage unity around him and him alone.[7] However accurate Ford's suggestion is, the centrality of Christ in John's Gospel and in this chapter in particular, is in no doubt. The final ringing call of Jesus in John 21 bears this out, 'Follow me' (21:19, 22).

Seven other characters, five named and two unnamed disciples, feature in John 21. The Beloved Disciple along with Simon Peter feature most prominently. They become contrasting and yet also complementary figures whose actions, attitudes and futures become deeply suggestive for the shape of Christian discipleship. The vivid portraits of a born activist and classic contemplative and the interplay between the two will offer much. The other five of the seven disciples who return to Galilee are silent characters in the story.

Simon Peter features much less in John's Gospel than in the Synoptic Gospels and yet in this Gospel still appears more often than any of the other disciples. Though not the first to follow Jesus (brought to Jesus by his brother Andrew, 1:41-42), Peter soon emerges as the natural leader and the outspoken frontman of the Twelve. It is Peter, for example, who offers the remarkable confession, 'Lord to whom shall we go? You have the

6   The verb 'to reveal (*phaneroun*) is repeated twice in verse 1 and found again in v14. The word forms bookends to the first main section of Chapter 21. It is a characteristically Johannine word, used nine times in the Gospel.
7   Prof. David Ford, Cambridge, in a lecture given at New College, Edinburgh on Feb. 28th 2020, 'God in the Gospel of John'.

words of eternal life. We have come to believe and know that you are the Holy One of God' (6:68-69). And yet it is this same perceptive Simon Peter who denies his Lord so blatantly (18:15-27). No wonder the one who walks onto the stage of John 21 is both highly experienced and deeply broken.

The identity of the other key character of John 21, the Beloved Disciple, is one of the great unsolved mysteries of Johannine studies. He only appears (at least by this designation) from the eve of the crucifixion onwards, appearing seven times.[8] Whether he is to be identified with the unnamed disciple who accompanied Andrew in following Jesus at the beginning of the Gospel (1:37) and 'the other disciple' who went into the high priest's courtyard with Peter during Jesus arrest (18:15) is not clear – but it is likely.

What we do know is that this Beloved Disciple was the key eye-witness for the Gospel. In 19:35 testimony is given by someone present at the crucifixion 'the man who saw it has given testimony and his testimony is true' and from 19:26 we know that the Beloved Disciple was standing at the cross. Clearer still are the words of 21:24 where, having just referred to the Beloved Disciple following Jesus, it says 'This is the disciple who testifies to these things and who wrote them down'. 'These things' could refer just to the events of chapter 21 but more probably indicate him being the key witness for the whole Gospel.

Tradition has it that this Beloved Disciple was John, one of the Twelve, brother of James and son of Zebedee; and in many ways this view makes good sense. Here was a disciple who had followed Jesus from the beginning, one of an inner circle, someone who had witnessed many intimate moments and in so doing had first-hand knowledge and had grown to love Christ and be loved by him in a special way. The Beloved Disciple clearly had a close relationship with Peter. John, the son of Zebedee and fellow fisherman, would fit better than anyone.[9] But such a view is not uncontested. Some of the biblical data does not seem to quite fit. It is puzzling, for example, why, if the Beloved Disciple is John son of Zebedee and key eye-witness, such key moments as the Transfiguration and Gethsemane (where, according to the Synoptic Gospels, John was

---

8   John 13:23-25; 18:15-16; 19:26-27; 20:3-10; 21:7; 21:20-23; 21:24.

9 We know from Eusebius that as early as Irenaeus, Bishop of Lyon, (ca 180-200) this was believed to be the case. Indeed, Irenaeus had contact with Polycarp, Bishop of Smyrna, who had actually met and heard John.

clearly present) were not recorded in John.[10] The debate continues and here we will simply follow the text of Chapter 21 which, for its own reasons, respects this disciple's anonymity. We will refers to him simply as the 'Beloved Disciple'. Certainly, like Peter, he has much to teach us.

Key themes of the beach drama

Before we come to a detailed reflection, it may be helpful to highlight the key themes we are going to encounter. First, and inevitably in a resurrection narrative, there is the theme of hope and promise. One of the most attractive and striking features of the whole of John's Gospel is its depiction of the sheer generosity of God. The language of fullness – of water turned into gallons of vintage wine (2:10), of 'rivers of living water' continually bubbling up (7:38), of the promise of 'life to the full' (10:10), of a grain of wheat dying and so producing 'many seeds' (12:24), the 'greater works' (14:12) and 'much fruit' (15:5) – keeps reappearing throughout the narrative.[11] John 21 is no exception. This chapter, which opens with disappointment, almost immediately gives way to joy. An extraordinarily large and miraculous catch of fish reveals the One the disciples had been told they would meet in Galilee. Both the miracle and the meeting provide assurance of a new future and a new fruitfulness.

Second, John 21 highlights the importance of community for spiritual formation.[12] There are seven disciples present in this drama, 'doubtless a symbolic number representing the whole disciple group and indeed the whole Body of disciples, the Church.'[13] The dominant images of this chapter – discovering together, hauling in nets together, listening together, eating

---

10 Martin Hengel, *The Johannine Question* (London SCM Press: Philadelphia: Trinity Press International, 1989). Hengel gathers together an impressive amount of evidence to identify the Beloved Disciple and author of the Gospel as John the Elder, referred to by Papias. If the author of John's Gospel, however, already had in his possession the Synoptic Gospels then it could be that he deliberately chose to not include key moments in the life of Jesus in order to make a different and complementary emphasis.
11 This is a key emphasis of David Ford's brilliant commentary *The Gospel of John. A Theological Commentary* (Grand Rapids: Baker Academic, 2021). 'A Gospel of Abundance' he calls it, 1 and 293.
12 R.E. Brown comments that this is certainly an 'ecclesiastical chapter'. R.E Brown, *The Gospel According to John*. The Anchor Bible (London, Dublin, Melbourne: Geoffrey Chapman, 1971), 1082.
13 G.R Beasley-Murray, *John*. Word Bible Commentary (Waco, Texas: Word Books, 1987), 399.

together, walking together, questioning together – all centred around the risen Christ – become suggestive of shaping practices for the church. As has been said, a possible key aim of the chapter is the unity of the Christian communities to whom the Gospel was written. If, as is generally assumed, John's Gospel was finally shaped and distributed after the death of both Peter and the Beloved Disciple and, if the churches in Rome were looking particularly to Peter's legacy and the churches of Asia to that of the Beloved Disciple, then this chapter can be seen as addressing suspicion between the two.[14] Both key disciples are honoured in this chapter. The respecting of difference is being celebrated as a key part of unity.

Another key contour of John 21 is the way specific leadership issues arise and are reflected on. Central to this is the calling of Peter as shepherd, called to feed and care for the flock. But around this and arising from this are a whole cluster of fundamental leadership issues - issues of spiritual perception, mission expectation, ministry resources, failure, restoration, competitiveness and priorities. Though leadership is a key issue to be addressed in this book it is important to stress that by the word 'ministry' I am routinely referring to the ministry of all the people of God (see Chapter 3 in particular).

Finally, the clearest theme of this chapter is undoubtedly the importance of an obedient following of, and a humble dependence upon, the crucified and Risen Christ for all ministry and mission. John's Gospel is rightly known as the 'spiritual gospel'[15] not just because of its prominent theocentric horizon and its rich articulation of the Father-Son-Spirit relationship but particularly because of its focus on the trusting, loving, intimate and abiding relationship between Christ and his followers. The Gospel of John takes us to the heart of obedient Christian discipleship and to an understanding of what fruitful ministry and mission means. John 21, I hope to show, has a key part to play in all this.

---

14 J.L. Martyn, for example, sees the stories of expulsion from the synagogue in the Gospel as aiming to address the issues of a later Johannine community persecuted by Judaism. In particular he sees Peter's re-instatement by Jesus in John 21 as a way of encouraging a reintegration of the Johannine community with the wider apostolic church. Though his views are much debated, they are suggestive of an important theme. J.L. Martyn, *The Gospel of John in Christian History: Essays for Interpreters* (New York: Paulist Press 1978).

15 This was a description used certainly from the time of Clement of Alexandria in the second century, recorded in Eusebius, *Ecclesiastical History* 6.14.7.

Chapter One

The Night They Caught Nothing: Disorientation and Disappointment in Ministry

**So they went out and got into the boat,
but that night they caught nothing. (John 21:3)**

The Epilogue to the Fourth Gospel opens with characteristic Johannine colour and contrast. The soft light of an early Middle Eastern sunrise glistens on the waters of Galilee whilst the Risen Christ stands as an unrecognised solitary figure on the shoreline. For seven of Jesus' disciples the darkness of the night just endured symbolised so much, not just the frustration of fishing all night and catching nothing but, far more pervasive, the personal darkness of deep disorientation and disappointment. Three utterly life-changing years had suddenly come to an end. Yes, their Master and Lord had risen and they had met him but the light of resurrection hope had not yet fully dawned in their lives.

We have no clear idea why Peter and his colleagues had decided to leave Jerusalem after the early resurrection appearances of Jesus and 'escape' to Galilee, seventy-five miles north. Even less can we know what was going through their minds as they checked over the family fishing boat, repaired rotting nets and launched into familiar waters. The suggestions that a return to Galilee was a total abandonment of Peter's calling, 'complete apostasy' as Edwyn Hoskyns puts it,[1] or an 'aimless activity undertaken in desperation'[2] seem unduly harsh.

---

1   Edwyn Hoskyns, ed. by Noel Davey, *The Fourth Gospel* (London: Faber and Faber 1947), 552.
2   Raymond E Brown, *The Gospel According to John*. The Anchor Bible, Vol. 2, (London, Dublin, Melbourne: Geoffrey Chapman 1972), 1096.

After all, Peter had been told that the risen Christ would meet him in Galilee.[3] Peter had been through too much with Jesus to be in rebellion. He had been the first to confess Jesus as Messiah, one of a select group who had witnessed the transfiguration[4] and the empty tomb and had already personally met the Risen Lord at least twice.[5]

My hunch is that those seven disciples were seeking to be obedient but in the context of serious disorientation. They certainly needed time and space to compute all that had happened. Fishing was as good a displacement therapy as any for working through confusion, fear and an unknown future. They needed company but also quiet. Where else do you go but home when your whole worldview has just been turned upside down?

Ministry Disorientation

I vividly recall the multiple disorientations I experienced when I first began to lead a church. There was a sense of expectation, a 'having to deliver' that I had never quite experienced before. This, coupled with an unnerving lack of a blueprint (in spite of being a pastoral assistant for a while before) left me uncertain, even anxious. I guess what generated the most questions was encountering firmly held church practices that I deemed either unwise or simply unhelpful. When should I begin to advocate change? What constituted ministry compromise and what was a wise biding-my-time? What was more important, establishing trust and a peaceful presence or fighting key battles whilst goodwill was in ample supply? A ministry mentor helped but it did seem a bit like driving through a winter white-out with only the occasional snow pole to guide me.

Since then I have often walked alongside young (and not so young) colleagues seriously shaken by what they are experiencing of ministry. I remember having coffee with a young Romanian pastor clearly distressed by his early taste of pastoral leadership, both ambushed by and disheartened with resistance to his leadership. He was still studying at college in Budapest whilst pastoring a small elderly congregation. I was struck by both his idealist expectations and his loneliness in the ensuing disorientation. He had not been fishing long but the net appeared to him discouragingly

---

3   Mark 14:28 to Peter directly, 'But after I have risen, I will go ahead of you into Galilee' and Mark 16:7.
4   Recorded in the Synoptic Gospels but, interestingly, not in John's Gospel.
5   Luke 24:34 where Simon Peter is particularly referred to, and 24:36.

empty. Equally, I have often spent time with older colleagues seriously thrown by how to respond to the seismic cultural shifts going on around them. It is a bewilderment with which I too have struggled.

Christian service of all forms requires far more orientation than we often acknowledge. Eugene Peterson, commenting on John 21, puts it well, 'Jesus was radically reconfigured and redefined by resurrection. Now *they* (Peter and his friends) were being just as radically reconfigured and redefined. The familiar concept of life after death was totally recast as life in 'the land of the living' (Psalm 116:9).[6] Quite so, but what exactly does this reconfiguration look like for people in leadership today?

What is more, we are being called to serve and lead in churches in the West which *themselves* are deeply disorientated. The Christian faith has well and truly been removed from the high street of public life and politely relocated to the quiet backstreet of private interests. We serve a church still coming to terms with its marginalisation and society's profound secularisation. In a recent Scottish government consultation paper on future funeral provision there was not a single reference to the church! Of course, as is often commented on, being on society's edge is where the Christian church first began and it is no bad thing to return there, not least in helping us rediscover our radical missionary agenda. But this marginalisation, if we are not careful, can have a serious knock-on effect on our understanding of Christian leadership and service. Jonathan Sachs, the former Chief Rabbi, speaking of religious leaders generally, comments that 'the "guardian of the sacred" is now left stranded: the last amateur in a world of professionals, the last practitioner of the unquantifiable.'[7] But it is imperative that we are not left stranded.

There are two areas where perplexity in ministry is particularly experienced. The first has to do with coming to terms with the massive cultural shifts in our Western society. The second involves an understanding of the subtle but very real differences between leadership in the secular workplace and in a Christian community. Both challenges require fresh theological thought and deep spiritual rootedness. One recent sign of encouragement has been the swiftness, energy and creativity of the church's response to

---

6   Eugene H. Peterson, *As Kingfishers Catch Fire. A Conversation on the Ways of God Formed by the Word of God* (Hodder 2017), 353.
7   Jonathan Sacks, *The Persistence of Faith*, Reith Lectures 1990 (London: Weidenfeld and Nicolson 1991), 72.

the Coronavirus pandemic, 2020–22. It has given fresh confidence to our capacity for adaptability and a re-evaluating of essentials.

The Shifting Cultural Landscape

It is difficult to over-estimate the extent and speed of change occurring in Western culture. Many of these momentous developments – globalisation, sexual liberation, the fragmentation of society, the communication revolution – are easy to name and their effects all too easy to chart. More radical still is that the very nature of change has changed. Today's shifts often have little continuity with what has gone on before – they are unanticipated and disruptive.[8] Who would have predicted in early 2020, for example, that within a few months most of the world would be socially distancing and sporting face masks or that in early 2022 there would be a major European war impacting the whole globe? No one needs convincing that all human society is in massive flux and that, for those of us engaged in Christian ministry and mission, our approaches will need to be very different in the future. Not all these changes are negative and certainly not necessarily antithetical to the gospel. Indeed, just as the disorientation of Peter and his friends finally led to an unimagined catch of fish, so these cultural changes can offer unique opportunities.

One utterly profound underlying shift in our culture has been a growing indifference to all truth-claims. For sure, scepticism has always been around but today such suspicion has acquired a distinctively postmodern and somewhat cynical hue. As Charles Taylor puts it in his *A Secular Age* faith is now an 'embattled option'.[9] At least during the 18th century Enlightenment and into the modern period, when divine moral authority was replaced with human reasoning, there remained a continuing quest for truth and the hope of human progress. But now even that quest has largely been abandoned. 'Deconstruction', the dizzy watch-word of postmodernism, has led to widespread disengagement with a serious quest for meaning and truth. It is one thing to agree with Jacques Derrida, the French philosopher who coined the word 'deconstruction' in 1967, that our understanding of the world is always *interpreted* reality – we always see things from 'a context' – but quite another to extrapolate (which he

---

8   Alan J. Roxburgh and Fred Romanuk, *The Missional Leader. Equipping your Church to Reach a Changed World* (Jossey Bass 2006), 7.
9   Charles Taylor, *A SecularAge* (Cambridge, MA: Harvard University Press 2007), 3.

personally did not) that no interpretation can ever be declared as true and authoritative. But that is what the trickle-down effect to the street-level can lead to – an instinctive suspicion of all claims to be authoritative.[10]

Of course this is not to say that therefore apathy reigns. Young people, in particular, are deeply committed to causes of global justice such as climate change, racism, animal rights and, as the Covid-19 pandemic showed, commitment to local community support. But such issue-based activism (to be warmly welcomed) can be based on decidedly flimsy moral foundations. I once asked an animal rights activist, standing at a stall in George Street Glasgow, 'On what basis do animals have 'rights'?' (I consider animal welfare to be a non-negotiable human *responsibility*). My genuine question elicited only colourful west coast abuse! It highlighted for me a real danger, that when such activism is based on insecure moral foundations it can lead too readily to an over-defensiveness. This, in turn, as we are witnessing more and more, can lead to an ugly weaponisation where one issue-based group despises and 'no-platforms' another. As Douglas Murray describes it, 'a set of tripwires has been laid across our culture.'[11] He well sums up our present moral crisis,

> The metaphysics that a new generation is imbibing and everyone else is being force-fed has many points of instability and is grounded in a desire to express certainty about things we do not know and be wildly dismissive and relativistic about things that we actually do know.[12]

Another major shift that has huge implications for ministry is what has been termed the radical 'turn to the self'. As the scaffolding of traditional institutions, particularly marriage and family life, have been systematically dismantled and as moral givens (often the result of a Christian heritage) are questioned, so we have become more and more left to our own resources. We have been persuaded to view ourselves as rational, autonomous individuals free to define how we live and even who we are, 'expressive individualism' as Charles Taylor calls it. We each need to choose our own values, identity, role, relationship patterns and beliefs. Rather than look

---

10 See the helpful chapter in James K.A. Smith, *Who's Afraid of Postmodernism?* (Grand Rapids: Baker Academic 2006), Chap. 2, 'Nothing outside the text?', 31-58.
11 Douglas Murray, *The Madness of Crowds. Gender, Race and Identity* (London: Bloomsbury Continuum 2019), 5.
12 Ibid., 233.

outside of ourselves for a moral compass we are encouraged simply to look within, to nurture our own inner moral dispositions, our own felt authenticity and write our own scripts.

As one writer well puts it,

> We are our own little story-tellers, living among the ruins of our former grand narratives. We tell stories purely for pleasure. Today we tell one story and tomorrow we tell another. Stories are fashionable; we change them with the seasons, as we change our clothes.[13]

I well remember the day I challenged a young couple about their 'lifestyle choice'. The young woman (whom I had recently baptised) went purple with rage when I had dared to question a key lifestyle choice she was making. 'This is my story, this is my song' and who are you to question it? The emotional and social consequences of all this can be tragic. As we look inwards, without any external referent, too often we find fragility not freedom, self-despair not self-worth. We discover that writing our own story is an existential load too great to bear. Our deep anxieties lead to online escapism and our painful angst to a restless reinventing of ourselves. It also all leads to a loss of real community and connectedness. Many have commented on the painful paradox that at the very time online connectedness has never been so good, emotional disconnectedness has never been so acute. In a recent Barna Report '*The Connected Generation*' (2019), 31% of young adults in the U.K felt they were lonely or isolated.[14]

Part of this turn to the self is well expressed in today's search for 'spirituality' It is a turn inwards rather than upwards – a '*Going Within*', to use the title of Shirley MacLaine's book on New Age spirituality.[15] Such an inner searching is fuelled by a deep disenchantment with both Western rationalism and institutional religion. Instead it looks for inspiration to an amalgam of such ancient resources as Gnosticism and such global resources as eastern mysticism.[16] As Shirley MacLaine puts it,

---

13 Gerald Loughlin, *Telling God's Story, Bible, Church and Narrative Theology* (Cambridge University Press 1996), 9.
14 See *Transform*, Magazine of the Scottish Bible Society, Issue 82, Spring 2020, 6.
15 Shirley Maclaine, *Going Within* (London: Bantam 1990).
16 See John Drane, *Cultural Change and Biblical Faith* (Paternoster Press 2000) especially Chap. 3 'Ancient Gnosticism for a New Millennium: Nag Hammadi and the New Age', 36ff.

> A great awakening is taking place. Individuals across the world are tapping in to their internal power to understand who they are and using that knowledge to elevate their lives and their circumstances to a higher octave of happiness and productivity.[17]

Again, all this requires significant readjustment to our pastoral approach. Those around us who are into Wicca, Gaia, spiritual 'channelling' and carrying around their protective healing crystals[18] may be on dangerous territory but the challenge is to learn to listen to and affirm their longings but then re-direct them towards the gospel.

Deeply related to all this is another hugely formative feature of contemporary Western society, that of a market economy and unfettered consumerism. The right of individual choice for the sake of personal satisfaction is the unquestioned assumption of our time. Indeed, Alan Storkey, rightly I think, argues that when all our clever talk about Derrida and others is done, postmodernism is consumerism:

> The deconstruction and fragmentation which he has often identified with changes in approaches to text and philosophy is actually buying, advertisements, TV culture, in-your-face entertainment, shopping, pressure, things filled living – in a word, consumption.[19]

How well we know that this choice-driven mentality has a habit of not only profoundly shaping our general lifestyle but our attitude to the local church. The way the local church, people chosen and gathered by God for his glory, has often become 'my community of choice', for 'my benefit', is deeply ironic. The pressure to perform as a church leader, in order to meet the high expectations of ecclesial shoppers, is very real. I do not wish to overplay this because it has often struck me how loyal folk can be to a local fellowship. My sense, however, certainly post-Covid 19 where on-line worship services came into their own, is that consumer pressure continues to grow. Spoken: 'Thank you for yesterday's helpful sermon'. Unspoken: 'It's just a shame it didn't quite have the clarity,

---

17 Shirley MacLaine, 56-57, quoted in John Drane, op.cit., 50.
18 The trend of 'spirituality-themed' beauty products infused with crystals.
19 Alan Storkey 'Postmodernism is Consumption' in *Christ and Consumerism. A critical Analysis of the Spirit of our Age*, ed. Craig Bartholomew and Thorsten Moritz (Paternoster Press 2000), 115.

theological panache and global illustrations of Tim Keller who I listened to afterwards at Redeemer Church, New York'.

A final cultural change that I have particularly had to wrestle with is today's insatiable demand for instant results; the world of immediate customer service, same-day-delivery, instant messaging, and super-fast internet highways. Waiting for all of 4.5 minutes in a telephone queue for an insurance claim just seems like the stealing of my whole day! It's what American journalist and social critic Paul Roberts calls 'the impulse society'.[20]

Christian ministry, in contrast, calls for the deeply counter-cultural discipline of a daily, dogged persevering spirituality. Serving Christ demands the dedicated patience of the all-night fisherman and the upland shepherd who has no watch but the sun. Compassion walks at a very gentle pace. The One we serve is the 'Three Mile an Hour God',[21] God walking at the pace of his incarnate Son through Palestine. Only at that pace can we discern the real needs around us. Only then can we truly encourage growth in holiness. Only then can we transition whole communities to a new and better culture. People and churches are not projects to be 'fixed' but fellow travellers to be understood, accompanied and patiently loved. God's plans take time and, as his co-workers, a long-term perspective is required. How we long, of course, for those 'whoosh moments' when the Spirit comes, powerfully and suddenly, like 'flash floods in the Negev' (Psalm 126:4). But routinely all discipleship, pastoral care, church leadership and evangelism involves a back-breaking 'sowing in tears' (Psalm 126:5).

Put all this together and there is a *massive complexity* that needs to be navigated in contemporary ministry. Whether it is working through an appropriate pastoral response to LGBTQ members of the congregation, complying with statutory regulations on safe-guarding or simply knowing where how to care for a highly mobile and work-stressed congregation,

---

20 Paul Roberts, *The Impulse Society: What's Wrong With Getting What We Want?* (Bloomsbury 2014).

21 An influential book by the Japanese theologian, Kosuke Koyama, *The Three Mile an Hour God* (SCM Press 1979). 'Love has its speed. It is a different kind of speed from the technological speed to which we are accustomed . . . It goes on in the depth of life at 3 miles per hour . . . It is the speed we walk and therefore the speed the love of God walks', 7.

great wisdom is required. Disorientation, for me, has never been far away. The most needed spiritual gift for our time is *discernment*.[22]

Disorientation and Vocational Perspectives

Alongside these huge cultural shifts, all forms of Christian leadership also require careful reflection on *expectations*. Indeed, I have long advocated the need for an 'expectation exchange' before a new pastor or ministry leader is appointed. This involves 'both sides' declaring their understanding of the role and then addressing ahead of time any disparity that has emerged. Too often, for example, the difference between the shape of secular employment and church ministry is not sufficiently acknowledged. I listened recently to a young leader speak of the unnerving disorientation she felt, moving from the highly structured, supervised and hierarchical world of social work to the almost unsupervised role of being a pastor. Not least, she commented, 'I felt very alone'.

Equally, the very language and mentality of 'contractual employment' though still relevant in church ministry particularly in legal terms, demands careful reflection. It's not that time sheets, outcome appraisals and job descriptors are necessarily inappropriate. Boundary-keeping is vital; family time, leisure time, study time and Sabbath time need careful guarding. But at the heart of all Christian discipleship and ministry (which should mark all Christians in the secular workplace, for sure) is serving with an ethos of overflowing grace. It will mean a glad willingness to go the extra mile; 'fishing all night' can indeed sum it up at times!

An associated issue is the reality of the service offered in local church life. Everyone involved has to be invited, encouraged, motivated and convinced! Transitioning from a life in management where people are told what to do (and paid for it) to a community of grace where Christ-like self-giving is everything is not easy. Too often we forget that the fundamental economy of the church is generosity and that her only currency is trust. There is a whole skill-set to be learnt in how to inspire, recruit, empower and resource those we work alongside.

Two perennial dangers stalk this reality. The first is the temptation to manipulate. Far too often hard-pressed and under-staffed church leaders,

---

22 John Drane, podcast 2021.

consciously or unconsciously, manoeuvre people, 'use' people and sadly even coerce people into areas of church life. Once, when my wife and I were checking out a potential new church having just moved to the area to study, we were not-too-subtly hemmed in at the door by a well-practised pincer-movement of pastor and wife! Their aim, it became clear, was not to welcome us, to get to know us and help us but to enlist us as children's workers!

The second temptation is to become overly driven ourselves. With no clear supervision or timetable, ministry leaders too often seek to prove themselves by overwork. It is what family system analysts term 'over-functioning'.[23] I remember realising to my shock and shame that when I left my first pastorate it required withdrawing from fourteen organisations *outside* the church! My wife commented, with a touch of weary resignation, that it explained a lot!

A further arena for potential disorientation is the art of holding separate and yet together our private devotional life and our public offering of ministry. What was once an eagerly anticipated daily space of quiet companionship with God – the reading of Scripture, the silence of prayer, time with others in worship and support – becomes a pressured space to formulate the next talk and identify who needs our urgent attention. It is the experience of the carefree rambler enjoying her haunts who, on becoming the National Park warden, finds those same haunts somewhat less romantic! The challenge is to negotiate how our personal spiritual life can both feed and inform our public ministry yet remain primarily an oasis for personal growth.

A final area of struggle I identify here is working out how much room should be given to secular views of pastoral care and leadership in shaping our vocation. What is the appropriate relationship between a thoroughly biblical and theological understanding of Christian ministry and insights from the world of management, psychology and counselling? I have discovered that it is a journey that requires both a critical and an appreciative eye.

On the one hand, it is clear the New Testament writers were nervous about using the current Greco-Roman language of leadership, with

---

23 See Bob Burns, Tasha D. Chapman and Donald C. Guthrie, *Resilient Ministry. What Pastors told us about Surviving and Thriving* (IVP Books 2013), 34-35.

all its hierarchical and status-conscious baggage.[24] Yet, on the other hand, there are times when 'the people of this world are shrewder in dealing with their own kind than are the people of the light.' (Luke 16:8). I can still remember the huge relief that descended on us as a church leadership when we engaged with the Belbin Team Role Inventory, a tool to help identify how people behave in teams. We immediately saw why 'the Plant' (the person who generates creative ideas) and the 'Completer-Finisher' (the person who works out meticulously how a proposal will work) both left our meetings with dangerously high blood pressures! Insights from MBA curricula are not necessarily from the dark side. Critical dialogue between biblical and secular insights can be deeply clarifying and enriching.[25]

Ministry Disappointment

Fishing on Galilee in the hours before sunrise was deemed to be the best time to fish. It also allowed a fresh catch to be ready for an early morning fish market. But not so that night. As the empty boat bobbed up and down and the Seven turned towards the shore there must have been long moments of silence as they remembered the good old times of record catches, wild fishing tales and particularly the last three amazing years with Jesus. Now what weighed them down was not a hold full of fish but deep disappointment.

It is a rare church leader or disciple-maker who has never wrestled with disappointment.[26] It comes at almost every turn, disappointment with church members and mentees, with leadership colleagues and denominational leaders, disappointment with self and, yes, disappointment with God. We all, in theory at least, have signed up to the Parable of the Sower and have learnt to be realistic in our expectations but when our high hopes don't materialise few of us find it easy. We long

---

24 See Andrew D. Clarke, *A Pauline Theology of Church Leadership* (Bloomsbury: T&T Clark 2013).

25 Here I am indebted to a very helpful essay by John Fitzmaurice, 'The developing philosophy of ministry' in *The Study of Ministry: A comprehensive Survey of Theory and Best Practice,* ed. Martyn Percy with Ian S. Markham, Emma Percy and Francesca Po (SPCK 2019), 15-27.

26 See the helpful Grove Booklet by James Newcome, *Facing Disappointment. The Challenge for Church Leaders* (Ridley Hall, Cambridge 2016).

for congregational growth, and some are privileged to experience it, but here in the West the undeniable overall narrative is one of deep cultural resistance to the gospel.

Disappointments become personal. We give our all to preparing a presentation that seemed particularly inspired and our hearers politely thank us and leave hastily. We plead with God for conversions and no fresh faces turn up for our guest event. We work so hard on the leadership agenda and some insignificant disagreement over the minutes sours the whole gathering. I wonder if Peter ever reflected on why *all* eleven disciples hadn't joined him. Was it because his own recent leadership failure had disappointed them? I guess for me the biggest disappointments I have struggled with are disappointments about myself – that email which should never have been sent, that sermon that needed far more homework, that pastoral visit where I failed to address the pain that was clearly lurking under the surface. For sure, we all know what it is to be too hard on ourselves and that often our high expectations are a product of our pride but still, disappointment can be deeply debilitating.

The danger of serial disappointment, of course, is that it can either lead to frustration and eventual anger or to erecting a protective shield around our emotions and a withdrawing from others. We can begin to see only setbacks and miss the many victories that are still taking place. I well remember the deep disappointment of approaching a very gifted person for a leadership role and finding that it actually precipitated her family leaving the church! So dismayed was I that for a while I became blind to all the good that was still going on around me.

Disappointment is important to acknowledge. Again and again the Psalmist lamented how badly he had been let down by friends, even close ones (Psalm 55:13) and seemingly by the Lord himself (Psalm 60:1). But even more crucial than owning disappointment is finding a true perspective.[27] It was true for those first disciples and equally vital for us. David Smith, the missiologist, in an essay on revival and renewal, tells the story of the profound disappointment of William Carey and his early colleagues in India. He quotes William Ward, 'the restricted progress of Christianity' formed 'one of the most mysterious dispensations of

---

27 J. Newcome, op. cit.,18.

Providence that has ever occupied human attention.'[28] Smith comments
that their urgent need was to find new models of church and mission and
a theological account of 'the absence of revival and the strange lack of
converts' and argues that such is our task too. 'Our churches look far more
like those of Revelation 2-3 than the exploding missionary community of
the book of Acts'.[29] Indeed he ponders whether our fascination with revival
'is in danger of acting as a form of religious ideology which conceals the
reality of the condition of Western Christianity and prevents believers
from facing the challenges of discipleship and mission in a post-Christian
culture.'[30]

The Stranger who Waits and Calls

As the boat drew nearer the shore, the sight of a solitary Stranger
on the beach caught the eye of the disciples. At first they didn't see the
charcoal fire, the rising smoke and the sizzling fish. They just saw a figure
vaguely familiar in his stance, watching them intently. How long he had
been there they didn't know; but it perhaps seemed odd that someone
should be waiting for them so early in the morning. The prophetic words
of John the Baptist at the beginning of the Gospel 'among you stands one
you do not know' (1:26) find fresh, poignant meaning here at the end of
the Gospel. The words, actions and gestures of this Stranger on the beach
are to be the focus of John 21 from now on.

The foundation to all Christian existence and ministry is God, in
Christ, who always takes the initiative and, in restoring love, comes to
where we are. The divine pursuing grace that first brought the Word into
the world is now the grace embodied in this waiting Stranger. In our
disorientation and disappointment Jesus stands waiting, watching and
calling.

Dag Hammarskjold was the second United Nations General Secretary,
a highly gifted Swedish economist and diplomat, who died in a tragic
air disaster on September 17th 1961. He was a man of deep faith and
mystical reflection as recorded in his personal diary, *Markings*, found

28 David Smith, 'The Work of the Spirit in Revival and Renewal' in *Spirit of Truth and Power Studies in Christian Doctrine and Experience,* ed. David F. Wright (Rutherford House 2007), 183.
29 Ibid., 185.
30 Ibid., 186.

and published after his death. Hammarskjold movingly describes his journey to faith in these terms,

> I don't know who – or what – put the question, I don't know what was put. I don't even remember answering. But at some moment I did answer Yes to Someone – or Something – and from that hour I was certain that existence is meaningful and that, therefore, my life in self-surrender, had a goal . . . As I continued on the Way, I learnt step by step, word by word, that behind every saying in the Gospels stands one man and one man's experience.[31]

That early morning encounter for Peter and his friends had a striking similarity to what had happened a short time before. Mary Magdalene, alone in a Jerusalem garden cemetery, had stood outside the empty tomb of her crucified Lord, crying and confused. (John 20:11) She too was disorientated and disappointed. Yet for her also the Stranger (the municipal gardener she thought) was standing and waiting and about to speak.

The One on the beach calls out, 'Friends, haven't you caught any fish?' It is the classic 'innocent' pastoral question! It is the Good Shepherd searching for his lost sheep among fishermen (and not the last time that these two metaphors will clash!) It is the beginning of an engagement that will lead to nothing less than reorientation and recommissioning. At the heart of all Christian service is hearing this Voice on the beach. Without a deep inner conviction that the Risen Lord has called us to Christian service it is impossible to sustain ministry. Pursing a 'career' involves an intentional mapping out of our future (career, French *carriere* – highway). A 'call' on the other hand has been described as 'staying close enough to hear the Voice of the one who will lead us step by step'.[32] Only that Voice can bring true orientation and encouragement. The great miracle of John 21 is not the miraculous catch of fish but the presence of the Stranger on the beach.

---

31 D. Hammarskjold, *Markings* trans. Leif Sjoberg and W.H Auden (New York: Ballantine 1967), 180 quoted in Richard Foster, *Streams of Living Water: Celebrating the Great Traditions of Christin Faith* (Trowbridge: Eagle Publishing 1999) 214.
32 Ben Patterson in P. Cedar, K. Hughes and B.Patterson, *Mastering the Pastoral Role* (Portland, Oregon: Multnomah 1991) Chap. 2 'A Call or Career?' 25.

Chapter Two

Ministry: Participating in a Miracle

**They were unable to haul the net in because
of the large number of fish. (John 21:6)**

The hidden reality of Christian service, for all its pressures and often unromantic quotidian ordinariness, is *miraculous grace*. We enter Christian service in all its variety with the fundamental conviction that our calling is to be heralds of an Easter message and leaders of an Easter People, made possible only by God's Easter power. At least that's the theory; but on a daily basis that's hardly how it seems! When we are sweating over the homily that just isn't coming together, when we see no chink of progress in our attempt to resolve a long-running leadership conflict, when in visiting we are greeted with comments about how disappointingly infrequent is our input, the word 'miracle' is hardly the first word that comes to mind. The only miracle we see is that we are still hanging in there!

It's in this context that John's account of the miraculous catch of fish is so evocative. It stands not only as the prelude and foundation to all that follows in Chapter 21 but as the window through which all subsequent Christian ministry is to be viewed. For John, what happened that morning as the Stranger offered instruction (21:6-7) was not just a supernatural event but, as with all the miracles he records, the giving of a sign and the telling of a parable. It was a powerful depiction to a group of fisherman who had toiled all night and caught nothing that fruitful service is not just difficult to undertake – but, without God's aid, is impossible. The only hope for each one of us, in the midst of all our challenges, is to operate in the joy and power of the Risen Christ working through us.

The Unique Sign of John 21

C.H. Dodd famously identified that lying at the heart of John's Gospel is what he called 'the book of signs'.[1] S.S.Smalley, building on this, sees this as consisting of six signs: turning water into wine (2:1-11); healing of the nobleman's son (4:46-54); healing of the invalid by the Pool of Bethesda (5:2-9); feeding of the five thousand (6:1-4); healing of the man born blind (9:1-7); raising to life of Lazarus (11:1-44).

What is more, these six are enclosed within the two great defining miracles of the incarnation (1:1-18) and the resurrection (20:1-31). All the signs reveal the glory of Christ but supremely it is revealed through these two 'bookend' miracles, the incarnation and resurrection. On this basis Smalley then concludes that the miraculous catch of fish in Ch. 21 is to be seen as the seventh sign, the one that 'completes the collection by standing in a unique and structurally important position.' It builds on and summarises the rest. He adds, 'It is also unique in being the only miracle recorded during the resurrection appearances.'[2] Smalley helpfully lays it out as follows:

Incarnation (Ch. 1)

1 Marriage at Cana (Ch. 2)

2 Nobleman's son (Ch. 4)

3 Sick man (Ch. 5)

4 Feeding of 5000 (Ch. 6)

5 Blind man (Ch. 9)

6 Lazarus (Ch. 11)

Resurrection (Ch. 21)

7 Catch of 153 fish (Ch. 21)

Part of the distinctiveness of this seventh sign is that, unlike the first six which had an initial Jewish audience, this miracle as a post-resurrection epilogue has a much wider, more inclusive *Christian* audience.[3] Similarly Bauckham sees this miracle not so much as a sign that points to the significance of the Person of Christ, as is the case of the first six signs, but

---

1 C.H. Dodd, *Interpretation of the Fourth Gospel* (Cambridge University Press 1968), 289.
2 Stephen S. Smalley 'The Sign in John XX1' in *New Testament Studies* Vol. XX 1973-1974, 277-8.
3 Ibid., 283.

as a vivid symbol of the coming universal mission of the church.[4] Jesus' resurrection power is now available to all and is the perspective with which we are to view all Christian living and service.

The Morning Bonanza

The voice of the Stranger, with its familiar and authoritative tone, must have been startling. 'Friends, haven't you any fish?' 'No' was the somewhat stony reply. Jesus went on, 'Throw your net on the right side of the boat and you will find some' (21:6). These were the experts, even if a little rusty! They, of all people, could 'read' the sea. They had their family fishing secrets, their own instinctive 'sonar' methods of detecting the shoals of Galilee tilapia, their folk traditions of how to track the clouds of sardines. They were certainly not in the habit of being given advice. What is more, from one side of the boat to the other was only a few feet; it just didn't make sense!

But that morning there was something deeply arresting about the Stranger's command and, almost certainly against their better judgment, they felt impelled to obey. Suddenly the boat lurched, the ropes cracked, the net tightened and the water began to boil as a massive shoal of lively fish were captured. The usual way to fish on Galilee was to deploy two boats and suspend a large trammel net between the two. Once a shoal was spotted they would surround it so there was no escape and then throw another net, a cast, over the shoal to draw them in. It was a skilled and labour intensive process. That morning it took all their powers simply to draw in this astonishing catch.

Recent archaeological excavations around the assumed site of ancient Bethsaida (Peter and Andrew's original home) has shown it to be an area where the fishing industry was thriving. More than twenty first-century harbours, breakwaters and fishponds have been found in the region, along with evidence of boatbuilding. In nearby Magdala excavations have revealed both a harbour capable of serving a large number of fishing boats and a mosaic at the entrance to a first-century villa depicting a fishing galley.[5]

The most spectacular find was in 1986 when a few miles north of this site a largely intact first-century Galilee fishing boat was unearthed. Now

---

4   Richard Bauckham, *Jesus and the Eyewitnesses. The Gospels as Eyewitness Testimony* (Grand Rapids: Eerdmans 2006), 366.

5   Sean Freyne 'The Fisherman from Bethsaida' in *Peter in Early Christianity*, ed. Helen K. Bond and Larry W. Hurtado (Grand Rapids, Michigan, Cambridge UK: Eerdmans 2015), 19-29.

on display in the Yigal Allon Museum in Kibbutz Ginosar,[6] the vessel is thought to be typical of the boats used on Galilee at the time of Jesus. The dimensions of the boat offer an insight into the struggle of those disciples after the miraculous catch of fish. The remains of the boat, 27 feet long, 7.5 feet wide, just over 4 feet high, depict a boat which would be more than a little cramped for seven disciples. Such a small boat would certainly have struggled with a net of 153 fish in tow.

It was highly unlikely that Jesus would have seen the shoal of fish from his vantage point on the shore. John's account is clearly intended to portray a display of supernatural knowledge and miraculous timing by Jesus. It was a sign meant to arrest the attention of Peter and the others in the same way that a similar miracle had done when Peter was first called (Luke 5:1-11).

Ministry in the Power of the Resurrection

Over and above John's Gospel being 'a book of signs' the whole narrative is like a majestic symphony in which two great theme tunes interweave and shape the whole. The first is the reality of God Himself, his power, love and glory. The second is the reality of this present created world of time and space. The dramatic centre to this Gospel is that these two realities coincide in Jesus Christ: the Word becomes flesh and the glory of the invisible God is seen, heard and handled.[7] Discipleship in John is far more than following Christ's example and obeying his teaching; it is nothing less than our space-and-time-bound lives being radically transformed by an eternal reality beyond. This vivid image of exhausted disciples hauling in an unprecedented catch of fish is paradigmatic of all Christian living and serving. 'If you remain in me and I in you, you will bear much fruit; apart from me you can do nothing' (15:5). Indeed in John 15:1-16 the verb 'abide' occurs eleven times and the phrase 'bear fruit' eight times; dependency on Christ and effectiveness are clearly bound together.

Karl Barth insisted that each moment of discipleship is to be viewed as 'an event', a grace event pointing us away from ourselves to God's power and promises.[8] All Christian living and serving is a participation

---

6   See article https://en.m.wikipedia.org/wiki/Sea of Galilee Boat.

7   J.A.T. Robinson 'The Use of the Fourth Gospel in Christology Today' in B. Lindars and S.S. Smalley, *Christ and the Spirit in the New Testament* (Camb. Uni. Press 1973), 64.

8   Karl Barth, *Church Dogmatics* 1/2 (Edinburgh T&T Clark 1956), 393. By 'event' Barth is not implying a set of disconnected discrete moments; God's covenant faithfulness brings continuity.

in the continuing ministry of the now risen and ascended Lord. Dr Martin Niemoller (1892-1984), a German friend, Lutheran pastor and colleague of Barth, spoke in similar terms. On the Fourth Sunday in Lent, 1933, he told his comfortable congregation in Dahlem, a fashionable suburb of Berlin, 'We have nothing to give and we Christians have nothing ourselves. We live by a miracle and this miracle is called Christ. He has everything, he does everything and he is everything. Our only duty is to see that men and women meet the miracle called Christ.' It was this conviction that would sustain him through seven years in Sachsenhausen and Dachau concentration camps.

Ministry as Obedient Discipleship

Such high views of Christian service only become a reality when rooted in the daily, costly business of listening to, abiding in and obeying Jesus. The miraculous catch of fish happened as the disciples obeyed the Stranger's instruction, 'Throw your net on the right side of the boat and you will find some' (21:6). How easily those experts of the sea could have rolled their eyes, muttered a sarcastic comment, cracked a fishing joke and continued pulling their empty boat into shore! But they didn't; their obedience was unquestioning, serious and immediate.

No Christian ministry takes us beyond a simple, faithful following of Jesus. Both our self-identity and our vocation are grounded in discipleship. We never move beyond being vulnerable sheep following the True Shepherd. Ministry is simply 'exemplary discipleship.'[9] We could almost define Christian leadership as authentic discipleship modelled, mentored and multiplied.[10] (It is important to note that if this is an accurate definition of Christian leadership then it certainly includes women. The women disciples of the Gospels are portrayed as exemplary, not least as the ones who didn't desert Jesus at his crucifixion.)[11] One striking feature of John's

9   See Chapter 6 'Focused Discipleship' in Paul W. Goodliff, *Shaped for Service. Ministry Formation and Virtue Ethics* (Eugene, Oregon Pickwick Publications 2017), 94ff.

10   C.f. Eugene Peterson, 'Nothing a pastor does is different in kind from what all Christians do, but sometimes it is more focussed, more visible'. 'The Gift: Reflections on Christian Ministry' in compendium *Life at its Best* (Grand Rapids, Michigan: Zondervan 1980), 410.

11   See Dorothy A. Lee, 'If women are models of leadership in Jesus teaching, how can they subsequently be excluded?' *The Ministry of Women in the New Testament. Reclaiming the Biblical Vision for Church Leadership* (Baker Academic 2021), 34.

Gospel is that each time there is an expression of 'fullness of life' (water into wine, the feeding of the five thousand, the lavish anointing of Jesus) it is invariably accompanied by humble obedience: Mary's words to the wedding servants, 'Do whatever he tells you' (2:5), the small boy's offer of five small barley loaves and two small fish (6:8) and Mary's sacrificial anointing (12:3).

This is highlighted by the description in John's Gospel of Christ's own attitude of obedience to his Father, famously expressed in the words of Jesus, 'I tell you the truth, the Son can do nothing by himself; he can only do what he sees his Father doing; because whatever the Father does the Son does' (5:19). It is a remarkable image. It is the picture of a craftsman and his apprentice; carpenter Joseph in his Nazareth workshop and his apprentice son Jesus. Patiently Joseph shows his son how to work with the grain of the wood, turn a piece of wood, chisel a tricky joint. In each case the son carefully follows suit.

Equally the Father in Heaven shows his only Son what he should be doing. Jesus, even as a twelve year old boy, gently rebukes his frantic parents, 'Didn't you know I had to be in my Father's house?' (Luke 2:49). The first priority of Jesus was not to serve the world, but to serve the Father who sent him into the world. Jesus could have healed far more than he did, he could have preached twice as much, he could have travelled internationally and, dare we suggest, he could have delayed his crucifixion by a few years. The fact he didn't was precisely because his life was not governed by need but by keeping his focus on his Father. Ray Anderson in his book *The Soul of Ministry* pulls no punches:

> The so called burn-out phenomenon among so many Christian pastors is not due so much to an over-investment in one's work as it is a symptom of theological anaemia. The problem is not that one is over-worked, but one is serving the wrong master, and this reflects an anaemic, sick theology. A healthy understanding based on the inner logic of Jesus ministry to the Father rather than to the world, will go a long way towards healing the sickness of personal burn-out. Jesus knew who his master was. He was not called to love the world more than the Father who sent him into the world.[12]

---

12   Ray S. Anderson, *The Soul of Ministry: Forming Leaders for God's People* (Louisville, Kentucky, Westminster, John Knox Press 1997), 82.

Such habitual obedience is what constitutes godly character and safe leadership. Pastoral skills and competencies, though important, always play second fiddle to the virtue of faithfulness. Christian ministries rarely crash because of a lack of creativity or competence. They do seriously flounder when Christ-like graces and basic discipleship faithfulness are deemed less important than gifting. During the funeral service for Dr Billy Graham on March 2nd 2018 all five children paid moving tributes to their father. One of his sons commented, 'The person who preached in stadiums around the world, and the person who was my father was the same man. I want you to know that there was only one Billy Graham'.[13] Integrity and simple obedience are everything.

Ministry as Resurrection Life Revealed in Brokenness

I will never forget Good Friday morning 1991. I found myself standing in the pulpit on a very cold April morning wearing the lightest of cotton shirts. It was all I could bear, such was the raw pain of a nasty outbreak of shingles. The shingles had been triggered by an almost indescribably dark pastoral experience a few days before involving hurt, division and a tragic suicide. I was in shock and out of my depth. The disorientation was intense. But that Good Friday morning as I opened the Scriptures feeling extraordinarily vulnerable, a powerful sense of the presence of the Risen Christ came to me and to the congregation. I preached on the words of the Roman centurion standing in the shadow of the cross, 'Surely, this man was the Son of God'. As I spoke, it seemed that something of the revelation that was his, coming in three hours of darkness, became our revelation. Together in the bleakness of that Good Friday we glimpsed a light that no darkness could overcome. It was an experience I will never forget and a moment that has deeply shaped my understanding of following and serving Jesus. Christian ministry of all forms is the enormous privilege of the risen Christ taking our brokenness and using it to bring something of his wholeness to church and world. Our calling as disciples is to allow the shape of our lives to be etched by the contours of Christ's life, death and resurrection.

Peter and his colleagues were bereft and broken men. An exhausting night of futile activity simply underlined the fact. But it was precisely *through* such

---

13 Reported by Revd David Coffey present at the funeral service in the BMS World Mission magazine Engage, March 2018.

brokenness that the Risen Lord was able to reveal his power. This too was to be paradigmatic for all future Christian service. The classic exposition of this is in Paul's Second Letter to the Corinthians. For Paul suffering in ministry is not only the norm but is the very means by which Christ's resurrection life is revealed. 'We always carry around in our bodies the death of Jesus, *so that* the life of Jesus may be revealed in our body. For we who are alive are always being given over to death for Jesus sake, *so that* his life may be revealed in our mortal body' (2 Corinthians 4:10-11). He uses the vivid image of cracked pots; the more pronounced the cracks the more the light shines out! 'We have this treasure in jars of clay to show that this all-surpassing power is from God, and not from us' (2 Corinthians 4:7).

In the ancient world, clay pots were part of everyday life, used mainly for storage of common cooking ingredients. Occasionally, however, precious things were also stored in them (for example, the Dead Sea scrolls were discovered in such earthenware jars) – and this is Paul's image. It's the startling contrast between the invaluable treasure of God's Good News invested in very ordinary and fragile lives. Ministry is simply living out this reality. Scott Hafemann comments, 'The greatest display of God's power is not the absence of pain or the presence of a miracle, but Paul's faithful endurance in the midst of adversity, through which God makes many (others) rich.'[14] The shared testimony of God's servants is that when we feel most out of *our* depth the true depth of *God's* love and power begins to show through. And that's how it is meant to be – so that all the glory is his.

Walking in Step with the Spirit

I have little doubt that Peter and his colleagues, following the Day of Pentecost and the rapid growth of the church, would often have reflected on that miraculous catch of fish and just how prophetic a sign it was. Who would have thought that after a futile night of fishing such a catch of fish would be netted; who would have thought after all Peter's failures three thousand folk would be converted on the Day of Pentecost? In a remarkable post-apostolic letter written by Clement to the Corinthian Church towards the end of the first century Clement describes the apostle Peter along with Paul as 'athletic contenders', 'noble examples', 'the greatest and most upright

---

14   Scott J. Hafemann, *2 Corinthians*. The NIV Application Commentary (Grand Rapids, Michigan: Zondervan 2000), 271.

pillars'[15] – epitaphs as far removed as you can imagine from the mind of Peter on the beach that day! Something clearly changed. It was lives filled with the Spirit of the Risen Christ that made all the difference.

I grew up in the city of York and came to faith in Christ just before a young Anglican curate-in-charge, David Watson, arrived from Cambridge in 1965, courageously taking on an almost redundant church of only twelve elderly members. The story of the subsequent renewal at St Cuthbert's (later St Michael's) is well known and documented.[16] It was not the church I attended but the impact of God's power at work there touched many of us well beyond the immediate congregation.

Later on, as a student at Oxford, I shared in the planning of a university-wide mission led by David Watson. (After many months of agonising over a catchy strapline for the mission we came up with the modest title '*Jesus Christ Today*'!) What constantly impressed me was not so much David Watson's brilliant communication and charismatic leadership skills, nor the remarkable church growth under his watch – but his vulnerability. His disciplined prayer life and humble attitude bore out his deep conviction that all ministry is about the life of the Risen Christ, in the power of the Spirit, being revealed through weakness. He suffered physically with severe asthma, regular exhaustion and died of cancer on February 18th 1984 at the young age of 51. His wife, Anne, struggled with depression. Their brave experiments with extended-family communal living included painful episodes. Together they had more than a few sceptics around. Yet through it all there was a powerful move of the Spirit that inspired many of us. Using his own bronchial weakness as an illustration he often talked about the church's chronic asthmatic condition, gasping for the Breath of Life.[17] But such Holy Spirit power is our only hope in ministry. It is our most essential resource. All Christian service and leadership is a miracle or it is nothing. As with those first disciples on the beach, power comes as we listen to Christ's call, obey his voice and trust his promises.

---

15   Todd D. Still, 'Images of Peter in the Apostolic Fathers' in op.cit. *Peter in Early Christianity* 162.

16   David Watson, *You are my God; An Autobiography* (London: Hodder and Stoughton 1983).

17   David Watson, *Discipleship* (London, Hodder and Stoughton 1981), 95.

Chapter Three

Christ: the Centre, Shape and Sustenance of Ministry

Then the disciple whom Jesus loved said to Peter, 'It is the Lord!' (John 21:7)

'It is the Lord!' The moment of recognition must have rocked the Beloved Disciple just as dramatically as the miraculous catch had rocked the boat. It was a cry of utter amazement and wonder – and its significance cannot be overestimated. It was an impromptu confession all as weighty as Mary's exclamation, 'I have seen the Lord' (20:18) and Thomas' later declaration in the upper room, 'My Lord and my God' (20:28). It seems the Gospel writer deliberately wants to underline this. First he immediately repeats it, 'As soon as Peter heard him say *'It is the Lord'*, he wrapped his outer garment around him . . . and jumped into the water' and then, a few minutes later on shore, he records 'none of the disciples dare ask him, 'Who are you?' They knew *it was the Lord'* (21:12). Throughout most of Jesus public ministry when he was addressed as 'lord' it was simply a term of respect. Now, however, it becomes filled with much greater significance.

It is this ringing exclamation which should shape and empower all aspects of Christian service. The story is told of Rowan Williams being present at one Easter Day cathedral service when a rather hesitant resurrection sermon was preached. On his way out he whispered to his professorial colleague Oliver O'Donovan, 'Christ is risen, he is *possibly* risen indeed!'[1] The historic truth of the resurrection of Christ was, and is, foundational to any understanding of Christian faith and ministry.

---

1   Quoted in Rupert Shortt, *Rowan's Rule* (Hodder and Stoughton 2008), 137.

The resurrection of Christ is something wonderfully new breaking into the old creation. As T.F. Torrance argues, it was a real event in space and time and yet an event that reconfigured both. 'Whilst the resurrection is an event that happened once and for all, it remains a *continuous live happening* within history, and therefore must be interpreted as running against the pattered stream of history of the secular framework of our space and time.'[2] Christ is our contemporary – and that changes everything, most certainly our perspective on ministry.

Hoisting the Christological Sail

Perhaps my favourite quote about Christian ministry, somewhat fitting with the image of the fishing boat struggling to the shore with its miraculous catch, was offered by the late Baptist scholar Neville Clarke. He wrote, 'That frail craft which is the church is always exposed to the danger of being blown helplessly in any direction by hurricane winds. If she is to catch the wind of the Spirit she must always hoist the Christological sail.'[3] Raising that sail is the aim of this chapter.

The theological starting point for any understanding of ministry is the redeeming and reconciling ministry of the triune God to our fallen world. The Father's overflowing love in sending his Son in the power of the Spirit is not only where it all begins but where all ministry must continue to be grounded and sourced. 'Before it is the church's ministry all ministry is first of all God's ministry in, through and as Jesus Christ in the power of the Holy Spirit.'[4] In particular, Christ's own serving and saving ministry is to be our focus. Jesus Christ not only perfectly *models* ministry but is the very *means* of all service in his name. The Spirit does not give us 'another ministry' but rather unites us to the ministry of the now exalted Christ. We participate in his continuing ministry. The Apostle Paul, for example, having summarised the Gospel as 'God reconciling the world to himself in Christ' then, in the same breath, declares that he has committed to us that very ministry of reconciliation.[5]

---

2   T.F. Torrance, *Atonement. The Person and Work of Christ*, ed. Robert T. Walker (Paternoster, IVP Academic 2009), 247.

3   Neville Clarke, 'The Ministry. A Review and an Assessment' in *The Baptist Quarterly*, Vol. XX1V Oct 1971 No. 4, 150.

4   Andrew Purves, *Reconstructing Pastoral Theology: A Christological Foundation* (Louisville, London: Westminster John Knox Press 2004), 3.

5   2 Corinthians 5:18-19.

Consider for a moment those high profile footballers who now have progressed to managing prestigious teams – the likes of a Steven Gerrard or a Frank Lampard. No longer on the field dominating play they now stand on the side-lines, guiding, goading, gesticulating and often groaning! No longer can their own brilliant mid-field defending, passing and shooting be directly part of the game. They still lead but no longer participate in the actual play. Not so with Jesus Christ. The ascended Christ doesn't just 'manage' the church from the side-lines, willing its members on to emulate how he used to 'play'. The church is the very Body of Christ on earth. Through the power of the Spirit the risen Christ continues *his* messianic ministry – amazingly, through our frailty, failures, suffering and weakness. The real presence of Jesus is to be encountered not just in communion but in every act of ministry. 'We always carry around in our body the death of Jesus, so that the life of Jesus may also be revealed in our body.'[6]

T.W. Manson, in four influential lectures given in 1948 entitled 'The Church's Ministry', hammered home this point again and again. There is only one 'essential ministry' he kept stressing. The ministry which began in Galilee and Judea is the ministry which continues today in and through the church. 'The Body of Christ is the organism which he uses to carry out His purposes in the world in the same way that He used his physical body in the days of his ministry in Galilee and Judea.'[7] This emphasis is so vital – and so easily forgotten. We do not simply work hard *for* Christ in gratitude for all he has done. We serve *with* him. Every time we preach, lead worship, counsel, chair meetings, mentor and pray we, like the Beloved Disciple, keep declaring 'It is the Lord!' Paul comments on his own ministry, 'I will not venture to speak of anything *except what Christ has accomplished* through me in leading the Gentiles to obey God by what I have said and done.'[8]

A Three-fold Christological Focus

There are three central themes that triangulate to form a full biblical view of ministry and all are centred on Jesus Christ. First, Christian service of all kinds begins with the call of Christ to follow him. We follow him, as the Servant of the Lord, in his messianic career of being servant *par excellence*. As with the original Twelve we are called to be with him and

---

6   2 Corinthians 4:10.
7   T.W. Manson, *The Church's Ministry* (London: Hodder and Stoughton 1948), 21.
8   Romans 15:18.

then sent, in his name, to serve his world, declaring and demonstrating that the Kingdom of God is near.[9] Our baptism celebrates not only our conversion but our ordination into a life-time of service within the messianic community. The function of every believer is *diakonia* (service); all are called to ministry. For me over the years, one of the most moving privileges has been to see young believers noticeably becoming less self-absorbed. They immediately evidence that to follow Christ is to follow the one who came 'not to be served but to serve.'[10]

Second, precisely because our conversion to Christ is also our incorporation into his Body, the focus must always be that it is the *whole church* which ministers. There are many different ministries within the church but they are all expressions of the one ministry of Christ through his Body. Everyone is thus indispensable for the church's ministry, everyone is part of the one overall ministry. Far too often this emphasis is underplayed. This is strikingly underlined in the New Testament by its declaration that precisely because Jesus Christ, and Jesus Christ alone, is *the priest* of the church by our participating in him through the Spirit, we *together* – in solidarity – become 'a royal priesthood.'[11] As Tom Greggs well expresses it 'To be a priesthood is to be God's *people* – not God's *person*.'[12] It is often pointed out (rightly) that no church leader is ever termed a 'priest' in the New Testament but it is less frequently emphasised that the 'priesthood of all believers' is not about individual privileges but about the essential *corporate* nature of our priesthood.[13] By participating in Christ's priesthood we are turned not only God-wards but towards each other in sacrificial ministry and *together* towards the world in humble witness.

It is this reality which renders distinctions such as 'leader and led', 'pastor and members', 'clergy and laity' secondary at best. Christ is present in the gifts of each member and our individual gifts are for the building

---

9   Mark 3: 13-14.
10   Mark 10:45.
11   1 Peter 2:9.
12   Tom Greggs, *Dogmatic Ecclesiology. The Priestly Catholicity of the Church*, Vol. 1 (Grand Rapids: Baker Academic 2019), 104. Greggs superb exposition of this theme of the priestly nature of the church is in Chapters 2 and 3.
13   The priesthood of the church is mentioned only three times in the New Testament and, in each case, it is about its corporate nature: 1 Peter 2:9, Revelation 1:6, Revelation 5:10.

up of the whole. The church is thus to be structured not as a hierarchy but more as a polycentric, inter-dependent, participative community where every member bears responsibility for confessing and representing Christ. As Miroslav Volf puts it, 'All members of the church create the "plausibility structures" in which the mediation of faith and life in faith become possible in the first place.'[14] Looking back over my years of local church ministry I would judge (in the midst of lots of not very fruitful enterprises!) that one of my most significant legacies has been to advocate, organise, shape and support 'ministry teams'. The goal has been to see every member of the congregation identifying with, and actively participating in, at least one ministry team.

Third, emphasis on *the ministry of all* does not exclude the importance of the *ordering* of such ministry within the Body of Christ. Such ordering must be determined, of course, by our understanding of the church, its nature and mission. As John Webster well puts it, 'Church order is the social shape of the converting power and activity of Christ present as Spirit.'[15] Given this, there is clearly a key place for *pastoral leadership*; that is, those called and gifted to ensure the church is shaped by Gospel truths and values. The crucial nature of leadership lies in its ability to envision, release, equip and empower the *whole congregation* to be a united Christ-centred and mission-focused community. This comes through teaching, preaching, modelling, guiding, persuading and overseeing (full-time, part-time, paid, unpaid).

This Gospel ordering may, of course, look somewhat different in practice according to different circumstance and situations. It is not surprising that within the New Testament no one pattern or blueprint of church 'orders' is to be found. The church leadership at Antioch, for example, with its prophets and teachers seems to have a different shape and feel to the leadership at Philippi with its overseers and deacons.[16] There were also leaders – apostles, prophets and teachers – who had important trans-local ministries. Culture, context and missional demands seem to have been

---

14   Miroslav Volf, *After Our Likeness. The Church as the Image of the Trinity* (Grand Rapids: Eerdmans 1998), 226-7.
15   See John Webster. 'The Self-Organising Power of the Gospel of Christ: Episcopacy and Community Formation' in W*ord and Church: Essays in Christian Dogmatics.* (Edinburgh, New York: T&T Clark 2001), 198.
16   Acts 13:1, Philippians 1:1.

important in shaping leadership structures. But still, central to the role of all leadership is a focus on the oversight *(episcope)* of the whole church. Each of the members may contribute to a given sector of the church's life but the distinctive calling of leaders is an *ordering of the whole*[17] for the sake of maintaining integrity in fulfilling the gospel mandate.

If leadership focuses on the big picture then, of course, the critical issue becomes '*Where* are we leading God's people?' What is the actual *telos*, the goal, of Christian leadership? It is the most basic of questions but, puzzlingly, not asked frequently enough! The unequivocal New Testament answer is that Christian leadership is about enabling people, in their experience, behaviour and relationships to move closer to Christ. It is, in Paul's famous words, 'to prepare God's people for works of service, so that the body of Christ may be built up, until we all reach unity in the faith and in the knowledge of the Son of God and become mature, attaining to the whole measure of the fullness of Christ.'[18] If this is not 'hoisting the Christological sail' I don't know what is! The ultimate mark of authentic Christian leadership is not efficient management or visionary drive but the determination, under God, to radically refocus people's lives on Christ and so to see a reorientation around Christ's saving grace and kingdom values.

Taking our Eyes off Christ – the Seductive Allure of Ministry

The emphasis of this chapter on Christ as the foundation and focus of all ministry may be seen as labouring the obvious. But I fear the point does need stressing. I am reminded of Oswald Chambers' famous comment, in a daily meditation entitled 'It is the Lord!': 'Beware of anything that competes with loyalty to Jesus Christ. The greatest competitor of devotion to Jesus is service for him.'[19]

I think he is correct. Ironically, there is something about Christian service that is seductive. In my experience it is all too easy to love theology rather than to love the God of which it speaks, too easy to conclude that success in the church is the same as health in the church, too easy to become almost addicted to the 'good feeling' that ministry can bring rather than simply the sense of privilege in serving Christ. The subtlety of the

---

17   Miroslav Volf, op. cit., 247.
18   Ephesians 4:12-13.
19   Oswald Chambers, *My Utmost for His Highest. Selections for the Year* (New York: Dodd, Mead and Co. 1935), 18.

distinction between 'hard work for Christ' and 'obedience to Christ' can easily be missed. When Mary anointed Jesus feet with expensive perfume and was criticised for not using the money for the poor Jesus made it clear she had got her priorities right.[20] Extravagant devotion to Jesus trumps all else.

Take a familiar scenario. Here are a group of church leaders, committed to discovering God's vision for their church. But soon they begin to experience tensions arising from divergent views. What follows is that, instead of Christ and his voice being the central concern, sides are taken, lobbying begins, restricted emails are sent and soon key stake holder interests eclipse all else. Or take another scenario, one I have encountered personally and read about too often. Here is a church which, for the sake of the church's reputation, begins to covers up past difficulties and even abuse. The leaders keep things to themselves, ostensibly to protect the flock, but the net result is that the crucial issues are never properly exposed and certainly not addressed. What has happened in both these cases is that the light, truth and freedom of Christ has been overshadowed. Misplaced loyalty has occurred. The simplicity of 'It is the Lord' has been subtly replaced. I find myself challenged by the shrewd observation of Diane Langberg, a prominent Christian psychologist who has been involved in trauma counselling around the globe, when she writes,

> I have learned during my decades as a psychologist that you can tell what is most important to someone by what they protect most vociferously . . . We love and worship the system of the church more than we love and worship Jesus Christ.[21]

The Glory of Christ – our Passion in Ministry

When the Beloved Disciple exclaimed to his fishing companion 'It is the Lord' it was not only a moment of surprise and revelation but of unconcealed joy. I find the image of those early followers, overcome with wonder on realising that this Stranger was none other than their Rabbi and Lord, deeply moving. It recalls the words of John the Baptist, 'The friend who attends the bridegroom waits and listens for him and is full of joy when he hears the

---

20   John 12:1-8.
21   This is powerfully spelt out in Diane Langberg, *Redeeming Power. Understanding Authority and Abuse in the Church* (Grand Rapids: Brazos Press 2020), 187.

bridegroom's voice.'[22] For the readers of the Gospel this recognition scene becomes a moment of worship.[23] It also invites a journey of discovery.

Slow as I have often been to see it, I now conceive the very heart of ministry as being about a continuous discovery of more and more of the grace and majesty of Christ and seeking to share that with others. The ringing phrase of Ephesians, 'to the praise of his glory'[24] is our anthem. Indeed, if it is true that the one directing the fishing that early morning was the very Word of God 'through whom all things were made',[25] then this journey of discovery will never end. Our greatest effectiveness as leaders will flow from an almost unconscious modelling of our delight in Christ.

If ever we cease to be overawed by the beauty of Christ and the extravagance of his grace, then we have badly lost our way. A retired Methodist minister, struggling with a degenerative illness, used to sit at the back of the church where we now worship. Never a Sunday went by without a loud and heartfelt 'Hallelujah' coming from his wheelchair. For all the rough and tumble of his life and service, his excitement that 'it is the Lord' has never left him. Karl Barth wrote,

> If you have heard the Easter message, you can no longer run around with a tragic face and lead the humourless existence of a man *(sic)* who has no hope. One thing still holds, and only this one thing is really serious, that Jesus is the Victor . . . we are invited and summoned to take seriously the victory of God's glory in this man Jesus and to be joyful in him.[26]

Far too often we frame our understanding of ministry by its challenges and difficulties and quickly find ourselves beginning to see it through the eyes of the elder brother in Jesus' parable, 'All these years I've been slaving for you and never disobeyed your orders.'[27] Ministry, for all its daily duties and disappointments, is the exhilarating, joyful privilege of again and again recognising 'it is the Lord'. The joy of the Lord is our strength in our preaching, in our everyday pastoral conversations, in our leadership

---

22 John 3:29.
23 C.K. Barrett sees worship as a central purpose of the Gospel of John. Quoted in M. Thompson, *The God of the Gospel of John* (Grand Rapids: Eerdmans 2001), 189.
24 Ephesians 1:6,12,14.
25 John 1:3.
26 Karl Barth, *Dogmatics in Outline*, tr. G.T. Thompson (London, SCM Press 1949, 123.
27 Luke 15:29.

decisions, in our seeing people come to faith and most clearly in our corporate worship. 'The Kingdom of God is not a matter of eating and drinking but of righteousness, peace and joy in the Holy Spirit.'[28] I love the story of John Owen, the great Puritan scholar, who was visited by a minister friend, William Payne on the morning of August 24th 1683 just before Owen died. Payne commented with enthusiasm on how Owen's latest book, *The Glory of Christ* was about to be published. Owen replied, apparently his last words,

> I am glad to hear it; but, O brother Payne! The long wished for day is come at last, in which I shall see that glory in another manner than I have ever done, or was capable of doing in this world.[29]

Participation in Christ – our Energy in Ministry

There is something deeply releasing in the truth with which this chapter opened, namely that the one essential ministry is Christ's and all our service is a participation in his. When our focus is the continuing ministry of the ascended Lord in the power of the Spirit, then we can relax. Christ is the Head of the church, the 'government is on his shoulders' and all the resources we will ever need are in him. Such an emphasis counteracts the constant gravitational pull of conceiving ministry as being about 'what we can achieve for God – with his helping hand'! Dietrich Bonhoeffer describes it well when reflecting on preaching, 'The proclaimed word is not a medium of expression for something else, something which lies behind it, but rather it is the Christ himself walking through the congregation as the Word.'[30]

This theme of participation is central to a number of recent studies on ministry.[31] However, what is often missing is a clear working out of what this means in practice. Participation language can be misleading. At times one is left with the impression that such participation consists of a mere

---

28   Romans 14:17.
29   Quoted in Sinclair B. Ferguson, *Some Pastors And Teachers. Reflecting a biblical vision of what every minister is called to be* (The Banner of Truth Trust 2017), 227.
30   Dietrich Bonhoeffer, 'Worldly Preaching', quoted in David Hansen, *The Art of Pastoring. Ministry Without all the Answers* (IVP 1994) 155.
31   See, for example, Graham Buxton, *Dancing in the Dark. The Privilege of Participating in the Ministry of Christ* (Paternoster Press 2001); Andrew Purves, *Reconstructing Pastoral Theology* op. cit.; Paul S. Fiddes, *Participating in God. A Pastoral Doctrine of the Trinity* (Darton, Longman and Todd 2000).

passive 'surfing' on the crest of Christ's continuing ministry. The witness of the New Testament, however, suggests ministry is more like white water rafting! We are carried along, for sure, by a power far greater than our own and yet there is the utterly exhausting business of keeping afloat, paddling furiously and avoiding the rocks! Paul captures this 'double agency' well and indeed the asymmetry of it, when he writes, 'To this end I labour, struggling with all his energy, which so powerfully works in me.'[32] In pastoral care, for example, we listen attentively, bringing to bear our best insights and experience, yet ultimately we are seeking to discern the ways in which God himself is active in the situation. In our preaching, we prepare thoroughly, read our audience well and employ the best communication skills we have, yet we fully recognise that unless our words are 'with power, with the Holy Spirit and with deep conviction'[33] all is in vain.

This concept of 'double agency' is worth pausing over. Rowan Williams in his recent work *Christ, the Heart of Creation*, makes use of the insight of Austen Farrer (1904-1968), the great Anglican theologian, that the Infinite and the Finite 'never occupy the same space'. In other words, God is so utterly *different* to all created beings that divine and human agency are never two components *of the same kind* in an action, even less are they in competition. 'What infinite agency causes simply *is* the system of secondary causality within which we finite agents act'.[34] It is not a question of asking what is God's part and what is ours, (eighty percent God, twenty percent me!) as if these two parts were somehow on the same level of being. God is *non aliud* ('not another thing'). He is not a super-enlarged version of our finitude. Rather, the infinite, eternal God who in Christ sustains, upholds and guides all finite things, energises all ministry and yet, with no sense of conflict, we have our full part to play. As Williams puts it,

> If God is truly the source, the ground and the context of every limited, finite state of affairs, if God is the action or agency that makes everything else active, then God cannot be spoken of as one item in a list of the forces active in the world. God's action cannot be added to the action of some other agent in order to make a more effective force.[35]

---

32 Colossians 1:29.
33 1 Thessalonians 1:5.
34 Rowan Williams, *Christ the Heart of Creation* (Bloomsbury Continuum 2018), 2.
35 Rowan Williams, ibid., xii.

Williams sees the mystery of Jesus Christ, both fully divine and fully human, as the defining 'grammar' or paradigm for this. Jesus Christ, the Eternal Word of God, is the central reality, yet he is also a fully human individual born at a particular point in time. The divine and human are not two competing 'components' of one person, but two realities of a very different order, the infinite and the finite, that perfectly co-exist. It is *this* sense of double agency that is vital to affirm in our understanding of participation. Our life and service are nothing unless we are in union with Christ through the Spirit, the infinite divine agency at work within us. Yet in our human finitude we are constantly called to 'work it out'. 'Continue to work out your salvation with fear and trembling, for it is God who works in you to will and to act according to his good purpose.'[36] Thus all ministry is a participation in the ministry of Christ *precisely by*, for example, 'not grieving the Spirit',[37] 'walking in step with the Spirit',[38] 'putting off the old self and being made new in the attitude of our minds',[39] 'understanding what the Lords will is',[40] 'participating in Christ's suffering'[41] . . . and so much more! We are '*co-workers* with God'. There is a non-competitive unity in *our actions*, not simply passively being caught up in Christ's continuing priestly ministry.

Nurturing a Christ-shaped Community – our Goal in Ministry

The real legacy of any authentic Christian ministry is not a large church, a relevant church or a visionary church but rather *a Christ-shaped community*. The church is nothing less than the Body of Christ. The Eternal Word of God, embodied in his humanity, finds expression in his community, the church. Thus it follows that all ministry must not only be centred on Christ but, by the Spirit, reflect and reproduce the pattern of Christ's ministry. Rowan Williams expresses this sharply, 'The 'apostolic ministry' is that ministry whose special province is both to gather the believing community around the centre which is proclaims, the Living Lord, and in that gathering to make sure this community is critically aware of itself . . . The ordered ministry is there, most simply, to minister to the

---

36   Philippians 2:12.
37   Ephesians 4:30.
38   Galatians 5:25.
39   Ephesians 4:22.
40   Ephesians 5:17.
41   Philippians 3:10.

Church's very identity.'[42] Being Christ-centred is far more than preaching Christ-centred sermons, though that is crucial. It involves developing a 'critical awareness' of Christ as the crucial shaping factor in *all we are and do*. I illustrate by suggesting four key areas where it is vital to work this through.

First, as hinted at earlier, there is an urgent need to move beyond viewing corporate leadership as a 'decision-making body' to being a 'community of discernment'. The primary focus of the former is horizontal (choosing between options presented to us) whereas in the latter the focus is vertical, *being attentive to Jesus Christ* in our conversation. This transition is more demanding and radical than is often assumed. It requires more than adding a few minutes of extra prayer at the beginning of a meeting. It calls for a whole new mind-set, a changed disposition, a moving away from the cut and thrust of debate to the delicate art of discerning together the mind of Christ.[43] Such an openness to the Spirit comes through embracing a set of intentional practices.[44]

I write this having just come from a leaders' meeting looking at the next stage of our church's life. It began with worship and a time to listen to Scripture. This was followed by a period of silence in which we were invited to 'shed', as best we could, our pre-conceived opinions and seek for a 'holy indifference', for God's will, not ours. Then there was time to weigh the different views offered, to listen for the prophetic voice and ultimately to discern the *one voice* that counts. I love the practice of the Mennonites where in the middle of deliberations someone may 'call for the Gospel', where everyone stops and a key passage of Scripture is read and reflected on. In this whole process the Holy Spirit does not bypass or over-power the human mind but brings about what Andre Munzinger helpfully calls 'a renewed relationality and orientation of the whole self towards God' which leads to a 'new Christocentric rationality'.[45]

---

42 Rowan Williams, 'Women and Ministry' in Monica Furlong, ed., *Feminine in the Church* (London: SPCK 1984), 15.

43 A very helpful book here is Ruth Haley Barton, *Pursuing God's Will together. A Discernment Practice for Leadership Groups* (IVP 2012).

44 See Danny E. Morris and Charles M. Olson, *Discerning God's Will Together. A Spiritual Practice for the Church* (Nashville: Upper Room Books 1997).

45 Andre Munzinger, *Discerning the Spirits. Theological and Ethical Hermeneutics in Paul*, Society for New Testament Studies Monograph Series 140, (Cambridge University Press 2007), 166.

Second, shaping a congregation around Christ requires serious attention to the pervading local church culture. All communities have an organisational culture; those systemic dynamics that shape attitudes, expectations and behaviour; that send out subtle signals and messages. Institutional cultures hold the potential to be either deeply deforming or transforming.[46] The problem is, we do not routinely pay as much attention to this as we should. The dynamic is well captured in the image of an iceberg; the way a community is *run* is the one-tenth above the surface, the way a community is *shaped* (by its habitual attitudes and patterns of behaviour) is the nine-tenths below the surface. It is absolutely vital, for example, that time is taken to nourish and protect a culture of mutual trust and respect; mutual trust is the key currency of all community life. It is equally important to take steps to dispel a toxic culture of gossip, back-biting and negativity. It is salutary that in Jesus' home town of Nazareth 'he could not do any miracles there' precisely because of a culture of disbelief.[47] At the opposite extreme, I have encountered cultures of triumphalism where there is neither theological room nor pastoral space to admit failure or long-term problems. Only the light and warmth of Christ can melt the icebergs!

In all this it is crucial for leaders to have the humility to listen to how others perceive the spiritual ecology they inhabit and promote. Our calling is to work determinedly towards observable cultural transformation where a culture of Christ-like grace is our goal. Often the key to this is not massive policy change but simply being alert to those moments where 'the old culture' suddenly rears its head and needs firmly challenging. I have battle scars over such seemingly minor issues as advocating the serving of refreshments before as well as after a service, sitting in the round where possible, allowing young children to dance at the front in worship, challenging folk who too quickly criticise the contribution of others and encouraging as a norm one-to-one prayer after a service. For us these challenges constituted key symbolic moments in building a culture of welcome, grace, inclusivity and joy. Neil Hudson talks helpfully about 'one degree shifts' in cultural change.[48] If your sailing boat make a one degree compass shift then after a few miles you find yourself sailing in very different waters.

---

46 Ruth Haley Barton, op.cit., 82.
47 Mark 6:5-6.
48 Neil Hudson, *Imagine Church. Releasing Whole Life Disciples* (IVP 2012), 97.

Third, talking of battle scars, Christ must be at the centre of our church conflicts. Conflict is inevitable in any community, the early church being no exception. What is not inevitable is that conflict has to be destructive. For sure, it is always painful but it can be constructive. The foodbank tension between the Greek-speaking and Hebrew-speaking widows in the Jerusalem church led to both a clarity of roles among the leaders and further church growth.[49] Conflict can provide an opportunity for folk to learn how to listen more empathetically and how to better live with difference. Ultimately it can move a church on from being what Scott Peck calls a 'pseudo-community' to being a more authentic community.[50] I have been involved in mediation work over many years with many churches and certainly there are skills to be learnt. Careful listening, managing a safe process, helping to focus on the issues not the people involved and moving folk on from entrenched positions to shared interests are all important. I have discovered – in what is always an emotionally demanding journey – that a helpful diagnostic aid is to encourage the disputants to reflect on what actually they are praying for in the situation. Are they praying for personal vindication; for them 'to win'? Or are they seeking justice, clarity, humility and an experience of the reconciling power of Christ at work? 'Search me, O God, and know my heart'.[51] Some of my most privileged and moving moments in ministry have been times when I have witnessed the love of Christ demolish entrenched views and heal long-held resentments. I once was working with a gifted mediator who suddenly asked permission to sing a paraphrase of 1 Corinthians 13 to a group of divided leaders. The Spirit of God descended and hearts were melted! We don't choose to be in conflict but we can chose how to respond when it comes our way. Placing the Living Lord centre-stage and not simply relying on a mediation process is vital.

Fourth, to be a Christ-shaped community is to be a people who take our very humanity seriously. This emphasis too flows from our doctrine of Christ. If, as was expounded earlier, the divinity and humanity of Jesus Christ are never to be conceived of as in competition, but rather full divinity and full humanity co-inhere in perfect harmony, then God

---

49   Acts 6:1-7.

50   Scott Peck, *The Different Drum. The Creation of True Community – the First Steps to World Peace* (London: Rider 1987), 86.

51   Psalm 139:23.

always rejoices over our humanity. Because of the incarnate Word, we can be fully assured that God never views humanity as a competitor. It is God's delight always to see human flourishing and human wholeness. To be godly does not involve 'an amputation of parts of our humanity' but rather 'to serve God is perfect freedom' – freedom to be all that God has made us to be.[52] To participate in Christ is to become more human never less. Disconcertingly, too often the church is disinterested in the very areas that are so central to our humanity – the dignity of our work, our rootedness in family relationships, the joy of hospitality and friendship, the complexity of our sexuality, the sheer fun of leisure and play and the responsibility of good citizenship. Too often discipleship is characterised by what is banned rather than by what is blessed! Is it *necessarily* less Christ-centred to enjoy an afternoon quad biking than an afternoon on a prayer retreat? Is it really less Christ-centred to be working hard for that 12 hour NHS shift to cover a colleague than to miss an important church meeting? For sure, motivation is everything but centre-stage must be the reality that Christ became one of us to heal and liberate humanity, not to stifle it.

One memorable Easter, in a moment of uncharacteristic abandon, I managed (with surprisingly little difficulty) to convince a congregation that instead of a formal Easter Sunday evening service we hold a ceilidh and dance in praise of the resurrection! The Beloved Disciple and Peter would have approved! When the Beloved Disciple exclaimed with such joy, '*It is the Lord*' and when Peter dived in, little did they know that their words and action would symbolise the very essence and shape of all subsequent ministry.

---

52   Words from a Rowan Williams' lecture, St Pauls Cathedral, 28th March 2019.

Chapter Four

Characterising Discipleship: the Shared Witness of Peter and the Beloved Disciple

**As soon as Simon Peter heard him say 'It is the Lord'
he wrapped his outer garment around him (for he had taken
it off) and jumped into the water. (John 21:7)**

Of the seven disciples in John 21 it is Simon Peter and the Beloved Disciple who become the primary focus. It is their words that are heard, their actions that are recorded, their personalities that shine through and their destinies that are hinted at. And what contrasting and colourful figures they are! Opposites often attract and here are two charismatic and hugely influential figures, so different and yet close partners on a journey of discovery. They deserve our careful attention.

The characteristic difference between them is highlighted in the distinctive ways Peter and the Beloved Disciple respond to the call of the Stranger on the shore. As the seven disciples struggle to haul in the remarkable catch of fish suddenly the Beloved Disciple recognises who it is on the beach. Deep in his spirit he becomes aware of the presence of the One whose love has so changed his life and he exclaims, (as explored in the last chapter) 'It is the Lord!' (21:7). The Beloved Disciple somehow sees before others see, sees further than others see and certainly sees with greater spiritual perception than others. He is a classic contemplative. In contrast, Peter, so true to all that we know of him, immediately and impetuously responds. He hurriedly makes himself decent (Galilean fisherman routinely fished naked), dives into the water, splashes his way to the shore and is the first to greet Jesus. Here is the classic activist.

Such contrasting reactions mirror exactly what had happened just a short while before on resurrection morning. Early that morning Peter and 'the other disciple' (who we assume to be the Beloved Disciple), having been alerted by Mary Magdalene, had raced to the tomb of Jesus (20:3). Though Peter had lagged behind, immediately on arrival at the cave he had dived in without a moment's hesitation. Here again is the activist - who acts first. When the other disciple, who had outrun Peter, finally musters the courage to venture inside he 'saw and believed' (20:8). Welcome the contemplative – the one who really 'sees' first.

Partners not Rivals

Scholars have often proposed that the Gospel writer was seeking to portray Peter and the Beloved Disciple as rivals and, in turn, as representatives of two competing streams of early Christianity (Western and Eastern).[1] Oscar Cullman is typical of many. He argued that, in contrast to the positive appraisal of Peter in the Synoptic Gospels, in the Fourth Gospel Peter is portrayed in less positive terms and certainly so compared to the Beloved Disciple. He comments, 'the mysteriously unnamed 'Beloved Disciple' of Jesus enters into a certain competition with Peter.'[2] Many other scholars agree, even characterising Peter as the 'flawed disciple' and the beloved disciple as the 'ideal disciple'.[3] They then reason that a central purpose of John 21 was to describe the 'rehabilitation' of Peter (with a view to encouraging mutual respect between the Western and Eastern Church).

However, it seems to me that though Peter and the Beloved Disciple are clearly very different the idea of some sort of implied rivalry is misplaced. Certainly Peter has some rather obvious failings and certainly the Beloved Disciple has noble features but the trajectory of the Gospel is that *both* are being honoured. Peter, through his weaknesses, finds the grace of forgiveness and is thus called to follow Jesus in a new way (21:19) and the

---

1   J.H. Charlesworth, *The Beloved Disciple: Whose Witness Validates the Gospel of John?* (Valley Forge, Penn, Trinity Press International, 1984), 391 quoted in Bradford B. Blaine Jn., *Peter in the Gospel of John. The Making of an Authentic Disciple* (Atlanta, Society of Biblical Literature 2007), 153.

2   O. Cullmann, *Peter: Disciple, Apostle, Martyr* (tr. F.V. Filson; London: SCM Press 1953), 27.

3   See for example, Martin Hengel, *The Johannine Question* (London: SCM Press 1989), 78. '. . . the idea that 'the disciple whom Jesus loved' is an 'ideal disciple' must be taken seriously. He really embodies the ideal of the disciple who stands closest to Jesus.'

Beloved Disciple, through his faithful presence at Jesus' trial and cross, becomes the faithful witness.[4] Indeed, there is even a sense of the Beloved Disciple himself honouring Peter for, on realising who the Stranger was, he instinctively turns to Peter with his discovery (21:7). The dominant impression of this Gospel is thus more about Peter and the Beloved Disciple being a double-act than about being rivals. They sit together at the Last Supper (13:23), follow Jesus together to the high priest's house (18:15) race together to the tomb (20:3) and, as we are to see later, walk together along the beach with Jesus (21:20). They are more friends and fellow-followers than ever competitors. Thus it seems far better to understand the Fourth Gospel's assessment of Peter and the Beloved Disciple as two disciples offering different but *complementary* qualities. I find strong sympathy with Bradford Blaine's conclusion that 'the two characters are depicted . . . as composite halves of the ideal Johannine Christian.'[5]

Peter the Activist, the Beloved Disciple the Contemplative

The sight of Peter's hundred yard 'breaststroke' to the shore seems a fitting image for Peter's whole approach to following Jesus. Nothing is done in half measures. One could even be forgiven for suspecting a love for high energy drinks! Peter is 'the doer' *par excellence*. Throughout the Fourth Gospel Peter is the respected leader and spokesman (13:24), the loyal disciple when many others 'turned back' (6:66-68), the zealous, if at times misguided, apprentice (13:9), the one who even offers to lay down his life for Jesus (13:37). Though less clear than in the Synoptic Gospels John's Gospel portrays Peter as the one 'first out of the stalls', the one who first declares who Jesus is (6:69), who uses a sword to defend Jesus at his arrest (18:10), the first to rush into the empty tomb (20:6), the one who now drags the bursting net ashore (21:11). It is therefore no surprise that it is Peter who is given the high calling of under-shepherd of God's flock. The very last recorded words of Jesus in this Gospel are to Peter 'You must follow me' (21:22). He is, for this writer, a true disciple where active, sacrificial service is central.

But similar to the tell-tale nature of Peter's swim to the shore, so also is the Beloved Disciple's recognition of Jesus, 'It is the Lord', Peter *reacts,* the

---

4   See Richard Bauckham, 'The Beloved Disciple as Ideal Author', *Journal for the Study of the New Testament* (49, 1993), 38.

5   Bradford Blaine, *Peter in the Gospel of John. The Making of an Authentic Disciple* (Atlanta, Society of Biblical Literature 2007), 23.

Beloved Disciple *recognises*; Peter *dives in* but the Beloved Disciple *discerns*. True seeing is a hugely important theme in John's Gospel.[6] Only Jesus fully sees God with face-to-face immediacy (1:18) but by seeing Jesus, the one who fully and truly embodies the life, love and glory of God, we see the Father (14:9). Thus the Beloved Disciple's recognition is highly significant here, modelling something fundamental to this Gospel. Peter was soon to be asked, 'Do you truly *love* me more than these' (other disciples)? (21:15) but here is the Beloved Disciple 'seeing more than these'.

It is instructive to attempt to identify the factors that may have contributed to the Beloved Disciple's perceptiveness. First, as his designation 'the disciple whom Jesus loved' implies he clearly enjoyed particular close fellowship with Jesus. This is suggested by one of the earliest scenes of the Gospel where the unnamed disciple (who we take to be the Beloved Disciple) and Andrew are keen to spend time with Jesus, anxious to know where he was staying (1:38). We then encounter him reclining next to Jesus at the Last Supper (13:23) and having particular access to Jesus (13:23-25). Some even see in John's reclining 'close to the bosom (*kolpo*) of Jesus' (13:23) an echo of Jesus intimacy with his Father, 'the Son who is in the bosom (*kolpon*) of the Father' (1:18).[7] Most movingly we find the Beloved Disciple alone among the disciples at the foot of the cross where Jesus speaks to him and entrusts his mother's care to him (20:26).

A second possible reason for the Beloved Disciple's ability to be spiritually perceptive was his willingness to be available, not just at Jesus' darkest hour where he witnessed 'a sudden flow of blood and water' (19:34) but also at his initial interrogation by the high priest. Third, and closely linked with this, is the Beloved Disciple's spiritual attentiveness, his ability to be a 'perceptive witness'. Here is the disciple who has not only seen the unfolding events of Christ's ministry but has begun to understand them and, if he is indeed the author of John's Gospel, then the end product is this profoundly insightful text.

The complementary role models of these two disciples is, for me, delightfully captured in the very closing scene of this Gospel. Jesus and Peter are locked in deep discussion as they walk along the beach

---

6   Bradford Blaine, op. cit., 23.

7   Kevin Quast, 'Peter and the Beloved Disciple. Figures for a Community in Crisis' (*Journal for the Study of New Testament* Supplement Series 32, Sheffield, JSOT Press 1989), 58.

(21:18-19). The Beloved Disciple, not to be left out, is trailing some way behind (21:20). It says it all – Peter busy in animated conversation; the Beloved Disciple alone with his own thoughts, Peter ahead of the game in his actions, the Beloved Disciple not lagging behind in his perception. Richard Bauckham well summaries this complementarity:

> In Peter's case the Gospel emphasises his love for Jesus, in the beloved disciple's case it emphasises Jesus' love for him. The former emphasis is appropriate for the active role of discipleship as participation in Jesus activity of serving and sacrificing: it corresponds to Jesus love for his disciples. The latter emphasis is appropriate for the more receptive role of discipleship as witness and corresponds to Jesus's enjoyment of his Father's love.[8]

Active Service with a Still Centre

Though at times we may wish for something of Peter's energy and zeal, more challenging for many of us is our lack of the quiet perceptiveness of the Beloved Disciple. We echo the sentiment of Richard Foster, 'The desperate need today is not for a greater number of intelligent people, or gifted people, but for deep people.'[9] The aim of this chapter is to explore ways of finding a balance between 'being' and 'doing', capturing the best of the characteristics of both the Beloved Disciple and Peter. It is the quest for rhythms of life that allow a truly healthy interweaving of service and solitude, of caring for others and contemplating the 'Other'. Henri Nouwen, employs a suggestive image to combine these two and at the same time places the accent on 'being' before 'doing'. He talks of a sculptor who is constantly looking with great attentiveness at his or her subject and then slowly makes visible what has been observed. Similarly, our calling as disciples and leaders is to keep taking a long, hard look at Christ and then, in ministry, to make him visible to others.[10]

Resources to aid such a quest stretch a long way back. One of the earliest classic texts on pastoral care was written by the 4th century Cappadocian Father, Gregory of Nazianzus (330-389 AD). Gregory was educated in

---

8 Richard Bauckham, op.cit., 38.
9 Richard Foster, *Celebration of Discipline* (London: Hodder and Stoughton 1984), 1.
10 H. Nouwen, *Clowning in Rome: Reflections on Solitude, Celibacy, Prayer and Contemplation* (New York: Doubleday 1979), 87-88. Quoted in Ian Stackhouse, *The Gospel Driven Church* (Paternoster 2004), 231.

Athens but from a young age was deeply attracted to the monastic life. Along with his great friend, Basil of Caesarea, he wanted to set up his own monastery; but on Christmas Day 361 reluctantly he was ordained. Almost immediately he panicked and fled to Pontus to escape his church responsibilities and find a contemplative life! He later recanted, realising he needed to be with his people and wrote *In defence of the flight to Pontus* his moving reflections on the tensions between active service and the need for solitude.

Interestingly, his namesake almost two hundred years later, Pope Gregory the Great (540-604), the last of the popes favoured by John Calvin, had similar struggles and wrote in a similar vein. Born in Rome to a privileged family he too was deeply attracted to an ascetic way of life and struggled to forgo his office as abbot of St Andrew's monastery (Rome) to serve as successor to Pope Pelagius the Second. Though Gregory the Great became deeply committed to his vast pastoral and missionary responsibilities (including the sending of Augustine of Canterbury to evangelise England in 597) he never lost sight of his roots in the monastic tradition. In his famous book on pastoral care *Liber Regulae Pastoralis* (*Book of Pastoral Rule*, 590) he well describes this tension, words that have a remarkably contemporary ring.

> The spiritual director should not reduce his attention to the internal life because of external preoccupations, nor should he relinquish his care for external matters because of his anxiety for the internal life. Otherwise he will either ruin his meditation because he is occupied by external concerns or else he will not give his neighbours what he owes to them because he has devoted himself to the inner life only.[11]

The *via activa* and the *via contemplativa* are never to be played off against one another. (I love the way the monastic reformer Bernard of Clairvaux (1090-1153) emphasised this by talking of Lazarus the penitent, Martha the activist and Mary the contemplative 'all dwelling in the same house.')[12] One of the key discipleship lessons I have learnt over the years, as with the assessment of Peter and the Beloved Disciple, is not to see

---

11 St Gregory the Great, *The Book of Pastoral Rule,* tr. George E. Demacopoulos, (New York: St Vladimir's Seminary Press 2007) 2.7, 68.
12 Quoted in Thomas Merton, *Contemplative Prayer* (Darton, Longman and Todd 1973), 65.

'duty' and 'devotion' as rivals. It is often in the very ordinariness of active service that virtues are strengthened, characters formed and a devotion to Jesus nourished. As we visit the sick, write a card to the lonely, labour over a sermon, compile a committee agenda and rush to the next school assembly something transformative can happen within us.

In large part, of course, this is because caring for others is never just one-way traffic, us 'doing good' to others. Serving others always involves a mutuality, a reciprocal giving and receiving of grace.[13] Thus 'the barrenness of a busy life' (a motto I used to hear often) is not an inevitability. The busyness of kenotic activity can result in immense inner blessing; it can refresh and replenish our souls. Dag Hammarskjold, the first General Secretary of the United Nations (referred to in Chapter One) saw this clearly, 'In our era, the road to holiness necessarily passes through the world of action.'[14]

That said, it is so vital that beneath all the 'noise' of our Christian service there is indeed a still centre, an attentive, listening heart. The fruitful life comes from 'abiding'– an enjoyment of God, a resting in Christ, the healing silence of the Spirit. Henri Nouwen tells of a conversation he had with Mother Teresa asking her for advice. She commented with characteristic simplicity, 'Spend one hour a day in adoration of your Lord and never do anything you know is wrong, and you will be all right.'[15] How often have we sensed that our frenetic activity is more a symptom of our insecurity rather than a gauge of our spiritual stature? How often have we observed a dull colourlessness coming to our work because our lives are no longer immersed in the multi-coloured dye of God's grace?[16] God's first longing is not for our service but for ourselves. As the anonymous author of the *Cloud of Unknowing* (fourteenth century) put it, '(God) is a jealous lover, and will brook no rival; he will not work in your will if he has not sole charge; he does not ask for your help, he asks for you.'[17]

---

13 Stephen Cherry, *Barefoot Discipleship: Walking the Way of Passionate Humility* (Continuum 2011), 160.

14 D. Hammarskjold, *Markings*, quote in R. Foster, *Streams of Living Water* (Trowbridge, Eagle Publishing 1999), 210.

15 Henri J.M. Nouwen, *The Way of the Heart. Desert Spirituality and Contemporary Ministry* (London, Darton, Longman and Todd 1981), 31.

16 1 Peter 4:10.

17 *The Cloud of Unknowing* (Penguin 1961), 52.

I have always been an active, somewhat driven person and developing a still centre has been a constant struggle. Only slowly have I developed my own habits and rhythms. From my early days as a Christian I have always put a high priority on starting each day with quiet, Scripture and prayer. Over the years I have used many resources, liturgical and devotional, but always seeking to listen to God and allow his love to enfold me. For most of the years of ministry I have also carved out time each day for a second daily oasis, this time of theological reading. This has not been related to any sermon preparation and has deeply shaped me. It is based on the conviction that theology, properly understood, is 'engaged contemplation'.[18] It is to develop faith as a 'healthy intellect'.[19] Then, on evenings without meetings I will often try and find time to walk and pray. Routinely I will read a short passage of Scripture, take it on the walk with me and, in a *lectio divina* mode, seek to savour its richness. Sometimes on longer walks I will take my pocket Psalms and New Testament and read a whole epistle or psalm on one walk. I try not to appear too odd to passers-by! For a restless person like me, meditating and praying whilst walking has worked well. I write this chapter during the 2020-21 pandemic. With all the swirling emotions and yet monotony of lockdown to punctuate the day with a morning, noon and evening 'daily office' has much to commend it. Using set prayers at different times of day both accentuates the rhythm of the day's devotions and roots us into something deeper than our present subjective struggles.

Love – the Integrating Centre

The active life and the contemplative life are, however, not just complementary – they both grow from a single root. That root is the love of God. Thomas Aquinas put it beautifully, 'As all the boughs of a tree proceed from one root, so all the virtues are produced from one love, nor has the branch, i.e., the good work, any life, except it abide in the root of love.'[20] Unless God's love in Christ shed abroad by the Holy Spirit is

---

18 Cornelius Ernst, *Multiple Echo* (London 1979), 151 Quoted by John Webster in *Evangel* (October 1983), 8.
19 The phrase is from Herman Bavinck, the Dutch Reformed theologian, quoted in G.C. Berkouwer, *A Half Century of Theology. Movements and Motives,* tr. by Lewis B. Smedes (Eerdmans 1977), 157.
20 Thomas Aquinas, *Catena Aurea,* 4-284 quoted in David F. Ford, *The Gospel of John. A Theological Commentary* (Grand Rapids: Baker Academic 2019), 298.

the deep reservoir that feeds both our public ministries and our personal walk then what God joined together has become seriously separated. A few years ago I had the privilege of visiting Malawi, a beautiful landlocked country in Central Africa dominated by its 300-mile-long Lake Malawi. One day a group of us took off to a remote, poor village about twenty kilometres from Blantyre, gingerly crossing an almost collapsed bridge and navigating huge potholes. To my surprise, when we arrived the whole village turned out to meet us. To my even greater surprise I was suddenly asked to address the joyful assembly, village chief and all! In a moment of panic-induced inspiration I talked about how our restricting of God's love is like the ridiculousness of trying to pour the whole of Lake Malawi into a cooking pot! Thanks to the translator, it gained a smile! It is only when we are convinced of the endless resources of God's love that a smile comes on our ministry. Our vista will always be limited; indeed, before the full extent of that love 'all nature trembles, all scholars are fools, all saints and angels blind.'[21]

At the very heart of John's Gospel is the revelation of the eternal, mutual love of Father and Son. The Father loves the Son (3:35; 5:20; 10:17) and as we dwell in the Son so the Father's love enfolds us. Jesus prays to the Father 'that the love you have for me may be in them and that myself may be in them' (17:26). It is a love that flows out through Jesus to his disciples and so to the world. It is the source of all life and power. No wonder Jude tells us to 'Keep yourselves in God's love.' (Jude 21) I recall one glorious summer evening on the Scottish Island of Colonsay sitting on a coastal rock looking out to the neighbouring islands and enjoying the sun's warmth on my face. As the sun's rays moved on so I kept shuffling along the rock to 'keep myself' in the sun's warmth. That is the purpose of maintaining a still centre to our ministries. We are all 'the disciple whom Jesus loved'[22] and the very heart of our calling is to abide in his love (15:9).

One way of savouring something of this is to reflect on God's sheer *beauty*, a theme prominent in Scripture,[23] and which can be depicted as the

---

21 Cornelius Ernst, op. cit., 70.

22 David Ford, in an informal talk to the Gloucester Diocese (You Tube), suggested that perhaps the very reason the author of the Gospel of John kept the Beloved Disciple anonymous was to invite us all to be that much loved disciple.

23 In the Old Testament there are 13 different Hebrew words which can be translated in English as 'beauty'. There is, for example, a word for the beauty of God's being

outward radiation of God's love. This theme has, for me, become important in seeking to unite a contemplative and active life. I guess my prayer, feeble as it is, echoes that of the Psalmist, 'One thing I ask of the Lord, that is what I seek, that I may dwell in the house of the Lord all the days of my life to behold the beauty of the Lord' (Psalm 27:4). But that prayer to know God's beauty through *contemplation* is also answered through my ordinary, everyday living and *active* service, 'May the beauty of the Lord our God rest upon us; establish the work of our hands for us – yes, establish the work of our hands.' (Psalm 90:17)

Jonathan Edwards (1703-1758) is one of the most famous exponents of this theme. His whole mind and ministry were deeply shaped by the reality of divine beauty. Indeed it marked his very conversion. 'I remember', he writes in his *Personal Narrative*, 'the thought I used to have of holiness . . . It appeared to me that there was nothing in it but what was ravishingly lovely; the highest beauty and amiableness – a divine beauty.'[24] He was constantly enchanted with the beauty of the natural world, seeing it as an image and reflection of the Creator's own beauty. But far more than that, he saw all God's perfections and redemptive purposes as utterly beautiful. 'Beauty' is not just one attribute among the many of the perfections of God, but God is beauty itself, the very foundation and fountain of all beauty. It is, for him, a key interpretive tool for all that God has done in creation, providence and redemption and all that God calls us to be in our moral response.[25]

Similar, two centuries later, is the emphasis of Hans Urs von Balthasar (1905-1988), the Swiss Catholic theologian who wrote a massive seven volume work entitled *The Glory of the Lord. A Theological Aesthetic'*. 'Beauty is the word that shall be our first', he wrote. In a strikingly parallel way to Edwards, Balthasar viewed beauty, along with truth and goodness, as one of the fundamental 'transcendentals' grounded in the very being of God. Bravely he went on to explore how such beauty is to be understood in the face of the ugliness of the cross. He argues that beauty at its highest is expressed as passionate, personal self-giving love and indeed that God's

---

(used in the famous phrase 'the beauty of holiness') the beauty of the human form, the beauty of dress and jewellery.

24 Jonathan Edwards, *A Personal Narrative* (Works 1:16).

25 Ronald Andre Delattre, *Beauty and Sensibility in the Thought of Jonathan Edwards. An Essay in Aesthetics and Theological Ethics.* Wipf & Stock Publishers, Eugene Oregon 2006 (previously published Yale University Press 1968), 117.

beauty can never be understood apart from God's love demonstrated at Calvary. Such divine beauty radically critiques all worldly perceptions of beauty.[26]

These themes move me. They draw me into praise and they energise me for mission. The beauty of God's love is to be the root of both our contemplative worship and our active witness. As Edwards writes, 'God's bringing the world into such beautiful form out of chaos without form and void typifies his bringing the spiritual world to such divine excellency and beauty after the confusion, deformity and ruin of sin.'[27] The biblical message is not so much a set of propositions to be 'ticked' as a reality that fires our imagination, stirs our hearts and humbles our pride. What could be more inspiring for weary disciples and church leaders than to both glimpse something of such beauty and experience a touch of it as we seek to bring healing and hope to our communities?

Underlying Rhythms

The natural world is alive with rhythmic movement. The Creator's pulse is to be felt wherever we turn. From the daily rise and setting of the sun to the wonder of annual bird migration and the circadian rhythms of our own bodies, God's drumbeat is ingrained in the world he made. Many years ago, as a somewhat enthusiastic zoology student, I kept beadlet sea anemones in tanks in my bedroom! I was fascinated by their diurnal rhythm, 'remembering' to open up to feed at the times the tides would have come in even though the water was now still! We too were made for rhythm. The key to an integrated life of prayer and perspiration is to nurture healthy patterns. Though hardly a great self-disciplinarian, I have found that developing a regularity to basic Christian practices has been essential.

I have already referred to a daily devotional routine. Another is the importance of keeping a Sabbath, a day off simply to unwind, rest, enjoy God's world and pause to regain perspective. It is the day we deliberately 'take our hands off' to affirm the truth that 'unless the Lord builds the house its builders labour in vain.' (Psalm 127:1). For those involved in 'full-time' Christian service this can rarely be a Sunday. For me Tuesday has

---

26 Stephen Fields, 'The Beauty of the Ugly: Balthasar, the Crucifixion, Analogy and God', *International Journal of Theology*, (9-10, 2007-08), 172.

27 Edwards, *Miscellany*, 479.

worked well, allowing Monday to be a day to follow-up urgent matters from the day before. Eugene Peterson puts it strongly when he says, 'The single act of keeping a Sabbath does more than anything else to train pastors in the rhythm of action and response so that the two sets of demands are experienced synchronically instead of violently.'[28]

Annual rhythm is also important. The shape of the Jewish year has a vibrancy to it with its festivals and fasting, its times of looking back and its seasons of thanksgiving, climaxing on the Day of Atonement. The narrative of John's Gospel is very much shaped by these festivals. In similar fashion, the Christian calendar offers important resources, shaping not just our corporate worship but our personal spiritual journey. I have found Lent an ideal time to re-read a whole Gospel and enjoy a residential retreat. I tend to read a fresh theological text over Easter and look forward to re-reading Acts in the weeks after Pentecost. I enjoy reflecting on hope in Advent and am increasingly convinced that Ascension Day is a much neglected festival.

The Outcome: the Attentive Life

What the differing responses of Peter and the Beloved Disciple had in common was that they were both *attentive*; the Beloved Disciple expectant of the Stranger's voice, Peter alert to the specialness of the moment. The attentiveness of contemplation leads to the watchfulness of seizing the opportunity. Peace and clarity walk hand in hand. Discipleship, says Rowan Williams, is 'a state of awareness'. I love his image of the prayerful disciple being like an experienced birdwatcher 'sitting very still because something is liable to burst into view'.[29] A life of discernment does not come through attending a course or reading a book but gradually, through the slow, habitual practice of sitting (as it were) very still in the hide, binoculars trained, camera on its tripod, guidebook at hand – waiting, watching and then responding in line with what God reveals. The Beloved Disciple was the alert birdwatcher and Peter the responsive cameraman who shot into action. Someone had indeed burst into view.

---

28 E.H. Peterson, *Working the Angles. The Shape of Pastoral Integrity* (Grand Rapids: Eerdmans 1987), 66.
29 Rowan Williams, *Being Disciples* (SPCK 2016), 3 and 4.

Chapter Five

Hauling the Net Ashore: Resourcing a Missional Community

Simon Peter climbed aboard and dragged the net ashore.
It was full of large fish, 153.   (John 21:11)

Fishermen love to count! To my regular amusement here in the Scottish Border town where I now live, each week on the local hotel noticeboard is an announcement of the Selkirk Angling Association's 'best catch of the week'. As a fisherman I read it avidly – it really is that important! Simon Peter, who alone seems to have dragged the net ashore, now contemplates the catch. It's not difficult to imagine him, momentarily forgetting his heavy heart, eagerly counting out the fish and, with boyish glee, announcing to the world . . . 150, 151, 152 . . . (dramatic pause) . . . 153. A loud corporate cheer from the other six disciples! The number 153 has caused endless fascination with commentators over the centuries. It is an intriguing number, being a triangular number (in this case the sum of all the numbers from 1 to 17) and many therefore conclude it has some subtle symbolic meaning. A simpler reading is to view it as an authentic eye witness account;[1] a miraculous and therefore a memorable catch.

What seems unmissable is that this overall image of Peter hauling in a bulging net and counting out 153 prime specimens is a promissory sign of the missionary abundance that was to come. Whereas the miraculous signs of the first twenty chapters of John's Gospel all point to the significance of Jesus, here the miracle points more to the

---

1   Raymond Brown, *The Gospel According to John*. Anchor Bible, Vol. 2, (London: Geoffrey Chapman 1966), 1076.

fruitfulness to be experienced by the disciples.[2] It echoes Ezekiel's vision of a miraculous flow of water from the Temple transforming the Dead Sea into fresh water teaming with 'a large number of fish' (Ezekiel 47:9).

In fact, the *whole* of John 21 is deeply missional. This Gospel, which opens with such christological richness, the Word who is one with the Father and sent from the Father (John 1:14), now ends with the implications of all this for mission as spelt out in momentous words of Jesus in John 20:21, 'As the Father has sent me, I am sending you'. Indeed Michael Gorman, who sees the entire Gospel of John 'permeated with a missional ethos', argues, 'John 21 is best seen, not as an epilogue, but as a summary of the Gospel's missionary spirituality and a peroration to remain faithful to the mission of Jesus in dependence on him'.[3] Here Peter's 'drawing in the net' (the Greek verb *helko*) resonates with John 6:44, 'No one can come to me unless the Father who sent me *draws* him' and 12:32, 'But I, when I am lifted up from the earth, will *draw* all people to myself'.[4] The whole scene is an acted parable of mission.

Peter – Fisherman, Apostle, Mission Enabler

Early that morning on the beach Peter may have been the solitary lander of fish but he was to become a key apostolic enabler of mission for so many. It is deeply ironic that in Christian tradition there has been such focus on the authoritarian successors of Peter (the Bishops of Rome), whereas the New Testament witness is that his true legacy was that of a shaper of communities. His original calling to be 'a fisher of people' involved far more than bringing individuals to faith in Christ. It involved 'hauling in the shoals' – bringing whole communities to missional maturity particularly in the Jewish milieu.

Like the rest of the Twelve Peter had shared the privilege of a unique apprenticeship in mission and community empowerment. For three years he had imbibed Jesus teaching and witnessed him at work. He had seen

---

2   Richard Bauckham, 'The 153 Fish and the Unity of the Fourth Gospel', *Neot* 36 (2002) 77-88.

3   Michael J. Gorman, *Abide and Go. Missional Theosis in the Gospel of John*. The Didsbury Lectures 2016 (Eugene, Oregon: Cascade Books 2018), 147.

4   Bradford B. Blaine Jr, 'The verb *helko* is well suited in the Fourth Gospel for describing missionary work.' *Peter in the Gospel of John. The Making of an Authentic Disciple* (Atlanta: Society of Biblical Literature 2007), 155.

how Jesus had unhurried time for individuals. He had been a key part of how Jesus trained and bonded the Twelve and Seventy in mission. No doubt still fresh in Peter's mind was the recent Upper Room teaching (John 13-17) described by Gorman as 'a missional discourse'.[5] Now, as Peter hauls in the net and counts out the fish, all this training was about to come to fruition. The gift of the Spirit at Pentecost was to make it possible. Peter, however, was not just to become the *solo* preacher, pioneer missionary and heroic martyr; rather, from the very beginning he oversaw and empowered others.[6] He wrote later in life about 'each one using whatever gifts they have received to serve others'.[7] Peter modelled mission *enabling*.

The analysis of many is that the focus of contemporary mission *leadership* needs to shift radically. This involves recognising that *directional* leadership now has limited value. Society is changing at too fast a pace for individuals to discern accurately. Far more effective is the facilitator, the cultivator, the enabler – the person who has the grace, listening capacity and coordination skills to allow each member of a congregation to contribute to an understanding of how God wants to guide the church in mission.

It is so often the members, not the leaders, who have a clear perspective on the key local missional challenges and opportunities. Alan Roxburgh, the Canadian missiologist, puts it well: 'we need leaders with the capacity to cultivate an environment that releases the missional imagination of the people of God.'[8] He argues that there must not just be organisational change within the church but a change of *culture*. It involves a transformation of the prevailing attitude from being 'please sign up to our latest project' (and mission projects and events certainly have their place) to 'please *all of us* pray, dream, share, experiment and help us together be the people God wants us *to be*.' This requires not less but more leadership skill and certainly requires more inner security. This is the theme to be explored in this chapter.

A 'Proper Confidence' in the Gospel

Foundational to all mission-enabling is the shared conviction that the good news of Jesus has divine power to save. In Peter's Pentecost sermon,

---

5   Op. cit., 81.
6   Acts 2:42-47.
7   1 Peter 4:10.
8   Alan J. Roxburgh and Fred Romanuk, *The Missional Leader. Equipping your Church to Reach a Changing World* (Jossey-Bass 2006), 21.

having spoken of the death and resurrection of Jesus, he concludes with consummate assurance, 'Therefore let all Israel be assured of this: God has made this Jesus both Messiah and Lord'.[9] Starting here is important because, for all our evangelical credentials, I have come to the conclusion that it is all too easy to lose confidence in the unique transforming potential of the gospel. What, for example, underlies the constant tendency, which I detect in myself, to have my head turned by the latest ecclesial band-wagon? This can be a fresh model of church, an innovative approach to ministry, an episode of revival or a new success story from church planters.

A clear distinction needs to be made between mission flexibility, something so needed, and mission trendiness, a constant temptation. I fear that sometimes the constant desire for something new is a tell-tale sign that the prime locus of authority and the very wellspring of our life, namely God's gospel, is not quite as central as we like to imagine. Ian Stackhouse, in identifying such worrying 'faddism', comments, 'No longer fuelled by, or confident of, the power of the gospel itself, the Pelagian temper becomes all too apparent as the church wearies itself with yet another strategy.'[10]

A number of years ago I had the privilege of speaking at a missionary conference in Thailand. On the opening day, as delegates gathered from all over Asia, I remember being gripped with a deep sense of inadequacy. What had I to say to such an experienced and gifted gathering? Just before the opening session a tall, confident man introduced himself. He and his wife were serving in Nepal. He said 'Andrew, this conversation is really twenty years too late but there is something I want you to know. Twenty years ago I visited your church in Newcastle with my then girlfriend. That Sunday morning was the first time the gospel really made sense. I had a powerful encounter with Christ. Thank you.'

It was both a timely encouragement and a humbling jolt. What was I doing being so preoccupied with *my* inadequacy? When was I ever going to be adequate – or wise or original? What new thing had I come all this way to offer? My only calling was to be a faithful steward of God's truth found in Christ. P.T. Forsyth put it with characteristic pungency, 'The truest things you will say are those things that have already been said many

9 Acts 2:36.
10 Ian Stackhouse, *The Gospel Driven Church. Retrieving Classical Ministry for Contemporary Revivalism* (Paternoster 2004), 16.

times, but they are still the most original. Grace is the most original thing in the world.'[11] Quite so.

Such gospel confidence includes the conviction that this good news is not just for individuals but is the power that can re-imagine, transform and reconstitute families, communities and nations – a foretaste of the end when creation itself will be made new. It is the gospel that finds its true roots in God's covenant promise to Abraham that 'all peoples of the earth will be blessed through you.'[12] Through the particularity of God's gracious calling to one founding patriarch, to one nation and ultimately to one Saviour, a universal promise is offered. It lays claim to every sphere of life. Jesus is the Redeemer of the political arena as much as the personal; the Redeemer of education, the art and sciences and media as much as church life; the Redeemer of Eastern culture as much as Western culture. As such the gospel involves a proclamation and demonstration of salvation expansive enough to embrace issues of justice, creation care, peace-making and community building.

Perhaps no one in our day has argued this more persuasively than the mission scholar, Bishop Lesslie Newbigin (1909-1998). When he returned to the U.K after forty years of missionary service in South India he was taken aback with how timid and intimidated he found the church. His great plea was for a 'proper confidence' in the gospel.[13] In his subsequent analysis of what has shaped Western culture he particularly highlighted the fatal Enlightenment distinction between undisputed 'facts' and chosen 'private values', and that the gospel had been relegated to the latter. This he vigorously disputed. No facts, scientific or otherwise, are value free. Whether it is acknowledged or not, all empirical 'facts' are based on presuppositions. In turn, the gospel is far more than an expression of religious values; it is, he asserted, 'public truth'. Like all truth it is based

---

11 Harry Escott, *P.T Forsyth and the Cure of Souls. An Anthology* (George Allen and Unwin 1948), 134.

12 Genesis 12:3.

13 Lesslie Newbigin, *Proper Confidence: Faith, Doubt and Certainty in Christian Discipleship* (Grand Rapids: Eerdmans 1995). 'The confidence proper to a Christian is not the confidence of one who claims possession of demonstrable and indubitable knowledge. It is the confidence of one who has heard and answered the call that comes from the God through whom and for whom all things were made: "Follow me".' 105.

on presuppositions but precisely because the momentous presupposition here is One who is 'the Way, the Truth, the Life', it lays claim over the whole of existence. The 'real world' is not the world 'out there' with its stories, assumptions and worldviews. The true frame of reference is God's revelation in the whole narrative sweep of Scripture from creation to consummation, all centred on Christ. It is what Newbigin provocatively termed 'universal history'. He pressed the point:

> The question is whether the faith that finds its focus in Jesus is the faith with which we seek to understand the whole of history or whether we limit this faith to a private world of religion and hand over the public history of the world to other principles of explanation.[14]

How I need to be reminded of all this! As I read the opinion columns, as I listen to impressive TED Talks and podcasts, as powerful thinkers write and speak so persuasively and plausibly, I have to keep asking, 'How does the Bible story centred on Jesus challenge the underlying assumptions here?' How do I 'take every thought and make it captive to Christ'?[15] How do I embody this Good News in my approach to the workplace, my relationships, my finances, my community involvement, my reaction to the news, my voting?

Tasting Grace Each Day

Equally essential for mission enabling is experiencing the daily reality of this gospel in our own lives. Without it there will be obligation but not an overflowing. A central, shaping motif of John's Gospel is the theme of *witness,* the verb 'to witness' occurring thirty-three times. Our primary mission is to be able to offer fresh, up-to-date witness to the presence of the Kingdom of God among us in word and deed. Unless each new day we taste anew the sheer generosity of God we will never truly operate with the joy and urgency that today really is 'the day of salvation'.[16] The prophet Jonah struggled with his missionary calling not primarily because of his prejudiced and nationalistic mind-set but because he had a shrunken heart. He had to experience salvation all over again, in the form of a very

---

14 Lesslie Newbigin, *Foolishness to the Greeks. The Gospel and Western Culture* (SPCK 1986), 61.

15 2 Corinthians 10:5.

16 2 Corinthians 6:2.

watery three-day rescue, for his heart to be expansive enough for cross-cultural mission.

What is true for us as individuals must also be true for the wider church community. Unless there is a continuing conversion of the church in the form of ongoing formation and deep moments of transformation then mission will always remain programmatic and not a matter of joyful, spontaneous witness. Nowhere is this necessity more eloquently expressed than here in John's Gospel. All mission activity flows from a participation in the very life and love of the Triune God which reaches out to our lost world. John's Gospel is all about a missional spirituality. Arguably it is the greatest need of the contemporary church.

Many years ago I had a somewhat puzzling encounter with the Holy Spirit which I have often reflected on. John Wimber, the founder of the Vineyard Churches, was leading his first UK Church Leaders' Conference in Sheffield, 1985. A few thousand of us were present and there was a palpable sense of God's presence among us. At one point John Wimber invited all of us to stand and then explained, in his warm and relaxed style, that he was going to read out the five-fold offices of Ephesians 4: 11 – apostles, prophets, evangelists, pastors, teachers – and invite the Holy Spirit, in whatever way he chose, to confirm our particular calling.

It was this sort of simple, daring and expectant tone that marked the whole two days. For some reason he read the fivefold offices in a different order and when he read out 'pastor' I experienced nothing (to my slight alarm!) But when he read out 'evangelist' something unexpected happened. I found my undemonstrative-self gently crying with deep sobs and not a little embarrassment for a good twenty minutes! In fact a counsellor came up to ask if I needed help. They were not, however, tears of personal sadness. I actually felt strangely at peace and inwardly composed. My best explanation to date has been that it was a privileged and momentary entering into something deeper of the love and pain of the Triune God for his broken world. I have never considered myself 'an evangelist' and still do not but that experience refocussed my conviction that without a *passionate* missional dimension to leadership something is seriously amiss.

Recreating Credible Communities

Though the power of the gospel has not changed what is abundantly clear is that the mission topography of the UK is today almost unrecognisable from that of forty years ago. It is not just that Christian values have been slowly eroded and a Christian heritage eclipsed; it is that deep and jagged fault-lines have appeared between Christian claims and contemporary culture. For most of us, we are now seeking to reach local people who not only have had no Christian influence for at least two generations but who have inhaled a deep and toxic suspicion of all religious claims. Professor Steve Bruce, the sociologist of religion, recently summed up the state of play in the U.K., 'the typical Briton has gone from church-going Christian, to nominal Christian, to non-Christian who nevertheless thinks religion (in the abstract at least) is a good thing, to being someone who supposes that religion does more harm than good.'[17]

Christianity, for most in our culture, is now not only an odd but a problematic relic of the past. The institutional church is simply viewed as an indulgent ghetto for those too afraid to face the pluralism of our age. The idea of somehow being able to tap into people's latent Christian sympathies is today a pipedream. The percentage of the UK population who reply 'none' when asked about their religious affiliations has grown from just three percent in 1963 to 44.7 percent by 2015 and among adults 25 and under the figure is nearly two-thirds.[18]

Liam Fraser, a Church of Scotland minister, has argued persuasively that what has essentially collapsed is the *plausibility* of the Christian church and its claims. No longer does the culture around us legitimise Christianity.[19] Any societal affirmation and appreciation of Christian values, practices and institutions has long gone. Our credibility has drastically eroded. Yet, he points out that, at the same time, all around us are signs of a deep longing for meaning and a fascination with what authentic spirituality could look like. It leads to the phenomenon that unchurched folk are far more open than the de-churched.

The trauma of the recent pandemic has only heightened this quest by shaking peoples' previous certainties. Liam Fraser's great plea is that, in

---

17 Steve Bruce, *British Gods: Religion in Modern Britain* (Oxford: Oxford University Press 2020), 270.

18 As quoted in James Emery White, *Meet Generation Z. Understanding and Reaching the New Post-Christian World* (Grand Rapids: Baker Books 2017), 27 From a 2015 British Election Study of 20,000 people.

19 Liam J. Fraser, *Mission in Contemporary Scotland* (St Andrew Press 2021), xiv.

all this, our most urgent missional task is to create afresh 'local cultures of plausibility', that is, ways of being church which in their very simplicity and authenticity make faith in Jesus Christ easier, not harder! I'm sure he is right; we need to be plausible before we can be audible.

Missional Attentiveness

If it is true that all mission is God's mission – that the initiative, creativity and empowering are all his – then the only logical response is to give ourselves to a careful discerning of where God's Spirit is at work. Innovation is about more than being relevant; it is about being sensitive and obedient. Thus a key component of mission enabling is aiding our congregations to practice true attentiveness to God. As the church in the West declines, one of our great dangers is panic, leading to a frenetic mission hyper-activity and, by so doing, missing what the Spirit of God is actually wanting to say. The late David Watson was making this very point when he commented, 'Evangelism in the church today is often hindered, not through the laziness of Christians but through the busyness of Christians in the wrong direction.'[20] Peter on the beach was soon to be Peter (with John) encountering a crippled man outside one of the temple gates in Jerusalem.[21] Significantly, they were on their way to afternoon prayers and had come from a community devoted to prayer.[22] It seems that it was precisely because of such prayerfulness that they were able to sense that they should not just offer the expected almsgiving to this beggar (true, they had 'no change' but the early church had a fellowship fund on which they could have drawn.)[23] Rather they sensed they should speak good news in the name of Jesus, 'Rise up and walk'. Ray Anderson in his book *The Soul of Ministry* comments, 'Discernment is the sensory organ of love, registering the feelings of those who are broken and seeking the glue of grace.'[24]

It cannot be stressed enough that such prayerful attentiveness is one of the most crucial ways a missional community is formed. It is about helping each other to see the spaces we inhabit through Christ's eyes; living as

20 David Watson, *I believe in Evangelism* (London: Hodder and Stoughton 1976), 178.
21 Acts 3:2.
22 Acts 2:42.
23 Acts 2:45.
24 Ray S. Anderson, '*The Soul of Ministry. Forming Leaders for God's People* (Louisville, Kentucky: Westminster, John Knox Press 1997), 216.

spiritually sensitive, critically-discerning disciples in the world. Not too long ago some of our family enjoyed a pre-Christmas break to New York. We enjoyed the lights, the ice rinks, the crazily busy restaurants, the festive crowds. But my wife and I also felt the shallowness, the secularity, even the strange loneliness of it all. One evening, on the way back to our hotel, we suddenly spotted the *Times Square Church* founded by Dave Wilkerson of *Cross and the Switchblade* fame and to our delight discovered a prayer meeting in progress. We joined a prayer gathering of about a thousand! After some led prayers from the front, the choir leader started singing the simple worship chorus:

> We are standing on holy ground;
> For I know there are angels all around.
> Let us praise Jesus now.
> For we are standing in His presence on holy ground.

I found myself deeply moved. Here I was in Times Square, this glittering icon of global secularity, yet actually 'standing on holy ground.' Prayer is the opening of our eyes to see the tracks and traces of God's Spirit in the most secular of haunts.

In St Andrews a fresh ministry to Eastern European fruit-farm workers began through no planning of our own. God simply led the church, through a 'chance' Sunday lunch conversation, to work alongside a delightful Christian Romanian family employed on a nearby fruit-farm with nearly 300 migrant workers. It resulted in a whole wave of new openings for the gospel. We found ourselves being invited to offer English lessons and to host welcome ceilidhs, football tournaments and yes, outdoor worship times. It is the Holy Spirit who is the primary agent in mission, the only one who has the power to lead us to the people of peace, to open doors, convict of sin and bring new birth. As Jesus said, 'When the Advocate comes, whom I will send to you from the Father – the Spirit of truth who goes out from the Father – he will testify about me' (15:26). Only secondarily are we witnesses, 'And you also must testify' (16:27).

Adaptable and Experimental

Attentiveness to God and the context in which he has placed us must inevitably lead to missional flexibility. Mission enabling is about supporting

God's pilgrim people on an unknown journey. I have long been persuaded that all pastoral ministry today is about *transitioning*; we are either about planting a church *de novo*, or we about helping a church to change to be a truly credible and missional community. It will be messy, exhausting, conflict-generating – and exhilarating! I still remember seeking to convince a group of church leaders of the value of a cell-church model only to have a bemused consultant doctor whisper in my ear 'rogue cells inevitably produce antibodies!' One of the strange paradoxes of ministry is that, on the one hand our calling is to be a non-anxious presence in the midst of a world of change whilst, on the other hand, our role is prophetically to agitate for transition.

The great danger of all 'recommended' models and strategies for mission is that though they can provide invaluable clues they never offer a clear pathway. The profile of the congregation as well as the profile of the context means that there are too many variables for a simple missional equation. Beginning a new church plant in a dormitory area, for example, with a highly mobile middle-class group of people (who rarely spent significant time at home) is going to look very different to establishing a new work in a settled isolated rural community. Every congregation needs to find its own unique calling. Mission enabling will involve calming fears about 'failed' experiments and missional U-turns. To walk in step with the Spirit does not imply military precision.[25]

Simple Friendship and Hospitality

'As the Father has sent me, so (i.e. in the same way) I am sending you' (20:21) is perhaps the most defining mission statement of John's Gospel. Mission for us, as for Jesus, is incarnational. Just as God became one-with-us in Christ, so only in vulnerable solidarity with the real life struggles of those all around us will our witness ever be credible. Having friends is the most natural and obvious way this happens. But this raises a crucial issue. Too often we have lost the conviction that friendship is a central Christian practice. The sheer effort and skill of making friends has become something

---

25 I am indebted to Dr Hans Riphagen of the Netherlands for the insights of this paragraph in a webinar – https://scottishbaptistcollege.org/event/church-in-the-neighbourhood.

of a rare art.[26] To befriend merely to gain a hearing for the gospel is to reduce friendship to a vehicle rather than a virtue. For Aristotle genuine friendship was more than affection, (someone *we like*) and certainly more than someone who is *useful* to us; it was a moral commitment to the good of those around us.[27] Even more so in Christian terms, friendship must be conceived in non-utilitarian ways. Friendship with our 'neighbours' must arise simply because we see them as those valued and loved by God; it should certainly not be conditional on them showing an interest in our Christian beliefs. As is often commented on, but too rarely heeded, church life can become so all-consuming that there is precious little time to nourish real friendships, simply for friendship's-sake. It is one of the areas where I have failed most.

Related to this is the importance of hospitality. Again Christian hospitality is not to be seen primarily for mission purposes but simply because the welcome of strangers is a mark of the godly life, an imitating of a generous and hospitable God.[28] In each of the four gospels most of Jesus' key conversations occurred in homes and hospitality was undoubtedly a key component in the early spread of the gospel.[29] Whilst second nature in the non-western world, a lack of a natural and unconditional welcome in our homes is, arguably, one of the most significant impediments to the spread of the gospel in the West. Mission enabling, if anything, is about modelling and promoting welcome and warmth in our homes and at our tables.[30]

It is also about simply blessing whole communities, the importance of which many are discovering. As a local church last Christmas we decided to offer boxes of biscuits and chocolates to the local retailers as a simple way of saying we were thinking of them in the present hard times. Their surprise and gratitude was refreshing.

---

26 Lina Toth, *Friendship in Christian Practice: Personal, Communal, Missional*. Paper given at *Theology Live*, Jan 29th 2021. She suggests that the classic Aristotelian virtue of friendship, *philia*, was slowly lost sight of in the church through its being eclipsed by a focus on *agape*.

27 Alasdair MacIntyre, *After Virtue, a Study in Moral Theory* (Duckworth, Second Edition 1985), 156.

28 Deuteronomy 10:9.

29 Michael Green, *Evangelism in the Early Church*. (London: Hodder and Stoughton 1970). 'The sheer informality and relaxed atmosphere of the home, not to mention the hospitality which must have often gone with it, all helped to make this form of evangelism particularly successful.' 250.

30 1 Timothy 3:2; Titus 1:8.

Resourcing the Frontline

The critical action of missional communities happens, not in church, but at the school gate, in the coffee shop, during office hours, with the walking group, on the rugby training ground. The whole emphasis of 'resourcing our frontline' (the place where each of us encounters our non-Christians contacts) is so vital.[31] It involves modelling to others how our broken lives can touch the broken lives of others. Mission the Jesus way is time-consuming, respectful, costly, exhausting, risk-taking and practical. It is as people are intrigued by a *sense* of something different that they become open to an exploration of the *source* of that difference. Kingdom saltiness leads to thirst in others.

In John's Gospel it was the 'signs' of the Kingdom that allowed the 'secret' of the Kingdom to be made known. I recall a young single mum, estranged from an abusive partner, attracted by a friend's simple kindness. Only after months of growing, patient friendship did she slowly and nervously dip in to our morning worship. When she did, to her surprise and embarrassment, she invariably filled up with tears. She later concluded it was because she was encountering, in her words, 'a different sort of love, the like of which I have never experienced before'. As John puts it in his letter, 'No one has ever seen God; but if we love one another, God lives in us and his love is made complete in us.'[32]

One of the best things we ever did as a church in Edinburgh was when we broke the congregation up (after a church lunch) into vocational groups, including homemakers, child carers and retired, and asked them to identify their key discipleship challenges and their key opportunities for witness. It made an important point. Mission enablers need to model this. I admire colleagues who, more routinely than I have ever done, intentionally meet congregational members in their work place to talk and pray about pressures and opportunities. The church has traditionally been good at supporting Christians in the caring professions but support for those in the media, in politics and law, in education, in the arts, in technology and in social care is now critical. James Hunter Davison's conclusion to his book *To Change the World* is salutary:

---

31 Cf. the excellent material of the London Institute of Contemporary Christianity, Mark Greene, *Fruitfulness on the Frontline. Making a Difference Where You Are* (IVP 2014).
32 1 John 4:12.

Against the prevailing view, the main reason why Christian believers today (from various communities) have not had the influence in the culture to which they have aspired is not that they don't believe enough, or try hard enough, or care enough, or think Christianly enough, or have the right worldview, but rather *because they have been absent from the arenas in which the greatest influence in the culture is exerted.*[33]

A key part of our task as mission enabling leaders is therefore to pray specifically and intelligently for all the vocations of our congregation. Writing in this context, Richard Neuhaus lays down the challenge, 'The ministry of intercession is an integral part of our own pursuit of holiness, and is *the clearest evidence of our faith in the complementarity of all vocations* within the Body of Christ.[34]

Local and Global

One of the oft mentioned explanations of the 153 fish is that ancient zoologists believed there were a total of 153 species of fish in the oceans and thus is symbolic of the universality of mission. The idea largely stems from St Jerome (342–420 AD), who claimed that the long poem on fishing, *Halieutica*, by the second century Greco-Roman poet Oppian of Cilicia makes this point. In fact Jerome was inaccurate, Oppian listed 157 known species![35] However, what does seem plausible, given that 153 is a triangular number, the sum of all numbers from 1 to 17 (and indeed made up of 7 and 10 both symbols of completion) is that the number is meant to convey the global breadth of Christian mission.[36] Be that as it may, the Great Commission for Peter and all the church was to 'go and make disciples of *all* nations.' Local and global mission are one, there being a powerful synergism between the two. Effective mission enablers are aware of this. It is true for at least two reasons.

First, all mission today, local as well as overseas, is cross-cultural. It is increasingly the case that, as our society becomes more and more distant

---

33 James Davison Hunter, *To Change the World. The Irony, Tragedy and Possibility of Christianity in the late Modern World* (Oxford University Press 2010), 89. Italics as in the text.

34 Richard John Neuhaus, *Freedom for Ministry* (Grand Rapids: Eerdmans 1979), 236. Italics mine.

35 Raymond E. Brown, op. cit., 1074.

36 Ibid., 1075.

from its Christian heritage, basic mission skills abroad are vital here: careful and humble listening, learning to speak a different 'language', feeling vulnerable and disempowered, and finding common ground. One of the very happy consequences of the fruit-farm ministry to Eastern Europeans in St Andrews, mentioned earlier, was that it went hand-in-hand with a growing partnership with a Baptist church in Alexandria, Romania. Our visits there, seeing God at work in a very different context, were deeply energising. Second, though less tangible, there is something about the very nature of cross-cultural partnerships that deeply pleases the heart of the One who, in Christ, has brought about a new humanity. God's pleasure becomes ours. I have experienced global mission involvement reversing compassion fatigue.

The Bottom Line

I end on a note of pastoral realism; something rarely named but essential to be faced. The ultimate cause of mission lethargy lies not with a lack of confidence, credibility or creativity but with the church being 'curved in on itself', an ecclesial version of *cor incurvatum in se* as Luther termed it. Dietrich Bonhoeffer, with his Lutheran heritage, saw this with great clarity.[37] The God revealed to us in Jesus Christ is a God of utterly self-giving love. God is present in the very suffering, solidarity-with-the-marginalised and humiliation of Jesus Christ. The whole of Christ's life as the man-for-others decisively reveals the very nature of God. To share in God's life in Christ is thus to participate in a journey of transformation where all our human relationships become other-focussed. The sheer, unchallenged *self-absorption* of much of our congregational life is frightening. To share in his church, the very Body of Christ, is never to be part of a self-protecting institution, but truly to be part of a-community-for-others. All resourcing for mission is vacuous without this understanding at the very centre.

As Peter hauled in the miraculous catch of fish, excited again to be at the bidding of Jesus, his own self-absorption was re-orientated. Mission can only ever happen as Jesus Christ, by his Spirit, frees us from our profound preoccupations.

---

37 See the essay 'Death Together. Dietrich Bonhoeffer on Becoming the Church for Others', Joel D. Lawrence in *Bonhoeffer, Christ and Culture*, eds. Keith L Johnson and Timothy Larsen (Nottingham: Apollos 2013), 113-129.

Chapter Six

The Net that Never Broke: a Passion for Unity

**It was full of large fish, 153, but even so with so many
the net was not torn   (John 21:11)**

It is often difficult to know how 'theologically playful' the author of
John's Gospel is being. As with the tantalising note of 153 fish, is this
accompanying comment that 'the net was not torn' also meant to be
suggestive? The net being referred to was a large casting net (*diktuon*)
not the smaller seine net used by individual fishermen. Such casting
nets were delicate and liable to tear, not least when dragged up the
shore. The fact it did not rip was thus something quite unusual, a detail
that would be both memorable and suggest significance. It stands in
marked contrast to the miracle recorded in Luke where, after a similar
remarkable catch of fish, 'their nets began to break' (Luke 5:6).

So what is John expressing here? Could it be pointing to the
importance of future church unity as well as mission? What gives some
credence to this suggestion is that the Greek word *schizein* (torn) is
related to the word *schisma* (division), a word prominent in this Gospel
for the division of people into factions over Jesus (7:43; 9:16; 10:19).[1]
The word is also used by John when the soldiers under the cross decide
not to tear (*schizomen*) Jesus' undergarment. John comments, 'This
garment was seamless, woven in one piece from top to bottom' (19:23).
From Cyprian onwards (the third century bishop of Carthage), this
observation has often been interpreted as an evocative symbol of the
unity of the church.

---

1   R.E Brown, *The Gospel According to John*. The Anchor Bible (London:
Geoffrey Chapman 1966), 1097.

Few things dismay a fisherman more than a gaping hole in his net! Yet, sadly, the same pain is often not felt by church leaders when the torn net of disunity is encountered (particularly *between* churches). Evangelical tribalism and ecumenical indifference are too often the accepted norm. Our propensity to label one another, to be suspicious of each other, to decide who is 'in' and who is 'out' is endemic. In the sharpest of contrasts, for John's Gospel the unity of God's flock was central to Jesus mission, 'there shall be one flock and one shepherd' (10:16). Similarly, commenting on Caiaphas' expediency, 'It is better for you that one man die for the people' John reflects, 'He prophesied that Jesus would die for the Jewish nation and not only for that nation but also for the scattered people of God, to bring them together and make them one' (11:52). It was the focus too of Jesus' passionate prayer on the eve of his crucifixion, 'May they (all believers) be brought to complete unity to let the world know that you sent me' (17:23). Just as the saving work of Father and Son is always seen as *one and the same* movement of grace in John's Gospel, so our mission which flows from theirs must be characterised by our own unison.

The Cape Town Commitment of the Lausanne Movement, in October 2010, described Christian unity as both a 'fact' and a 'mandate' and went on starkly to declare, 'A divided church has no message for a divided world.' More fully it went on to say, 'Our love for the Church of God aches with grief over the ugliness among us that so disfigures the face of our dear Lord Jesus Christ and hides his beauty from the world, the world that so desperately needs to be drawn to him.'[2]

It was Peter, alone apparently, (21:11) who hauled in the unbroken net. And, significantly, it was this apostle who was to be the first to advocate and witness the beginning of the miraculous integration of both Jews and Gentiles. Peter probably felt remarkably alone as he 'hauled in the net' of Cornelius' relatives and close friends coming to faith.[3] But it was the beginning of a unity the world had never seen before. Markus Brockmuehl, in his book *Simon Peter in Scripture and Memory* comments, 'Beginning as a fisherman from Capernaum the apostle became a contrast, bridge-building and uniting figure in the early church.'[4]

---

2   *Cape Town Commitment. A Confession of Faith and a Call to Action.* (The Lausanne Movement 2011), 65.

3   Acts 10: 23-48.

4   Markus Bochmuehl, *Simon Peter in Scripture and Memory* (Baker Academic 2012), 180.

A Heart for Unity

I have never met a Christian leader who has confessed to being against church unity in principle! I don't expect I ever will. However, the reality is that unless we have a God-given intentionality and passion for visible Christian unity we will never give it its proper priority. At the congregational level a lack of unity will, of course, always become obvious and demand attention. It's hardly possible to avoid disgruntled members and bullying individuals. Developing cliques and tense relationships are hard to miss. At this local level we will work for unity not least for the quiet life! The real test as to whether we have a heart for Christian unity, however, is the extent to which we invest in building harmonious relationships with the other churches and church leaders around us, both within and beyond our own tradition.

I was privileged to grow up in an environment where wider Christian unity was modelled by my parents. My father began a Christian bookshop in York in the late 1950s long before most towns had one. He started a York-wide inter-church youth meeting on a Sunday night at 8.30, and an inter-church youth camp that still continues today. He knew folk from many church traditions, preached in many and his funeral was a great inter-church reunion.

He also knew how ugly division could be. One fateful day he and the other elders of his Gospel Hall (he was with the Brethren) decided to allow women to contribute to the worship before the Breaking of Bread! The next Sunday a shadowy group known as the 'trustees' (some of them good friends of dad until that moment) changed the church locks so none of the dissidents could get in. It nearly broke my parents' hearts. A few months later, having been part of planting a fresh congregation, my father went back to that Brethren Hall to take a funeral and to begin to re-build relationships.

Somewhere along the line, God, in his grace, gave me a heart for unity too. When I began pastoral ministry, I determined, with God's help, to make unity a priority at a congregational, denominational and city level. Jesus' beatitude from the Sermon on the Mount, 'Blessed are the peace-makers for they will be called the children of God' has been hugely formative for me, particularly in the years when, as a denominational ministry advisor, I was involved in a significant amount of conflict resolution. Unity is a heart issue because it is about reflecting the heart of our Father in heaven.

It is all too easy to find legitimate 'truth' reasons why we shouldn't be involved in some gesture of unity. But close up, my honest observation is that for all our talk of defending gospel truth and the danger of 'guilt by association', actually, worryingly, more often the true motivating factors are either personal insecurity (and all the fears and competitiveness that go with that) or simply a lack of a generous spirit and a cavalier attitude towards Ephesians 4:3 'make every effort (spare no effort) to maintain the unity of the Spirit'. Count Nicolaus Zinzendorf (1700-1760), the Moravian leader and an ecumenical theologian whose thinking was well before his time, observed, 'all fellowship which is only based on agreement of opinions and forms, *without a change of heart*, is a dangerous sect.' Unity begins with a transformation of the heart.

A heart and passion for unity, however, is far more than about simply seeking to counter-act the pain of disunity. The visible unity of God's diverse people in the creation of a new humanity is the very glory of the gospel. It is the fruit of Christ's death and resurrection which allows him, after 'the suffering of his soul', 'to see the light of life and be satisfied'.[5] There have been few things more exhilarating for me than, at one evening service, having the privilege to baptize nine people from such varied backgrounds as a young roofer from Fife, a university lecturer from Ukraine and an American student! To witness week by week professors, taxi-drivers, nurses and dinner ladies worshipping together, learning together, serving together, seeking to bring out the best in each other, is nothing short of breath-taking. For two years my wife had the privilege of being part of a Christian community in Gaborone, Botswana, with the delightfully accurate name 'Open Baptist Church'. There were 23 different African nationalities represented in the church as well as others, like my wife, from around the world. The almost sociological impossibility of such a community is a tantalizing taste of what is to come.

A Theology of Unity

A true passion for unity is nourished by a thought-through theology of the church 'beyond the local'. The starting point may be a local congregation with Christ in their midst, multiplied many times. Equally, the starting point may be with the one true church world-wide with Christ as its global

---

5   Isaiah 53:11.

Head and then seeing all local churches as concrete expressions of that one church. Either way, all biblical ecclesiology must take as its true foundation the gospel of Christ. The world-wide church is that community of those who are 'in Christ', redeemed by his death and resurrection and inhabited by the One Spirit.

In one very pointed comment by the author of John's Gospel, following Jesus' prediction of his death, he writes that Jesus would die not just for the nation 'but also for the scattered children of God, to bring them together *and make them one*' (11:52). More fully, both the universal and local church exist by the grace of the Triune God, the Father who elects and calls his people (the ecclesia), the Son who reconciles us to God and to each other (the new humanity), and the Spirit who incorporates us into Christ (the fellowship of the Spirit). Christian unity is never merely a 'coalition', as if we choose to voluntarily associate around a set of agreed doctrines, it is a gospel *creation*. The church is that 'new creation' community, still broken and struggling, but heralding the day when God's new heaven and new earth will come. To that extent, there is only one sort of unity; and that is evangelical unity, unity around the *evangel*.

This is what the Lord's Supper celebrates and why it is so central to the church's life. 'Because there is one loaf we, who are many, are one body, for we all partake of the one loaf'.[6] Thus, whether we characterize the wider church as a 'community of communities' or as 'local outcrops of the one true church' we need to insist that the Body of Christ is always both local and global. As P.T Forsyth put it, 'What the Gospel created was not a crowd of churches but the one Church in many places.'[7] Church leaders need to model this breadth in their relationships. To settle for less than this is to truncate the gospel. Indeed, Miroslav Volf goes as far as asserting that the openness of every church towards all other churches is an 'indispensable condition of ecclesiality'.[8] This, for me, raises the stakes to its proper gospel height.

Further, a full biblical understanding of the church's unity must also include our relationship to the countless number of the redeemed

---

6   1 Corinthians 10:17.

7   P.T. Forsyth, *The Church and the Sacraments* 1917 (London: Independent Press 1964), 68.

8   Miroslav Volf, *After Our Likeness. The Church as the Image of the Trinity* (Grand Rapids, Michigan, Cambridge UK: Eerdmans 1998), 156.

worshipping where Christ now is, in heaven.[9] The use of *'ecclesia'* in Ephesians and Colossians seems to include such a reality.[10] The importance of this is that such a perspective adds huge impetus to a passion for unity. If it is true that the church is essentially a 'community of anticipation', a first fruit of that ultimate gathering,[11] then our present attitude to other churches will naturally express that heart longing of what will be. God's covenant people are a pilgrim people whose attitudes and actions are shaped and defined by their ultimate destination. Tom Greggs puts it well,

> Unity lies ahead of us as we continue to experience the gracious work of God in the realities of space-time: it is something from which and towards which we journey *as the Holy Spirit actualises the unity of the church as an event.*[12]

As was mentioned in the last chapter on mission, it is interesting that the word John uses for 'hauling in the net' (*helkein*) (21:6,11) is the same verb (*helko*) he employs for speaking of Jesus who, 'when he is lifted up from the earth, will draw (*helkuso*) all people to himself' (John 12:33). In other words, our enthusiasm for 'drawing in' the unbroken net of the church will flow from our worship of, and obedience to, the one who is lifted up in death, resurrection and ascension and who himself draws in the net by the Spirit.

The significance of the work of the Holy Spirit in bringing unity cannot be over emphasized – and this for a number of reasons. First, of all the Gospel writers, it is John who emphasizes that the Spirit of God is the Spirit of truth.[13] Truth must be foundational to unity. Without a shared conviction over the 'one Lord, one faith, one baptism, one God and Father of all' (Ephesians 4:5), talk of Christian unity is vacuous and the Spirit of truth cannot own it. In saying this, however, it is vital to also acknowledge the distinction between primary gospel truths (over which we must agree for meaningful Christian unity) and secondary issues, the *adiaphora*, as the Reformers called them. It is the distinction between the 'essential' and the

---

9   Hebrews 12:22-23.

10   E.g. Ephesians 1:22; 3:10; 3:21; 5:23; 5:27; 5:32; Colossians 1:18; 1:24.

11   Miroslav Volf, op. cit., 140.

12   Tom Greggs, *Dogmatic Ecclesiology. The Priestly Catholicity of the Church.* Vol. 1 (Baker Academic 2019), 453. Italics original.

13   John 14:17; 16:13.

'expedient'. Admittedly, over the centuries this distinction has been hard to draw but an affirmation of the truths of the Apostles and Nicene creeds have stood the test of time as to what is primary and non-negotiable.[14] When folk humbly seek to live under the Lordship of Christ and the authority of Scripture I want to respect them and walk in fellowship with them even if we come to different interpretive conclusions over secondary matters.

Second, this same Spirit of Truth is also the One who pours God's love into our hearts. Unity comes as the 'flood' of the Spirit washes away our sinful prejudices and barriers. In the famous Psalm on unity 'How good and pleasant it is when God's people live together in unity' (Psalm 133) two vivid images are employed that both underline this uniting ministry of the Spirit of Love. God's gift of unity is like perfumed oil flowing down Aaron's beard; and it is like the meteorological miracle of refreshing, life-giving dew on Mount Hermon ending up hundreds of miles south on Mount Zion. What is even more striking in the poem is the three-fold repetition of the Hebrew word 'descending'; v.2 'oil running down' *(descending)* on the beard', *descending* on Aaron's beard and v.3 'It is like the dew of Hermon *'descending'* on Mount Zion'. All true unity, like all good gifts, comes down from above.

I will never forget a conference I attended in 1994 in Prague of a gathering of European church leaders. It was towards the end of the Croatian War of Independence. On the last morning, at the conclusion of a moving communion service, we stood in a circle to pray. Opposite me was a Serb brother and next to him a Croat believer holding hands, knowing that at that very moment their two nations were bombing each other. We prayed together and sensed a remarkable 'descending' of the Spirit. Only in Christ and by his Spirit is such unity possible.

Over the years there have been for me those in leadership who have stood out and touched me by modelling a generosity and graciousness of the Spirit that transcended denomination boundaries and inter-church rivalries. Growing up in York, I was deeply influenced by the ministry of the Anglican evangelist and pastor, David Watson, referred to in Chapter

---

14 Oscar Cullman *Unity through Diversity* (Philadelphia: Fortress Press 1987). 'In order to find an objective criterion for the precise establishment of the primary truths of the Bible I am accustomed to referring to the creedal statements which were already recorded in fixed form within early Christianity.' 23

Two. His capacity to reach out a hand to all who named the name of Christ deeply influenced me. In his book *I believe in the Church* he writes,

> One of the first requirements for the unity of the church in the first century was the manifest presence of the Holy Spirit. Through the cross of Christ, such unity was possible; and through the life of the Spirit, such unity became real.[15]

This theology he modelled, sometimes at much personal cost. In painful contrast, I have occasionally encountered colleagues who, in the name of preserving gospel faithfulness, have, ironically, been deeply unfaithful to the gospel in their lack of interest in anything that doesn't quite forward their particular views. The primary fruit of the Spirit is self-less love.

Third, the Holy Spirit is also the eschatological Spirit, the one who brings something of the glorious future into the present. We live now in the power of the Spirit but we live knowing there is a greater fullness still to come. This underlines the biblical distinction between our *present* quest for unity, which will always be partial and that *final* and perfect heavenly harmony for which we still await. Such a bi-polar understanding is clearly portrayed in Ephesians 4:1-16.

The passage opens with the present, practical realism of a fragile congregation, where the urgent need is to rely on the Holy Spirit who has *both* brought unity and will make it more real through the ripening of the fruit of the Spirit, 'be completely humble and gentle; be patient, bearing with each other in love' (Eph 4:2). In stark contrast, the passage concludes with a majestic vision of the future consummation of God's plan, characterized as 'attaining the unity of the faith and knowledge of the Son of God and become mature, attaining to the whole measure of the fullness of Christ' (Eph 4:13)., Larry Hurtado comments:

> This unity of the faith is not presented here as something that can be devised by councils and doctrinal committees, but is instead a component of the eschatological resolution of all ambiguities in the bright light of God's full revelation and final victory.[16]

---

15 David Watson, *I Believe in the Church* (London, Hodder and Stoughton 1978), 336.
16 L.W. Hurtado 'You've got to "Accentuate the Positive". Thinking about difference biblically', *Scottish Bulletin of Evangelical Theology*, Vol. 30, No. 1, Spring 2012, 26.

Thus, we work hard at *maintaining* the present unity of the Spirit and indeed pray for it to deepen, but we can only *await* the full and complete 'unity of the faith and knowledge of the Son of God'. We patiently work towards the day when that great multitude from every nation, tribe, people and language will stand before the throne and the Lamb in complete unity of mind and heart. Until then we live with the realism that, because of our partial sight, our present unity will never be based on complete doctrinal agreement – but rather on a Spirit-empowered *bond of peace* that allows us to choose not to go to war over secondary differences. Hurtado observes that we have tended to reverse this clear sequence of Ephesians 4:1-16, placing full doctrinal agreement centre-stage rather than a reliance on the Spirit.[17]

The Cost of Unity

Eugene Peterson in *The Message* paraphrases Ephesians 4:3, 'Pour yourselves out for each other in acts of love, alert at noticing differences and quick at mending fences.' Over the years it has seemed to me that we have been very quick to say 'no unity at any cost' but much slower in affirming 'unity at great cost'. Mending fences (and fishing nets!) is often thankless, back-breaking work. The quest for Christian unity does indeed require a 'pouring out of ourselves'. It involves personal sacrifice at the congregational level, at the city level and national level. It costs in time, listening generously and learning humbly; it costs in terms of possible misunderstanding as people see us associating beyond certain limits; it costs in energy and thought. It is worth pondering why, in the early church, the many divisive tendencies never led to a real break. Part of the answer, perhaps, is the way the apostles and leaders gave themselves at great personal cost both to resisting the factional elements and to practical expressions of love in inter-church aid, particularly to the poor in Jerusalem.

Most of all, the quest for unity costs the death of our egos. Bishop Lesslie Newbigin, who very much led the way in founding the United Church of South India, lamented superficial forms of unity which 'demand no death and resurrection as the price of unity.'[18] There has to be a dying to personal

17 Ibid., 27.
18 Lesslie Newbigin, in *Lesslie Newbigin Missionary Theologian. A Reader compiled by Paul Weston,* Chap. 8 'The Nature and Calling of the Church' (SPCK 2006), 123.

insecurities, ungenerous dispositions, proud traditions, preferences and prejudices and a rising to a joyful affirmation of all who truly are in Christ.

Nurturing Local Congregational Unity

Local church unity does not come automatically. Simply to call the church to 'be one' and expect it to happen is naïve. Given our fallen human nature and the attacks of the Enemy, our unity in Christ must be both protected and deepened. Maintaining unity involves 'every effort'; the sweat, tears, toil and wisdom of skilled shepherds. Over the years four convictions have guided my own approach. First and foremost, unity comes as Christ is exalted through worship and the preaching of his Word. When folk are in love with Jesus Christ, kneeling each day at the foot of his cross and seeking to follow him in obedience to his commands, then unity around him will be the joyful result. Unity comes not by a pleading for unity but by a proclamation of Christ.

Second, unity comes through the intentional and prayerful creation of a culture of kindness, generosity, mutual respect and a respecting of difference. This is a tone and ethos that first needs to be modelled by the local church leadership. Jürgen Moltmann talks helpfully of gospel unity being 'unity in freedom', a vision that celebrates, rather than is threatened by, diversity-in-unity.[19] Far too often leaders perceive a range of views in their congregation as a potential threat; they want the security of unanimity, even uniformity. In contrast, happy the church leader who has the rootedness to model a holding lightly of what is peripheral and an uncompromising passion for what is primary. I remember a group of young, zealous, somewhat charismatic women who were more than a little disturbed to discover other young women in the church happily going to yoga classes. It caused considerable tension. The charismatic group assumed the others were blindly exposing themselves to anti-Christian philosophy and unhelpful spiritual influences. In fact the 'yoga lot' were meditating on Scripture throughout their exercises. Both groups slowly learnt to respect the perspective of the other and to keep Christ central.

Third, a key pastoral skill is to *anticipate* potential division. So many divisions can be avoided by thoughtful preventative measures. For me, this has meant, for example, spending extra time with folk who have displayed

---

19 Jurgen Moltmann, *The Church in the Power of the Spirit* (SCM Press 1975), 343.

the potential angularity to cause disunity. It has meant having conversations with folk whom I have anticipated will not be comfortable with a proposal in a church meeting – not to persuade them to a particular viewpoint but to give them the dignity of expressing their fears. It has involved drawing alongside folk who feel spiritually and socially on the church margins. It has particularly included anticipating controversial matters and getting the corporate leadership to agree a course of action *before* a major crisis hits.

I well remember talking through with the church leaders a very problematic and potentially divisive marriage issue. When finally confronted with having to make a controversial decision the leaders already had established an agreed way forward. As I listened to a radio interview recently with a senior aviation engineer about the two Boeing 737 Max airline crashes over Jakarta and five months later, Addis Ababa, I was struck by a phrase he used. He commented that the main cause of airline disasters was 'an atrophy of vigilance' with computer software. Such an 'atrophy of vigilance' is often the cause of church disunity.

Fourth, maintaining congregational unity involves not being afraid to confront divisive people. Conflict is inevitable in any community and happy the church leader who has taken some time to be equipped in basic conflict resolution skills. I wish I had acquired them a lot earlier in my ministry! A primary lesson, which I learnt the hard way, is *never* to seek to confront by letter, e-mail or telephone! Face-to-face conversations in a safe place and usually with a friend who is trusted by both parties is crucial. What has been revolutionary for me is seeing conflict resolution as a *process*. This invariably involves hosting a number of meetings rather than a one-off plea for resolution. Though confronting a person's inappropriate behaviour is at times necessary, there can be great value when seeking to resolve conflict in helping both sides identify the *common issue* rather than focusing, as we so often do, on the 'annoying other'.

Encouraging Inter-Church Unity

It has been a priority of mine over the years to not only meet with neighbouring leaders of my own tradition but church leaders from across the denominational spectrum. To not only take an interest in others but to invest time, energy and emotion in the wider church is a serious challenge. As Jurgen Moltmann puts it, 'A community which does not see the suffering and testimony of other communities as its own suffering and testimony is denying the One Christ, who suffers and acts in all places and at all times.'[20] But it is also deeply enriching. So often I have sensed, as we have shared together and in particular prayed together, that the pleasure and power of God has descended.

A practical distinction I find helpful is the distinction between personal unity and institutional unity. The reality is that in terms of global ecumenical conversations stalemate exists. Most painfully, whilst the official Roman Catholic Church continues to believe she is the one true visible church she simply cannot treat other separated bodies of Christians as full churches. For them and many others, there is the sincere conviction that where a body has no bishop there can be no church. To move from saying 'episcopacy is of the essence of the church' to saying 'it is very valuable to the church' is a step many just cannot take without their whole ecclesiology collapsing. So full visible *institutional* unity is at present stalled, at so many levels. But, that said, we surely can *personally* fellowship with, learn from and prayerfully support colleagues from very different traditions who love and serve Christ and his gospel. Partnering with them in particular projects may not always be realistic but standing with them as sisters and brothers in Christ is not an option but a duty.

The unbroken net on the beach that day was, as we have said, unexpected with such a large catch of fish. It was noteworthy for the Gospel writer. Far more noteworthy and newsworthy, in our deeply fractured world, is when a local church enjoys rich unity-in-diversity and when local churches joyfully come together in prayer, worship and mission. This is what Jesus prayed for. It is what he died and rose for. It is what he looks for. The one who called us to be 'fishers of people' never intended a torn net.

---

20   J. Moltmann, ibid., 343.

Chapter Seven

The Beach Party – Leadership, Power and Space to Grow

Jesus said to them, 'Come and have breakfast' (John 21:12)

The risen Jesus on the beach that morning was in no rush. A charcoal fire had been lit, a meal prepared and now an inviting aroma greets seven hungry, tired and somewhat dazed men. The waiting Stranger becomes the welcoming Host; Jesus quite deliberately creating space and time. It was an opportunity for an unhurried reunion and how they would welcome that! They sat face–to-face with the risen Christ.[1] At first they were tongue-tied, 'None of the disciples dared ask him 'Who are you?' They knew it was the Lord' (21:12), yet they had so many questions, so many unresolved issues, so many unarticulated emotions. The Risen Christ, compassionate as always, created the context to re-assure them.

This happened in a number of ways. First, as he fanned the charcoal fire, rotated the baking fish and ate breakfast with them he was underlining the sheer physicality of his resurrection body. He really was alive again, glorified for sure, but still the same Lord who ate fish and had charcoal dust on his hands. Second, it seems that by deliberately including some of the 153 fish the seven had just caught (v.10) – the fish couldn't have been fresher! – Jesus was intending to make it quite clear that the miraculous catch was equally no illusion. And third, he wanted them to savour the joyful reality of renewed

---

1   David Ford in his *The Drama of Living. Becoming Wise in the Spirit* (Canterbury Press 2014), Chapter 3, writes movingly of the importance of face-to-face encounters. He quotes the Jewish philosopher, Emmanuel Levinas and his concept of the 'hospitality of the face'.

fellowship. 'He took the bread and gave it to them and did the same with the fish' (v.13).

The suggestion by some that this meal was eucharistic may be wide of the mark, yet they see something important. It was reminiscent of so many intimate moments, meals and miracles they had experienced together over the past three years. It is significant that though the New Testament tells us little of what happened between resurrection and ascension, one thing that is made clear is that eating together was a prominent feature (Acts 1:4; 10:41). Space and time to be together was crucial. One can only imagine the content of the many conversations they had together about the Kingdom of God (Acts 1:3) and, equally, one can only speculate about the relief, the laughter, the tears, the puzzlement and the sheer joy of those 'resurrection times' together.

Space for Individual Freedom *and* Communal Commitment

This striking scene of the risen Lord having a leisurely beach breakfast with his disciples is, for me, an important and formative image of pastoral ministry. Jesus that morning was deliberately *making room* for doubts, questions, exploration and growth. He no doubt listened as much as he spoke. Each of the seven, as they sat around that beach fire, had been individually chosen, called and mentored by Jesus; in turn, they had freely chosen to follow Jesus. This beach reunion celebrated their being bound together in community and yet the freedom and space to be themselves.

In this chapter I want to explore *the importance of space* within the dynamics of a community of grace. Paul Fiddes puts the reason for this exploration well; the Kingdom of God is not 'an area held by a controlling power; the 'kingdom' is rather a kind of 'space' in which persons have the freedom to grow and develop.'[2] Thus at the heart of all pastoral ministry, in the context of discipleship-in-community, is a deep respect for the freedom of conscience of every individual. Every person in fellowship together must be granted space for free, personal choice – space to hear and respond to God, intellectual room to express doubts and ask questions, opportunity to explore their unique gifts, space to be themselves before God. The unique personality and contribution of every individual is to be carefully guarded,

---

2   Paul S. Fiddes, *Participating in God, A Pastoral Doctrine of the Trinity* (Darton, Longman and Todd 2000), 97.

honoured and valued. As Andrew Root emphasises, 'pastoral ministry can be seen as nothing more and nothing less than making space for people to encounter the very presence of God.'[3]

In the account of the rich young ruler who came to Jesus asking how to inherit eternal life, it is particularly telling that when he chose *not* to take up Jesus challenge and went away sad (Mark 10:22) Jesus didn't pursue him, even less coerce him. Fundamental to Jesus loving him (Mark 10:21) was granting him the dignity of freedom to decide. How I love the moment in John's Gospel when Jesus writes on the ground with his finger before the angry crowd and the accused woman! It is the unforgettable moment when Jesus both forever condemns all space-less, knee-jerk reactions and demonstrates the power of forgiving love (8:6). In my own Baptist tradition 'making space' includes allowing all members of a congregation, however immature or seemingly ill-equipped, to participate in discerning God's will for the future direction and mission of the local church.

Such 'space', of course, is never freedom to 'do our own thing'. Rather it is the space that allows the risen Christ, as with those first seven, to so transform us *individually* that *together* we become more of the 'contrast community' that Christ calls us to be. Holiness becomes meaningful only in the discipline of community life. Only in real and accountable relationships can the fruit of the Spirit fully ripen. Patricia Took captures the synergism of these two poles, individuality and community, very well.

> My own experience of the saints of God is that the closer they are to the Lord the more distinctive and, it has to be said, eccentric, they become. It is as if the flavour of the person is distilled in some way and they are liberated to be truly themselves, but they are themselves on behalf of the others.[4]

---

3   Andrew Root, *The Relational Pastor. Sharing Christ by Sharing Ourselves* (IVP 2013), 10. The emphasis of the whole book is that so often we treat people as individual tools for our ministry purposes rather honour them as persons loved and valued by God. This is vital. But Root's central thesis that 'we are our relationships' (18) and that human relationships in and of themselves are how we encounter God seems somewhat over-played.

4   Patricia M. Took, '*It shall not be so among you*'. *Power and Love in the Community of Christ*' (Hertford Baptist Association Booklet; Signposts for a New Century 2000), 13.

Such an individual-communal dialectic is ultimately rooted in our understanding of God himself. John's Gospel, of all the Gospels, celebrates God as a communion of three mutually-indwelling persons, Father Son and Spirit. (John 16:14-15). The Cappadocian Fathers of the latter half of the Fourth Century sought to explore and develop this theme, emphasising that the very Godhead is *both* the particularity of each divine Person, with space allowing that particularity to be expressed, *and* a fundamental unity of being, constituted by the loving inter-penetration of the three-in-one. The church, in spite of all its creaturely limits, is called to reflect and echo something of this pattern. Through the ministry of the Holy Spirit dwelling within us both particularity and communion are nurtured.[5]

Such a theme is explored movingly in Miroslav Volf's book *Exclusion and Embrace,* based on his own personal experiences of the painful, ethnic divisions and bloodshed of the war in the former Yugoslavia. Volf wrestles with how the different 'other' (Croat and Serb) can so easily become a threat that leads to exclusion. In contrast, he sees the heart of the gospel as being the 'embrace of Christ', the one who, as God incarnate, welcomes difference with warm, open, forgiving arms. Christ's embrace is the basis for all peace, breaking down the walls of hostility, defining moral boundaries and honouring our distinctive persons.

What is particularly apposite is Volf's pastoral insight that 'creating ecclesial space for difference' cannot occur without space being created *in ourselves.* Volf movingly talks about the 'the two dimensions of the passion of Christ: self-giving love which overcomes human enmity and the creation of space in himself to receive estranged humanity.'[6] It follows that it behoves all in pastoral ministry to reflect honestly on exactly how much room we truly can give to the sometimes challenging particularity of others. Only as we experience the embrace of Christ ourselves, he argues, do we find the ability to create space for others. 'Embrace,' says Volf, 'is grace and grace is always risk.'[7]

---

5   See especially Colin E. Gunton, *The One, The Three and the Many. God, Creation and the Culture of Modernity. The 1992 Bampton Lectures.* (Cambridge University Press 1993), Chapter 7, 180-209.
6   Miroslav Volf, *Exclusion and Embrace: A Theological Exploration of Identity, Otherness and Reconciliation* (Nashville: Abingdon Press 1996), 126.
7   Ibid., 147.

Imaginative as it may be, the image of an inviting expanse of Galilean beach, the fresh morning air and a leisurely conversation between Jesus and his disciples becomes an evocative parable of ministry. Safe church is where there is both pastoral attentiveness and pastoral space. It is only possible, as it was that morning, when Christ is truly at the centre of a community. His resurrection power is marked by self-giving and life-giving love.

The Shrinkage of Space and the Unsafe Church

Pastoral ministry thus involves vigilance about space. It demands a constant attentiveness to the fine line between godly persuasion and undue pressure. The sight of seeing that watershed crossed into manipulation and intimidation can be ugly indeed. Many of us, no doubt, have had brushes with 'unsafe' church. You can almost sense the need for a hard hat as you walk into them! Sometimes you sense the church is simply 'rudderless' – the vision and values seem unclear, the ministries un-coordinated, discipleship expectations unarticulated, moral boundaries uncertain and what holds people together seems more about familiarity and comradery than the supernatural diversity-in-unity of the Spirit. There is almost too much space! But perhaps more concerning is the church where there is a shrinkage of space, where an unspoken conformity is expected and spiritual claustrophobia is the result. It is the church where the leadership has a distinctive 'surveillance' feel to it and where everyone appears to think, talk and pray with an unnerving similarity. It is the church where the authority of the biblical interpreter seems to eclipse the authority of the Word itself and where expectations are not only clear but come with subtle sanctions for any dissent.

It is worryingly possible to be part of a church (and I reflect on my own ministry) which celebrates the doctrines of grace and yet where guilt is a prime tool of the leadership. The reality is that the fine line that exists between healthy directional leadership and controlling leadership can so easily be crossed. In a survey conducted in 2013 by the *Evangelical Alliance,* 13 percent of respondents believed their church leader to be overly controlling or dominating and a key reason folk were leaving their church.[8] In an earlier study of those who have left the church and are now 'churchless

---

8 *Life in the Church?* Evangelical Alliance Report (2013) quoted in L. Oakley and J. Humphreys (SPCK, Thirty One: Eight 2019), 43.

believers' one of the main reasons cited for their disaffection (29 percent of those interviewed) was a lack of opportunity to ask questions and disagree.[9]

Leadership, Power and Space

Lurking behind these concerns is the issue of power. Power, somewhat simply put, is 'the ability to effect change', the capacity to influence the thoughts, values and behaviours of others.[10] Though power itself is morally neutral, the reality is that it can be used for good or ill. Within our theme, power is having the wherewithal to either create space for personal and community well-being or to reduce space for personal and institutional control. The typology of power adopted by Rollo May, the American psychologist, is particularly helpful – and salutary.[11] He views different forms of power as on a continuum, moving from expressions of destructive to productive power. He identifies five forms: *exploitative* power, *manipulative* power, *competitive* power, *nutritive* power, and finally and most positively, *integrative* power. The latter is when power is used to enable a person to fully flourish in an integrated way within a community.

Few people in our time have explored the issue of power and its influence more searchingly than the French cultural historian and philosopher Michel Foucault (1926-84).[12] Though hardly a Christian in his lifestyle and convictions and though in the hands of more than a few social scientists his ideas totally dominate,[13] Foucault does offer important, almost prophetic,

---

9   Francis L.J. and Richter P. *'Gone for Good? Church-leaving and returning in the 21st century* (Peterborough: Epworth Press 2007), 102.

10   Power is 'the ability to act or effect something strongly', *Shorter Oxford English Dictionary* (Oxford University Press, Fifth Edition 2002). A definition of power is a contested issue; the above would be a 'thin' definition.

11   R. May 1972, *Power and Innocence, a Search for the Sources of Violence.* (New York: W.W. Norton 1972), 105-110.

12   I am grateful to Roy Kearsley and his book *Church, Community and Power* (Ashgate 2008) for much of what follows and for setting me on a fascinating trail of Foucault's work.

13   Douglas Murray in his *The Madness of Crowds* (London: Bloomsbury Continuum, 2019), commenting on today's post-Marxist perspective that underlines a lot of present wokism talks of the 'distorting prism of Foucault'. 'For a certain type of person who is intent on finding blame rather than forgiveness in the world, Foucault helps to explain everything.' 53.

insights for the Christian community. One of his central observations is the sheer ubiquity of power. Power is not a separate concept but intimately related to, and shaping of, all relationships, so much so that he habitually talks of 'power-relations'. As such, power is often played out in subtle, unseen, complex and diverse ways.

In this he was turning his back on what he saw as the all-too simplistic 'oppressor-oppressed' bi-polarity of the Marxism with which he grew up. Foucault helpfully identifies different sorts of power; for example 'sovereign power' – power that is obvious, directional and unquestioned; 'disciplinary power' where institutions more subtly impose conformity; and 'micro-power', the complex power dynamics of small communities where the interplay is unpredictable and often unnoticed.[14] Power, he argues, can creep into a community with a sort of 'capillary effect'; it is 'the microphysics of power'.[15] Once named, all these categories of power are not difficult to identify in the Christian community yet, as Foucault warns, 'relations of power are perhaps among the best hidden things in the social body.'[16] For the Christian community this is a stark reminder that power is an unavoidable reality and it is naïve in the extreme for churches to think they somehow inhabit a power-free zone. Indeed the greatest danger is when power issues are unrecognised or unacknowledged. Wherever there are differences in gender, in social status, in educational ability and financial means then power issues will inevitably be at play. At times the dynamics of power will be obvious and their misuse blatant. At other times the play of power will be much more subtle. This is why pastoral vigilance is so vital.

Michel Foucault's particular approach was to analyse (often in meticulous detail) the ways in which institutions and society's conceptualisation of issues have been shaped by power. Many of his books are explorations of how societal changes have, in the name of progress and liberation, actually been more about subtle shifts in social control. For example, in his history of the penal system, *Discipline and Punish*, he

---

14 These distinctions are first introduced in his *Discipline and Punish. The Birth of the Prison* (Penguin Books, ET 1977).

15 M. Foucault, ibid., 26.

16 M. Foucault, *Politics, Philosophy, Culture: Interviews and Other Writings 1977-1984*, 118, quoted in Christopher Watkin, *Michael Foucault* (Great Thinkers Series, P&R Publishing, New Jersey 2018), 36.

shows how the move away from execution and public torture in the early modern period to the rise of the prison was simply about power, previously targeted at the body, now being aimed at the mind and soul.[17] Such histories were of value to him precisely because they serve as mirrors, accurately and vividly reflecting power-play in our culture more generally.[18] Such all-pervasive power, Foucault argued, is shaping in two particular ways. First it can shape our perception of truth itself because truth and power, he argued, although not to be identified, are intimately connected to the extent that he can talk of 'power-knowledge'.[19] It is not just that power can distort truth but access to truth is often determined by power. Second power can be deeply shaping of our understanding of ourselves and all human relationships.[20] How many of our life struggles flow out of a dominant parent, an institutional prejudice or impenetrable social cliques?

Alarm Bells for the Church

Michel Foucault's writings, disturbing, wild and often accepted too uncritically, do sound important warning bells for the church and its ministries. The concept of 'power-knowledge', for example, is sobering. How easy for preaching to be used to forward an agenda other than simply allowing God's Word and Spirit to do its own work. The story of how the Dutch Reformed Church of South Africa used scripture to justify apartheid is well-known but still remains a salutary reminder. As mentioned earlier, is it the authority of inspired Holy Scripture that really rules or is it that of the interpreter? [21]

Equally, Foucault helpfully alerts us to the very real possibility of power-damaging relationships. Pastoral abuse cases tend to focus on high

---

17 Michel Foucault, *Discipline and Punish, op. cit.,* 101.

18 Paul Strathern, 'History was not recording the truth of the past but revealing the truth of the present.' *The Essential Foucault* (Virgin Books 2002), 7.

19 Michel Foucault, *Discipline and Punish,* op.cit., 'There is no power relation without the correlative constitution of a field of knowledge'. 27.

20 Foucault saw 'self' as a social construct and believed in self-transformation, 'through limit experiences', a far cry from a Christian vision of self. See the excellent article by John Collins, 'Life after the Death of God. Michel Foucault and Postmodern Atheism' in *Cambridge Papers,* Vol. 5 No. 4 Dec. 1996.

21 Martyn Percy, 'The Dynamics of Power in Churches' in *The Study of Ministry: A comprehensive Survey of Theory and Best Practice* Ed. Martyn Percy with Ian S. Markham, Emma Percy and Francesca Po, (SPCK 2019), 526.

profile instances of Foucauldian 'sovereign power' – bullying, favouritism, a dominant church family, the threat of withdrawing church giving. I recall the shock of having to advise a church where a millionaire-elder, who employed several church members in his company, had used his position to pressure those employees into supporting a controversial church policy. However, it is the much more subtle expressions of 'micro-power' that we often allow to go unnoticed and unchallenged. We can employ strategies as varied as silent non-engagement over an agenda item to a less-than-transparent selective sending of emails to press our own cause. As Roy Kearsley warns, 'Put bluntly, vigilance is possibly even more necessary in a healthy church, for the richer the mix the greater the combustible chemistry.'[22]

One form of power abuse, hinted at earlier, is where space simply 'to be' is subtly denied through a 'surveillance culture'. Foucault famously captured this by making use of the image of the panopticon.[23] This was a hypothetical prison design by the utilitarian philosopher Jeremy Bentham (1748-1832), in which an observation tower is placed strategically at the centre of a circle of prison cells. From this intimidating vantage point a prison supervisor would be able to see into, and through, each cell. The idea was that such surveillance would be so invasive as to cause prisoners instinctively to conform out of fear.[24] Though a somewhat extreme image, it points up the uncomfortably fine line that sometimes exists between pastoral oversight and inappropriate control. Foucault actually talks at one point of 'pastoral power' and uses the idea of the Catholic confessional as a sort of symbol for how our secular society attempts at times to control people by what they have revealed of themselves. How many disclosures on social media have led to power-play and grief? In the church context I have known cases of leaders confessing painful things to their colleagues in confidence, only to find those very confidences being used against them in later, more troubling years. All this is food for thought.

Lisa Oakley and J. Humphreys in their sobering book *Escaping the Maze of Spiritual Abuse* argue that, based on a number of extensive surveys in the UK church, misuse of power is widespread. At the heart of what they term 'spiritual abuse' is 'a systematic pattern of coercive and

22 R.Kearsley, op. cit., 215.
23 Ibid., 195.
24 Ibid., 228.

controlling behaviour in a religious context', sometimes non-intentional, often involving over-supervision and a misuse of Scripture, usually very subtle and *always* damaging.[25] Many victim's voices are allowed to speak in the book, one saying 'I remember feeling pressurised and pushed into action. Disciplining had become a yolk to me. I felt scrutinised. Checked out. Every move I took seemed to be watched and judged upon.'[26] (It is important to note that they go out of their way to stress that leaders can be victims as well as perpetrators.)

Space and Boundary Keeping

Another area where vigilance about space is required is in the respecting of boundaries in pastoral care and counsel. Marilyn Peterson, in her book on boundary violations *At Personal Risk*,[27] makes the robust point that the person in the best position to *help* is often the person most at risk to *hurt*. Pastoral carers are most at risk of unethical behaviour when the magnitude of their power is underestimated. Peterson comments 'Boundary violations grow out of our struggles with power and our negation of its significance.'[28] It is all too easy to be dismissive of the reality that *every* pastoral encounter has an inherent power-differential. Vulnerable people hand power to us *on trust* and if ever that 'covenant' of trust is violated immense damage occurs.

The purpose of boundaries is to guard the space of that power difference and for that to happen we need to be very self-aware of intention and motivation. Our sole concern has to be the well-being of the person we are seeking to support. Once we detect in ourselves even a hint of the need for the other person's affirmation (or more) we are sliding into dangerous territory. Peterson, a psychotherapist and trainer, catalogues many disturbing cases of how a 'process of disconnection'[29] has led the counsellor to forgetting the privileged position he or she holds which, in turn, has led to an indulging in inappropriate remarks and favours. Equally a key part of the safe environment that needs to be offered is for the 'client'

---

25 Oakey and Humphreys, op. cit., 31.
26 Ibid., 46.
27 M. Peterson, *At Personal Risk. Boundary Violations in Professional-Client Relationships* (New York, London: W.W. Norton 1992).
28 Ibid., 70.
29 Ibid., 3.

to be absolutely assured of freedom to receive or reject any advice offered without the relationship being at all in jeopardy. Whenever a counsellor's personal convictions override and ignore the counselee's own state of mind and heart – then a sacred boundary of respect has been crossed.

Celebrating Life-giving, Space-creating Leadership

The cautionary tone of the above is hardly the whole picture. Jesus sat among his disciples that morning as the powerful Lord of life, the true 'Shepherd and Overseer'[30] of his people. His aim was the formation of an apostolic band that would be foundational for all future leadership. It has to be recognised that although Michel Foucault's insights need to be heeded, the influence of postmodern suspicion has cut both ways, creating not only a healthy awareness of power- relations but at the same time fuelling an almost instinctive distrust of leadership generally. In contrast, the New Testament, whilst warning of the dangers of worldly power, encourages leaders to be honoured both in society and the church.[31] Leaders are called to lead! Creating space for growth is one thing, allowing a leadership vacuum is quite another. As Jonathan Langley well says 'We must not kid ourselves that a withdrawal of power leaves an egalitarian utopia. Remove the government from Somalia and the warlords rush in.'[32] There *is* a crying need in the church for strong leadership.

Jesus models how such leadership should look. In Foucauldian terms, his 'sovereign power' is regal precisely because it is releasing; his 'disciplinary power' is formative, shaping us into his image and his 'micro-power' is healing because it is his loving sensitivity to the details of our lives. Crucial is the recognition that Jesus' power is always power *given away* for the redemption of the world. All the miracle-signs of John's Gospel, for example, not only point to the significance of the Person who has unique divine power but also point to the *sheer selflessness* of such power. Unlike all fallen human power, power wedded to our egos, God's power, revealed in Jesus, is defined by its goal. It is self-renouncing, consistently deployed for the loving and liberating, the re-creating and restoring of the 'other'.

---

30 1 Peter 2:25.

31 1 Peter 2:13; Hebrews 13:7,17.

32 Jonathan Langley, *Mission Catalyst* Editorial, 'Are We the Masters of the Universe?' Issue 1, 2020, 2.

This is memorably portrayed when, in an Upper Room, the all-powerful Jesus stoops to wash his disciples' dirty feet. With great effect, John juxtaposes the comment, 'Jesus knew that the Father had put all things under his power, and that he had come from God and was returning to God' (13:4) with the '*so* he got up from the meal, took off his outer clothing, and wrapped a towel round his waist.' (13:5). It is a parabolic act that foreshadows the cross. Five times in John 10 we are told that the mark of the Good Shepherd is that he 'lays down his life for the sheep' (10: 11,15,17, two times, 18). Christ's power is the self-emptying power of love. It defines how power is to be deployed.[33]

Foundational to such humility and selflessness is an alertness to the somewhat basic distinction in all Christian service between God's role and our role. Ministry is, in its very nature, the inter-play of the two – God's power always primary but, in ministry, always mediated and incarnational. This we explored in Chapter 3. The danger comes when the distinction between *opus Dei* and *opus hominum*, divine and human agency, becomes blurred.[34] When, for example, the 'anointed' preacher becomes the unquestioned mouthpiece of God or the exhortations of a charismatic worship leader become automatically endued with prophetic authority, then there is a collapsing of distinctions which can lead to a damaging self-focus. There is thus an essential *asymmetry* to the perception of this inter-play, a gracious God always being the prime mover, and the central expression of this being the creation of space for the Risen Lord to do his own work.

Such authentic, space-creating Christian leadership involves a number of things. First, there must be space within church to question and explore. 'Be merciful to those who doubt', says Jude (v. 22). Too frequently the comment is heard, 'I don't feel safe enough to ask the sort of questions that matter to me.' It is hugely important for seekers to feel they have a secure place from which they can explore the faith. A case in point was

---

33 Watkin, ibid., 'Christ subverts the perennial dichotomy between the lord and the servant; between the humbled and the glorified: the Lord is forever the Servant, and the Servant is forever the Lord.' He goes on, 'In the work of Foucault and Nietzsche, we see ruptures within the history of power, but in the great reversal (through Christ) we see a rupture in the prerequisites and structure of power relations themselves.' 89.
34 This is a criticism Martyn Percy makes of fundamentalism but is, in my view, more generally applicable to evangelicalism. Percy, op.cit., 72.

when a spiritually-uncertain church attender was given permission (after some considerable leadership discussion!) to join one of our worship groups. What a delight, months later, to witness her coming to faith during communion whilst playing at the front. Too often, in a laudable desire to be a 'contrast community' we can suffocate rather than facilitate genuine moral exploration and growth. The church community is, as it were, not called to be as a circle (bounded and fixed in shape) but cross-shaped, (where its arms can extend without altering its shape).[35] This is particularly true in our welcome of same-sex attracted friends. I am not suggesting a capitulation to moral heterodoxy but simply registering a concern that unless adequate safe space be risked for some missional moral ambiguity, (all of us sinners on the journey to redemption) then two dangers follow. One is that the true welcome of Jesus is not experienced. The other is that we do not trust the Holy Spirit to do his work of conviction and conversion.

Second, there is need for space to grow, not least in the discovery and practice of the varied gifts of the Spirt God has given to each of us. It has been well said that 'the vocation of the church is to sustain many vocations.'[36] The gifts of the Spirit are for the work place and wider community as well as the church. True team leadership (eldership or its equivalent) is vital for this to develop, a team modelling a diversity of gifts and mentoring the whole congregation. I find the passion of Gareth Malone, the choirmaster and broadcaster, taking highly unlikely groups of people (military wives included!) and moulding them into more-than-decent choirs, an inspiring model for leadership. We too need our ecclesial 'auditions', creating small group contexts for people to learn about and begin to exercise their gifts. We too need much 'rehearsal time', in mission and ministry, where mistakes can be made and learnt from.

The freedom to use the gifts of the Spirit within a congregation will only be in proportion to our forgiving capacity as a congregation! If we fear failure we will never fly. Leaders are called to be skilled 'conductors', enabling everyone to find their place in the Body through multiple ministry teams. The crazy idea of the medical lawyer and novelist Alexander McCall Smith to advocate *Really Terrible Orchestras* appeals to me, where the tone

---

35 This image comes from G.K. Chesterton, *Orthodoxy* (London: John Lane, The Bodley Head 1908, Reprint: Milwaukee, Wisconsin: Cavalier Books 2015), 28.
36 Richard John Neuhaus, *Freedom for Ministry* (Grand Rapids: Eerdmans 1979), 229.

of the occasion is as important as the harmony of the music. He initiated the movement after concluding children's orchestra experiences were often far too serious and unrelaxed. I have had for many years a secret aspiration to be the pastor of the *Really Terrible* Church!

One of the best prayer meetings I have ever attended was taken by one of our home groups. The person who played the piano was a shy girl just coming back to the Lord after an illicit affair; the person who introduced the prayer meeting was a young man with learning difficulties; someone took part who had recently been made redundant; the person who gave a devotional had never spoken publicly before. And the actual home-group leaders said nothing all night! But they had planned it very carefully, to encourage and draw the others out. Spiritual growth, of course, is far more than finding our place and gifting within the Body of Christ. Fundamentally it is about character development, the shaping of those virtues that allow us to be a true community and allow an attractive, Christ-like lifestyle to be offered to a watching world.

Third, leadership involves creating space for the congregation as a whole to be part of discerning God's will for the ministry and mission of the church. There is a great need for leadership wisdom to discern when they *themselves* should offer clear direction (and that does need to happen) and when they should be encouraging all the people of God to be part of a listening process. It is far easier for a leadership team to declare and implement *their* decisions than to invite the whole congregation on a journey of discovery. Some of my most exhilarating moments in leadership have been times in a church meeting or in a small 'discernment group' when the most unlikely of people have offered something patently prophetic and it has altered the thinking and planning of leaders and all. Alan Roxburgh and Fred Romanuk in their book *Missional Leadership* write refreshingly, 'God's future is already being cultivated in the church among the ordinariness of one another.'[37]

Fourth, and most critically, space needs to be created for a congregation simply to be with God. Silence, biblical meditation, unhurried worship, reflective prayer and the valuing of the church sacraments are key. Both baptism and communion are material spaces which magnify the primacy

---

37 Alun J. Roxburgh, Fred Romanuk, *The Missional Leader. Equipping your Church to Reach a Changing World* (Jossy Bass 2006), 145.

of divine grace and promise - and allow the Spirit to come. Too often we are so frenetic in our activity that space and time to allow God to be God are simply missing. No wonder it has been said that when people are searching for authentic spirituality the last place they look is the Christian church.

I cherish the image of those first disciples sprawled on the beach, utterly captivated by the life-giving power Jesus, with 153 fresh fish piled up behind them as evidence. For once these fishermen were in no hurry. They listened, they reflected, they asked questions, they ate the bread of friendship. True leadership is about empowerment. It is about creating space for Jesus to sit amongst us; making space for his resurrection power to overawe us and his love to fill us.

After finishing this chapter I was interested to discover that in Simon Walker's insightful trilogy 'The Undefended Leader', having explored many metaphors for leadership from 'hero' to 'servant' he concludes by opting for the same image as here, that of 'host'. He comments, leadership is about 'offering a repertoire of social and emotional skills that allow a host to create and sustain a healthy, enriching, dynamic and (most importantly) humane space in which people can grow and give their best.'[38] Such 'hospitable leadership' is costly but is all worth it when we sense the presence of Jesus ministering in our midst. How we need resurrection beach parties!

---

38 Simon P. Walker, *The Undefended Leader*, Vol. 1 'Leading with Nothing to Lose' (Piquant 2007), 152.

Chapter Eight

Ministry Starvation and its Remedy

Jesus came, took the bread and gave it to them,
and did the same with the fish.   (John 21:13)

The beach breakfast was not just about renewed fellowship and space to talk and explore; it was about feeding seven ravenous fishermen. The image is striking. At the centre of this lakeside scene is the Resurrected Lord cooking, beckoning his disciples to breakfast (21:12) and then *personally* distributing bread and fish. Indeed, there is almost a hint in the text that the seven held back from Jesus' invitation to 'come and have breakfast' (21:12) and so he had to take the initiative and go to them, 'Jesus came . . . to them' (21:13). The word 'companion' literally means 'one who shares bread with another' and here is Jesus signalling his continued companionship as he serves each one individually. Unlike the story of Emmaus Road where the breaking of bread was the moment of recognition, here it is simply a time of refreshment. As with the feeding of the five thousand and four thousand, Jesus knew that hunger must be satisfied before hearts can be changed. It is interesting that in early artistic depictions of Christian meals with bread and fish there are often seven participants.[1] The action of Jesus that early morning was clearly memorable and meaningful. He is the generous, hospitable Giver of food.

Ministry with Morsels

There are times in ministry when we know we are offering a less than adequate spiritual diet. Recovery begins by owning our malnutrition.

---

1   Raymond E. Brown, *The Gospel According to John, X111-XX1*. The Anchor Bible (London: Geoffrey Chapman 1972), 1100.

Sermons have content but no conviction, teaching is sound but not fresh, pastoral visits offer care but with little spiritual nourishment, leadership meetings become more about business than discernment and mentoring involves offering advice rather than an infectious over-flowing of abundant life. We lead worship with a forced zeal and a cold heart. Such times are troubling because we are all too aware that the primary reason is that we ourselves have become spiritually under-nourished. The beauty of Isaiah 12:3, 'With joy you will draw from the wells of salvation' has become a distant memory. Our output has, for too long, out-stripped our input. Out of the lack-of-abundance of our hearts our mouths now speak.

Worryingly, we can persuade ourselves that such a way of Christian service is acceptable, even sustainable. When, however, in our spiritual emptiness, we are tempted to pull a sermon off the internet and, in a pastoral visit, have no sense of 'a word from God' to offer, then we know crisis looms. Ministry on auto-pilot is no ministry at all.

Dehydrated Humanity

Spiritual malnutrition is often accompanied by emotional exhaustion. The 'wells of salvation' are about hydrating who we are as whole people. When we are not enjoying the Living Water both an emotional and a spiritual shrivelling takes place. Concentration becomes difficult, former fun things seem unattractive, little things irritate, people (even friends) become draining and an appetite for discovery wanes. No longer are the ordinary things of life of much interest. My father had the annoying habit of almost relishing those moments when the car petrol gauge flickered onto red. Only then would we head for a garage – sometimes not quite making it. Seeing colleagues numbly go through the motions of ministry, with their emotional gauge distinctly on red, is troubling. Realising it is true of yourself is desperate.

It is salutary to note that it is often when our ministries are most flourishing that we are in most danger of allowing our humanity to diminish. For me this became alarming clear at the birth of our first child. Our daughter was born at dawn on an October Sunday morning, the very Sunday morning I had planned a special all-age, all-singing, all-dancing harvest festival service. Embarrassing as it now is to recount, it took more than one colleague to persuade me that it was more important for me be at the side of my wife at the birth of our first child than to be at the front of the church for a harvest service! It was put to me by an incredulous friend, 'Which harvest festival do you think you should be at?' Zach Eswine, in his moving book, *Sensing Jesus, Life and Ministry as a Human Being* talks about the tragedy of losing our humanity in the midst of ministry. He recounts this tale:

> I learned today of another friend leaving the ministry. We went to seminary together. He won awards. He was a standout leader in our class. He planted a new church that grew quickly and gave him accolades. He became one of those men whom others ask to speak at their conferences. There is no moral failure, no hidden and dark secret. He is simply dead inside, burned out by a way of life that gave him success in our eyes but dehydrated his humanity.'[2]

'Come to Me . . . my Burden is Light'

The cause of ministry starvation has its roots far deeper than in a lack of self-care and over-busyness. It begins to take hold when we start losing sight of the most basic of life-giving truths; the great Reformation re-discovery that God is *pro nobis, pro me* (for us, for me!). God's whole disposition is that he is there for us, seeking us, wooing us, unconditionally loving us and delighting in us. The Israelites starved in the wilderness (until the manna and quail take-away meals arrived) not because of exhaustion and over-busyness but because they kept forgetting God's covenant promises to them. When ministry takes on a transactional feel (*we need* to do this to please God, to live up to the expectations of congregation, colleagues and ourselves) exhaustion inevitably sets in.

I love the whole emphasis of Dave Hansen's beautifully written little book, *The Art of Pastoring* when he summarises his pastoral ministry disarmingly, 'I tell people I read the bible, pray and visit friends (his congregation). That's all I do.'[3] We are called to be 'parables of Jesus,'[4] he argues, simply allowing our lives to help people encounter the outrageous love of God and then stepping away. There is a simplicity to ministry. However costly our Christian service, Jesus never calls us to carry a yoke

2   Zach Eswine, *Sensing Jesus. Life and Ministry as a Human Being* (Wheaton, Illinois: Crossway 2013), 257.
3   David Hansen, *The Art of Pastoring. Ministry without all the Answers* (Downers Grove, Illinois: IVP 1994), 122.
4   Ibid., 130.

that is not 'easy' and a burden that is not 'light.'[5] It's about enjoying and infectiously sharing a relationship like no other. From this a number of things flow.

Jesus always took time to rest and insisted his followers do the same. On the beach that morning the seven disciples would almost certainly have found themselves recalling those times when Jesus had simply relaxed with them, ate with them, shared stories with them, encouraged them to go home and sleep. The prophet Elijah, after his show-down with the prophets of Baal at Mount Carmel, was rung out and depressed. God first allowed him to sleep. Then angels pointed him to 'warm bread on coals'[6] just as Jesus did on that beach.

Sleep is as much a discipline as work. Days off and holidays are to be as carefully planned as our sermons. Controlling our diaries is as important as controlling our tongues. Tiredness in ministry is like a long-distance drive in serious fog: we slow down to a crawl, we become irritable, we become scared of pastoral collisions, we can't see clearly, we just wish we were at the end of the journey. There are no short-cuts when it comes to rest; and refreshed bodies and minds are an essential prerequisite for renewed ministries. Over the years, with amusing predictability, I have had members of the congregation sidle up to me after a holiday and offer congratulations on my markedly improved preaching!

Friendship and rest go together. It is in the company of good friends that laughter happens and serious things find perspective. Close friends not only offer support but mentor without you realising it. They ensure we don't take ourselves too seriously and distract us from our work obsessions. Friendships with non-Christians particularly help here. The idea that leaders should have no close friends in a congregation is clearly both unrealistic and unhelpful; yet the issue of appropriate boundaries must not be ignored. I can think of a number of occasions where a close friendships between a pastor and a member of the congregation has led to poor judgment by the pastor in order to please the friend. But, that said, intimate friends are vital. They provide safe places to be with people who, as Henri Nouwen insightfully puts it, 'do not need us'. He writes 'I personally have been fortunate in having found such a place in L'Arche, with a group of friends who pay attention to

---

5   Matthew 11:30.
6   1 Kings 19:6.

my own often-hidden pains and keep me faithful to my vocation by their gentle criticisms and loving support.[7]

Play is also an essential part of rest, the ability to delight in activities with no obvious utilitarian end (other than relaxation). Days spent idling away absorbed in photography, improving your origami, propagating plants or just plain swimming are hardly wasted days. People seem puzzled when fly-fishermen put back the potential fish supper they have just caught. But there are things done for fun, not for food.

Play affirms the intrinsic worth of the created world. Recently I spent a crazy day entertaining two lively locked-down grandchildren and then, after dinner, immediately switched to chairing a tense church meeting on Zoom. Somehow spending a day arm-wrestling with a four year old put the evening's ecclesial arm-wrestling in perspective! The Kingdom of God is about becoming like little children! Play has the happy ability to keep in check our tendency to see *our* ministry as indispensable in God's purposes. Clearly what is play for one person may not be for another but the essence of play is a self-forgetfulness and a joyful stepping out of the oppressiveness of always feeling time is against us.[8] Indeed Peter Berger, the American sociologist, considers play to be one of the 'signals of transcendence', when somehow we become so absorbed in a joyful activity that time seems to stand still and there is a taste of eternity. 'When adults play with genuine joy', he says, 'they momentarily regain the deathlessness of childhood.'[9] Indeed the eschaton will include play.[10] As we saw in chapter three, the divine and the human are never competing for the same space. To love God in our prayers is never at the expense of enjoying him in our play. Lego building is a friend of Kingdom building.

Allowing Jesus to Feed Us

We characterised discipleship in Chapter Four as a rhythm of activity and contemplation. Here our focus is on times of crisis when personal

---

7 Henri J.M. Nouwen, *In the Name of Jesus. Reflections on Christian Leadership* (Darton, Longman and Todd 1989), 50.

8 I am grateful here for an on-line forum *Pastors in a Secular Age* and a conversation on play led by Dr Anne Tomlinson of the Scottish Episcopal Institute.

9 Peter Berger, *A Rumour of Angels: Modern Society and the Re-discovery of the Supernatural.* (Penguin 1970), 76-77.

10 Zechariah 8:5.

malnutrition has taken root. The invitation to 'come and have breakfast' served by Jesus is good news indeed. There is no substitute for taking prolonged and unhurried time simply and prayerfully to allow Jesus to feed us. He delights to do so as on that Galilean beach. For me, I look back to times when, exhausted, I have taken time to go on retreat, sometimes a day retreat, more often a residential retreat. (The first half of my life of ministry I went to conferences; the second half I went on retreats!). There is nothing like reading Scripture slowly and carefully (with no thought of a sermon and no commentary in sight); learning to truly *listen* to Scripture rather than to *raid* Scripture.

The church father Origen of Alexandria (c.184 – c.253) puts it simply in his commentary on Matthew's Gospel, 'Whenever someone draws near so as to make room for the Word, then the kingdom of Heaven draws near such a person.'[11] I have found reading through a whole gospel or epistle in one sitting immensely refreshing. I remember sitting in the chaos of Terminal 6 of Heathrow Airport during a snow storm, waiting for a delayed plane and reading John's Gospel from beginning to end. It was nothing short of exhilarating. Between the chapters I people watched. Swirling around me were masses of irate, frustrated and anxious world travellers. I could only just imagine their wildly diverse stories but here I was reading a narrative that included them all.

I fondly remember spending a whole morning, guided by a retreat director, simply meditating on Psalm 139. The intimacy of God's love which I experienced was powerful and renewing. David Hansen tells of a time in his own ministry where exhaustion hit. 'One summer twilight my head lay in my wife's arms: I wept bitterly and told her I was quitting the ministry.' He tells how, almost unaccountably, in the weeks that followed the clouds slowly cleared:

> I preached from Jeremiah that fall. I laughed with joy as I foraged the fire and brimstone of the weeping prophet. I gave up fighting with boards over money and my 'rights', stopped fighting against life in the wilderness. I began to feed on the Word.[12]

---

11 Origen Commentary on Matthew X.14 quoted in D.H. Williams *Evangelicals and Tradition* (Paternoster 2005), 76.
12 David Hansen, op. cit., 65.

Equally nourishing for me have been extended times of quiet prayer and solitude, often while walking. Many years ago I was on retreat at one of my favourite haunts, Holy Island, Lindisfarne. The Anglican sister who was warden of the centre asked me how I intended to use my time on the island. I showed her a book entitled *Dynamic Leadership* that I had been planning to read. In no uncertain terms she made it known that 'this was a place to wait on God, not to learn about dynamic leadership!' The book was banned – and I was blessed![13] Eugene Person summarises it all so well,

> There is a large, leisurely centre to existence where God must be pondered, lovingly believed. This demand is not for prayer-on-the-run or for prayer-on-request. It means entering realms of the Spirit where wonder and adoration have space to develop, where play and delight have time to flourish.[14]

'Come to this sacred table, not because you must but because you may' we say as we invite our congregation to the Lord's Supper. We pray with them, 'So feed us with the body and blood of Jesus Christ your Son, that we may forever live in him and he in us.' The nourishing power of the sacraments is far too often underplayed. Their renewing power lies in their pointing us away from ourselves to the promises of the Gospel; God in Christ really is 'for us'. I recall reading the testimony of a colleague who was totally immobilised by ministry burnout and deep depression. Attending normal services was simply too much, as was receiving direct prayer ministry. He would visit a close friend, play chess and celebrate communion. With no emotional demands the sheer objectivity and simplicity of the Lord's Supper was his main route back to spiritual health.

Allowing the Holy Spirit to Re-vitalise Us

The ministry of the Holy Spirit is central to John's Gospel and central to renewal. For John, the Spirit is the unseen wind that brings new birth[15]; the thirst-quenching living water that becomes 'a spring of water welling

---

13 Paul Beasley Murray, *Dynamic Leadership. Rising above the Chaos of the One-Man Band* (Tunbridge Wells: MARC 1990). It was a book that subsequently I read and found helpful and encouraging!
14 Eugene Peterson, *Working the Angles. The Shape of Pastoral Integrity* (Grand Rapids: Eerdmans 1987), 65.
15 John 3:8.

up to eternal life'[16]; the refreshing stream that will flow from within[17]; the Counsellor who will testify about Christ[18] and the power of the breath of the Risen Christ that will equip us for mission.[19] God the Spirit is the one who renews our exhausted, dehydrated selves and allows the Dead Sea of ministries that have nothing left to give to be made wonderfully fresh. 'Where the river flows everything will live' is the great vision of Ezekiel 47 as the trickle of water flowing from the temple becomes a great river, swarming with aquatic life.[20] I thank God for many times where in silent prayer, or with colleagues laying hands on me, the Holy Spirit has brought me back to the one who says 'If anyone is thirsty, let them come to me and drink.'[21]

Importantly the Spirit's ministry of restoration particularly comes in the context of his people, the new temple 'a dwelling where God lives by his Spirit'.[22] So often it is in worship and fellowship and shared mission that our replenishing comes. I recall a time when I preached on Ezekiel's vision of the River of Life at our partner church in Alexandria, South Romania. After preaching, a team of us offered to those present an opportunity to come forward and be anointed with oil as a symbol of the Spirit's presence and renewal. It was deeply moving to see all the congregation, some who had endured great hardship in the Ceausescu era, come forward. Not only were tired church leaders and weary members nourished – but so were we.

This, of course, raises the uncomfortable question of how is it that we become malnourished whilst being within the very Body of Christ. A key part of the answer, I suggest, is that spiritual and emotional emptiness often arises through underplaying the importance of the mutuality of ministry. I began pastoral ministry with the expectation of preaching twice on a Sunday and addressing at least one other meeting each week. It was and is unsustainable over a long period of time. In more recent years there has been huge personal blessing in being part of a multi-voiced church. Not

---

16 John 4:14.
17 John 7:38.
18 John 15:26.
19 John 20:22.
20 Ezekiel 47:9.
21 John 7:37.
22 Ephesians 2: 22.

only has a preaching team of women and men brought essential diversity of insight but it has allowed me, for one, regularly to sit under the teaching of others and be well fed.

It also puts a rightful focus on the intrinsic power of the written and Living Word, irrespective of preacher or teacher. Put bluntly, much ministry starvation comes from either personal pride – 'my bible teaching is best' – or from the lack of courage to insist on a polyphonic approach. Listening to gifted bible teachers online is a great bonus. The Spirit's ministries are manifold. For sure, we are irresponsible to utilise folk who have no gift or anointing for bible teaching but we are equally irresponsible to try and emulate John Wesley who preached, on average, fifteen sermons per week! Less is more when it comes to nourishing both ourselves and our congregation with a healthy spiritual diet.

To meet Jesus is to meet the Bread of Life. To serve Jesus is to share the Bread of life. To be starved in the process is a profound anomaly. 'Come and have breakfast' was a stunning invitation. Accepting the invitation is the only way through.

Chapter Nine

Ministry Failure and Restoration

**Simon, Son of John, do you truly love me
more than these?** (John 21:15)

The breakfast meal is now over. Jesus and Peter find themselves alone as they stroll down the Galilean shoreline, almost certainly at the beckoning of Jesus. Never, I suspect, had Peter felt so vulnerable and never less wanting to be alone with Jesus. Peter was a broken man; his three-fold denial of Jesus had shaken him to the very core. His breaking down and weeping bitterly on hearing the cock crow those weeks before (Mark 14:72) was perhaps just the first of many moments of raw and bitter regret. How could he possibly be forgiven for such a blatant moral meltdown? Jesus and his disciples had shared in an emotional farewell meal in an Upper Room where Peter had promised, in front of his colleagues, 'Even if I have to die with you, I will never disown you' (14:31). He had defended Jesus, albeit with misplaced bravado, in Gethsemane. How could he explain to himself, never mind to others, what had happened? And more to the point, how could he forgive himself?

Peter's joy that morning on encountering the risen Christ was, I suspect, a somewhat muted joy; shame and embarrassment, tainting his celebration. The very charcoal fire (*anthrakia*) on the beach would have reminded Peter of that *anthrakia* in the courtyard of the high priest where he had warmed his hands and spoken such cold words of betrayal.

Failure in Ministry

Failure in ministry takes many forms. For some it is stark, devastating and public – marital unfaithfulness, uncontrollable debts, inappropriate and persistent texting to minors, a hidden addiction exposed. Such moral collapse, like the sudden crumbling of an ill-constructed bridge, is always the result of many months of hidden erosion. The corrosive waters of excused moral compromise and habitual denial have been flowing for a long time. In such cases restoration will need to be slow, radical and intense. It will inevitably involve serious accountability and skilled pastoral care. Public ministry will wisely be put on hold. In walking alongside colleagues coping with such moral failure I have often encountered a brokenness like no other.

For others, ministry failure is less public but no less debilitating - for pastor and people. We fail people with our over-controlling leadership, with our neglect of even-handed pastoral duties, with our avoidance of dealing with conflict, with our inability to handle personal criticism. Here the failure is often not fully recognised or understood and can cause deep congregational hurt and confusion. It often results in misplaced guilt (i.e. guilt among the wrong people!) and a nebulous negativity where the congregational dynamic is unhealthy but undiagnosed. It takes discerning and experienced oversight to adequately name and address these issues. As Bishop Stephen Neill wrote, 'It is not failure that matters but refusal to recognise failure . . . If a man*(sic)* is willing to be honest, there is hardly anything that God cannot do for him.'[1]

In reflecting on 'ministry failure' sensitivity is needed in understanding what we are actually talking about. All of us involved in ministry, at whatever level, feel failures at times. If you are anything like me, it is all too easy to end a routine day more than a little disappointed with ourselves. We are conscious of how poor has been our time management and how our pastoral care has revealed hidden preferences and (well disguised) irritations. Our meditation on Scripture has been marred by distraction, our wider theological reading minimal and our prayer-life a little woeful. Of course we are alert enough to know that 'success' in ministry is hardly to be measured by crass statistics. We are smart enough to recognise that the church website we have just been browsing, which heralds a sixth church plant in two years, is not exactly a missional norm! Ministry appraisal, we well know, is, at best, a tricky business. Yet there are days when 'ministry failure' still seems a pretty sane and honest assessment.

This sort of 'low level' sense of failure becomes more acute, of course, when we are struggling with ill-health, and particularly mental ill-health.

---

1   Stephen Neill, *On the Ministry.* (London: SCM Press 1952), 43.

Classically, times of depression leave us feeling utter failures and a vicious circle is soon operating, with our sense of failure feeding our depression. Absence from work for a long period due to stress or a serious illness can leave us feeling guilty that we have let God and his people down. Then there is the (not-uncommon) painful scenario of a good and godly leader being hounded out of a church for standing up to bullies and challenging the status quo. These leaders too are made to feel failures. What is obvious, but cannot be stressed enough, is that all this is *not* the sort of moral failure being considered here. False guilt abounds in ministry and our enemy, the Accuser, delights in exploiting it.

There is something actually healthy about a sense of inadequacy which casts us back on to the faithfulness of God. For sure we need to keep examining our hearts and, yes, we are all moral failures in need of daily forgiveness but distinctions are needed. Mark Meynell, in his deeply moving and insightful book, *When Darkness Seems My Closest Friend. Reflections on life and ministry with depression*, concludes by arguing that profound personal struggles such as depression are to be seen, not as a ministry impediment, but as a ministry gift. Our weakness humbles us, makes us totally reliant on God's grace, deepens our empathy and increases our credibility. He quotes someone who commented, 'Never trust a leader without a limp'.[2] Maynell writes,

> If my experiences as a cave dweller (one of his evocative metaphors
> for depression) help me to 'carry each other's burdens and in this
> way (to) fulfil the law of Christ' (Galatians 6:2) then I can genuinely
> see them as a gift. I do not need to identify a divine causal link to
> my depression to sense a divine purpose in it. My tears now have
> redemptive meaning . . . I have come to believe that my depression has
> made me a better pastor.[3]

All of this is to be sharply distinguished from the moral failure that occurs when there is a tragic, persistent and serious flouting of biblical standards. Issues such as marital unfaithfulness, chronic debt and financial impropriety always come with deception and lead to an evaporation of trust and immense hurt. For the sensitive leader involved in these things

---

2   Mark Meynell, *When Darkness seems My Closest Friend. Reflections on life and Ministry with Depression* (London: Inter Varsity Press 2018), 178.
3   Ibid., 173.

the guilt that follows is crushing. Peter's failure was personal, (though it must have shaken the other disciples – they all, of course, deserted Jesus) and overwhelming. 'He wept bitterly,' reports Matthew.[4]

The good news of Jesus is that there is always hope. God's redeeming power knows no limit. Peter's restoration and recommissioning is powerful and instructive, not least because it involved a painful journey. Serious moral failure involves issues which are complex and the route to repentance and restoration can be long and challenging. Gordon MacDonald, back in the 1980s, was a highly acclaimed American pastor, speaker and author. Many of us were significantly helped and shaped by his book 'Ordering Your Private World' (1984). Then, two years on, at the helm of the American student movement Inter-Varsity Christian Fellowship, he resigned admitting adultery over many months. When asked why he had not informed the board when appointed he said, 'I have no good answer for that . . . The same distorted and deceived mind that got me into this (adulterous relationship) was causing me not to think clearly . . . I suppose I was in that very naïve perspective that says, 'This is going to be covered, it's going to go away.'[5] A few years later he bravely published a sequel 'Rebuilding Your Broken World' (1988). It is a moving testimony to God's restoring grace but also a sober reminder that the journey of repentance is multifaceted and costly. To one aspect of his reflections and advice we will return.

The Root of Failure

It is perhaps worth pausing for a moment to reflect on what may have been at the root of Peter's catastrophic failure. One possible candidate could be sheer physical tiredness. Luke makes it clear just how tired the disciples were at Gethsemane when he comments that they were 'exhausted from sorrow.'[6] We are all too aware, after a taxing weekend of ministry, how morally vulnerable we can be. Another candidate could have been Peter just dropping his guard and allowing an arrow of the enemy to get through. It could have been sheer fear. Matthew seems to imply that it was just as Jesus was beginning to be brutally tortured that Peter's moral collapse began (Matthew 26:67-68). In part, I suspect each of these things were going on.

---

4   Matthew 26:75.
5   Quote from *Christianity Today*, July 10th 1987 found on christianitytoday.com.
6   Luke 22:45; NEB 'worn out by grief.'

But, perhaps, at heart, some hidden, moral fault-line had been there a lot longer. Dominic Smart in his book, 'When we get it wrong: Peter, Christ and our Path through Failure' agrees and argues that Peter's denials sprang from a long-existing false security. Peter, he suggests, was sincere, energetic and passionate in his love for Christ but was too confident in himself. He sees as a clue Peter's bold words just hours before his denial, 'Lord, I am ready to go with you to prison and to death' (Luke 22:33). Peter 'the rock' still needed to learn that his only hope was in standing on the Rock which is Christ. Smart comments '(Peter) thinks that because he is sincere he is also secure. It's one of the biggest mistakes we can make in our discipleship'.[7] Peter, it seems, *underestimated* the momentous spiritual battle that was raging as Jesus made his way to crucifixion and *overestimated* his own moral fortitude.

I think Dominic Smart is right. Indeed, failure for all of us has at its ultimate cause a sense of self-sufficiency, a denial of our total dependency on the grace of God. Smart later makes the suggestive comment that Luke's words as Jesus was led into the house of the high priest, 'Peter followed at a distance' (Matt. 26:58; Luke 22:54) are revealing. Both our real failures and our frequent 'sense of failure' comes as we distance ourselves from the source of all our strength.

Closure and a New Chapter

Scholars are united that one of the main reasons John 21 was written was because of the unfinished business with Peter. The Good Shepherd had a particular lost sheep still to find, restore and re-direct. It's interesting that each of the first three Gospels, in their own way, all also hint at such closure and a renewed future. For Mark, the angel says 'But go tell his disciples – *and Peter*.'[8] For Matthew the reader has already heard Jesus say 'You are Peter and on this rock I will build my church'.[9] For Luke the two from Emmaus had rushed back and heard the disciples say 'It is true, the Lord has risen and has appeared to Simon.'[10] However, it is here in John 21 that this question of 'closure' is dealt with most fully. Peter, we are told, was

---

7 Dominic Smart, *When we get it wrong. Peter, Christ and our path through failure* (Paternoster Lifestyle 2001), 39.

8 Mark 16:7.

9 Matthew 16:18.

10 Luke 24:34.

hurt when Jesus asked him three times over, 'do you love me? (21:17). But we are meant to see this as the 'faithfulness of the wounds of a friend.'[11] It was the sting of an antiseptic, the pain of pushing a dislocated bone back into place. The repetition was deliberate so that healing could come and a new future enjoyed. Jesus is seeking 'not so much Peter's triple retraction of his denial, even less to embarrass him again before the other disciples; it is rather what awaits Peter in the future that prompts Jesus to reinforce his ties with him as never before.'[12]

The Restorative Question

It is striking that Jesus doesn't tackle Peter's denial head on. Jesus doesn't name what he clearly knows and then has a 'heart-to heart' with Peter. Jesus doesn't invite Peter, like a good trauma therapist, to rehearse the events of the past few days. As George Beasley Murray observes, there is something 'highly unusual' about Jesus' three-fold questioning.[13] There is no sense of Peter being counselled, even less rebuked or lectured but neither is it a purely tangential engagement. What is actually happening is a profound engagement through an approach that brings out the best of a broken man who is thinking the worst. A simple question is asked three times. It is asked with slight variation (most commentators agree that the word differences are more stylistic than substantial) 'Simon, Son of John, do you truly love me more than these?' John's Gospel is full of direct and penetrating questions by Jesus (seventeen in fact), but this is the most searching. With great psychological skill, the three-fold question both evokes the pain of Peter's threefold moral collapse and addresses it with redemptive possibility.

What is key, it seems to me, is where Jesus puts the emphasis in these questions. 'Do you love **me**?' The comparison is between the 'these' and 'me'. In other words, this is not Jesus putting Peter on the spot and assessing his strength of love compared to others. This is not Jesus seeing whether

---

11 Proverbs 27:6.

12 H.N. Ridderbos *The Gospel According to John; A Theological Commentary* Translated by J. Vriend (Grand Rapids: Eerdmans 1997), 667 quoted in Braford B. Blaine Jr *Peter in the Gospel of John. The Making of an Authentic Disciple*, Atlanta, Society of Biblical Literature 2007), 170.

13 George R. Beasley Murray, *John*. Word Biblical Commentary (Waco, Texas: Word 1987), 404.

Peter quotient of love has come back up to an acceptable level. Rather, this repeated questioning is a gracious invitation for Peter to readjust his focus. Do you love **me?** It is Jesus gently turning Peter's gaze to the one whose love is immeasurable. This is the key pastoral move Jesus is making. For Jesus, failure is never the last word.

This emphasis is perhaps hinted at in three particular ways. First, going back to the story of Peter's failure, Luke makes the memorable comment immediately after Peter's denials, 'the Lord turned and looked straight at Peter.' (Luke 22:61). Was it a knowing look of sadness and hurt? Or did that look also contain love and forgiveness? I'm sure it was both. It was certainly a 'wordless gaze'[14] that Peter would long remember. Second, here now on the beach, it seems, Jesus deliberately uses his original name, 'Simon, son of John' (v.15), rather than the new name given him when first called. Was this perhaps to jolt Peter into remembering all the Lord had done? Third, it is noticeable how the initial question is framed. 'Do you love me *more than these?* This is hardly likely to be Jesus inviting a comparison between Peter's level of love and that of his companions. If that were the case it would have been more natural grammatically for Jesus to have added the word, 'Do you love me more than these **do.**'[15] Further Jesus is very soon going to rebuke Peter for making comparisons (21:22). Much more likely, Jesus is wanting to turn Peter's attention away from all that was distracting him back to Jesus himself.

Peter, like so many of us, was totally caught up with himself. He was consumed with bitter regret. The sight of that charcoal fire on the beach would have been a distinctly uncomfortable reminder of his cowardice as he denied ever knowing Jesus to a servant girl over a similar charcoal fire. Here is Peter locked in painful introspection; and here is Jesus, with consummate skill and gentleness, moving him on, 'Peter do you love **me?'** 'Peter, stop looking backwards with regret; stop looking inwards with self-condemnation, stop looking around at what others are thinking – and look

---

14 Markus Bockmuehl, in an essay on how and when conversion (turning) happened for Peter, comments 'Strikingly, the only person who 'turns' in this context of denial is not Peter but the Lord who hauntingly turns and convicts the apostle with a wordless gaze'. Markus Bockmuehl, *Simon Peter in Scripture and Memory. The New Testament Apostle in the Early Church* (Baker Academic 2012), 157.
15 Rekha Chennattu, *Johannine Discipleship as a Covenant Relationship* (Michigan: Baker Academic 2005), 175.

to **me**!' Jesus is soon going to say 'Simon, follow **me**', (21:19). Of course, this '**me**' makes it an astonishingly egotistic question that can only make moral sense if Jesus is the divine I AM. Jesus is inviting Peter to find his hope and ground his trust in the only One who can 'take away the sin of the world' (1:29) and the only One who has authority to say 'So if the Son sets you free you will be free indeed' (8:38).

P.T. Forsyth, in his book *The Cure of Souls*, may not have been thinking about broken Peter when he wrote these words, but he could well have been: 'God is deeper than the deepest depth in man. He is holier than our deepest sin is deep . . . Think more of the depth of God than the depth of your cry.'[16] On the beach that morning, as we saw at the end of Chapter One, divine grace was relentlessly and lovingly pursuing this broken disciple. For many of us in ministry the antidote to our constant tendency to 'feel a failure' as well as our committing serious failure is to truly live by that grace in Christ that we are so often commending to others.

The pastoral move Jesus makes here is one we are also called to emulate. Repentance, essential to any restoration, involves in essence a radical turning around from looking at and pleasing self to gazing on and pleasing Christ. The great value of biblical ministry and pastoral care is that it keeps refocussing attention of what truly matters. Many a time have I gone into the pulpit feeling unsure, emotionally exhausted and spiritually self-doubting, caught up with myself. Fresh resilience has come as I have remembered the 'me' of 'do you love **me**? Preaching and ministry is simply an allowing of the Living Word of God, through the written Word of God, to meet and transform first my life and then that of others.

Beyond Words: Shame and the Look of Love

There can be no doubt that alongside Peter's guilt there must have been an enormous, crushing sense of shame. *Guilt* is essentially about recognising the wrong that we have done. Shame is much more about how we see ourselves as a result of wrong (done to us as well as by us). Guilt is a moral response to *actions*, shame an emotional response to *self*. Shame leads us to hide, to fear exposure, to cover our face, to step outside into the night as Peter had done. When the angel had announced to the women

---

16 P.T. Forsyth, *The Cure of Souls* (Grand Rapids: Eerdmans 1971), 128.

at the empty tomb, 'Go tell his disciples…and Peter'[17] was that because Peter had separated himself from the others through shame? Shame results in a dark distortion of self-esteem and an equally dark sense of personal hopelessness. All this must have haunted Peter. And all this was understood by Jesus.

If it is true that God's gracious response to guilt is *forgiveness* and God's gracious response to shame is *acceptance* then far more was going on with Jesus and Peter that day than is usually commented on. Jesus is not just posing questions to Peter, he is deliberately drawing him in to a face-to face-encounter. Jesus very body-language is one of warm acceptance. The face of love that Peter had seen (mentioned earlier) at the scene of his denials now looks again into Peter's eyes. On the open beach that morning, with Peter contemplating the terror of exposure, the light of the risen Christ dispels the darkness of shame. Peter can again look up and look forward; Peter can again envisage a vocation. All restoration for ministry failure involves far more than divine and human assurance of forgiveness. The body-language of acceptance by the Body of Christ is also crucial.

The Restorative Community

We have no indication in the Gospels of how the other disciples responded to Peter's failure. After all, in their own way they were all more than a little culpable by their desertion when it came to Christ's trial and crucifixion.[18] I like to think that the six of them who returned to Galilee with Peter did so, in part, out of support for Peter. What is crucial to leadership restoration in my experience is a forgiving, accepting and healing community. Without such, a way back is so much more difficult. What is striking about Gordon MacDonald's personal journey in his *Rebuilding Your Broken World* (referred to earlier) is how a restorative community became so vital to that story. He talks not only of the remarkable forgiveness of his wife and children, not only of a group of men who journeyed with him through a protracted period of self-examination and godly sorrow but of a much wider community of friends who reached out to him in love and extraordinary grace. He writes:

---

17 Mark 16:7
18 Matthew 26:31.

Gail and I will never forget two visits on the day our world publicly broke apart. Each visit was from two people. The first visit was from a young man and a young woman who had worked as my assistants for the two previous years. They sat and listened tearfully to what I had to tell them; how our lives were to be abruptly changed and how – as a result – their lives would be changed. And when I was through, they instinctively came across the room, laid hands upon Gail and me, and struggled through a prayer for us. These two, in their early twenties, gave more grace and kindness than we could ever have imagined.

The second visit came from two much older people: also a man and woman. Their gift came in their insistence in reflecting on a number of specific things they felt we had done for them and their colleagues. They insisted on going into detail so that we would not forget for a moment that, as far as they were concerned, history was not a black hole. Grace, mercy, peace and kindness filled the room that day.[19]

This communal response was no substitute for the painful personal journey that had to be undertaken. It involved stepping away from all public ministry for eighteen months. MacDonald outlines five key stages to his restoration: confession, reflection on the pre-history of his sin, the discipline of many accountable conversations, the receiving of comfort, the advocacy of his worth by others. I found this last point very telling. There were people who were willing to stand up for this 'broken-world person'. This is the quality of acceptance that heals shame. The fullest expression of this came from a small struggling congregation, Trinity Baptist Church in New York City.[20] When he sought to dissuade them from approaching him as a potential pastor they said, 'We're all broken people here . . . We've all had failures in our resumes. Come and talk to us about how you've dealt with it.' MacDonald concludes,

> My conviction is that revival will spring out of a rediscovery of the power of repentance and the granting of restorative grace. When sanctuaries become places where man or woman, having failed God and the community of Christ-followers, can open his or her heart and say in blunt language, 'I have sinned' then revival will start.[21]

Pentecost was soon to follow for Peter.

---

19 Gordon MacDonald, *Rebuilding your Broken World* (Godalming, Surrey: Highland Books 1988, updated edition 2004 with Epilogue), 232.
20 MacDonald refers to this in an Epilogue to a later edition (2003).
21 Ibid., 277-8.

Recommissioning: its Joy and Demands

Here on the beach restoration and recommissioning go hand-in-hand. Intentionally and beautifully Jesus intertwines his restorative question with wonderful words of affirmation. Jesus doesn't ask his question three times, and then, once truly assured that his disciple is safe again, recommission him. No, immediately on hearing Peter's first declaration of love the re-appointment begins. Such interlacing of question and commissioning is to highlight that our call to serve is always and only a call of divine grace. Incredibly, the one who has failed so much is about to be given oversight of no less than the pastoral care and mission of the early church, 'Feed my lambs', 'Take care of my sheep', 'Feed my sheep.' (21:15-17). Jesus' unspoken absolution is the immense trust Jesus now places in Peter. What could be a greater sign of acceptance? God, then and now, is the God of the second chance. This beach encounter with the risen Lord was for Peter the beginning of an unbelievable new journey. It was an adventure that would take him from the depths of failure to the heights of Pentecost; to an extraordinary mission to Cornelius house, to the Council of Jerusalem, to a ministry at the heart of the empire, to the pain and dignity of the martyrdom that Jesus is about to predict.

One of the most troubling issues for those who have failed in ministry is the anxiety that once moral collapse has happened there is susceptibility to further failure. Given this, there must have been something deeply assuring (rather than unnerving) for Peter by Jesus immediately going on to talk of Peter's distant future 'when you are old you will stretch out your hands' (21:18). The implication - this failed apostle would indeed make it to the end and make it with exemplary fidelity. It was a shrewd and additional restorative move by the Good Shepherd.[22]

Peter goes into the future a different man. First, there is a whole new orientation to his ministry. John in his Third Epistle reminds his friend Gaius of a church member called Diotrephes, unflatteringly described as one who '**who loves to be first**'.[23] It conjures up all sorts of pastoral nightmares, from that pedantic church administrator who always likes to be up front, to the church leader who assumes his directives are essentially uttered *ex cathedra*, to the elder who lives for his appointment to that key

---

22 I am grateful to Dave Redfern of St Andrews for making this observation.
23 3 John 9.

denominational committee, sitting around a shiny table and admiring his own reflection! In a more loveable and humble way, this was Peter all over! Peter loved to be first, first to attempt to confess who Jesus was, (and got it so right and so wrong), first to try his hand (his feet!) at walking on water, first to offer to be a martyr for Jesus, 'I will lay down my life for you', (13:37), the first to defend Jesus with a sword in Gethsemane, the first that morning to dive overboard and swim to Jesus. He couldn't help firing first; needing to be the hero leader. Now Jesus' question powerfully brings about a radical re-ordering. It effects a replacement of 'love to be first' with a 'love for Jesus'. For sure, Peter becomes the leader of the church in Jerusalem, but as one Catholic commentator – no less – notes, John 21 is 'not about Peter's primacy but about his penitence'. Peter knows that if he is anything, Shepherd and Apostle, it is only because of the undeserved grace of Christ. This beach encounter was his Jabbok and he goes into future ministry 'limping' as much as the patriarch Jacob had done.[24] The death of ego in ministry, as in all discipleship, is the daily, intentional laying down of our agendas at the foot of the cross and seeking to do 'only what the Father is doing' (John 5:19). It is only possible if our heartfelt passion is, as Jesus, 'not to please myself but him who sent me.' (John 5:30)

Second, for Peter there is also a renewed understanding of what truly matters in ministry. Jesus three-fold question may have had as its emphasis, 'Do you love **me**?' but the importance of love, captured by the different verbs used, is impossible to miss. 'Do you truly **love** me?' It's an emphasis that will never leave him. He writes in his Epistle 'Though you have not seen him, you love him' (1 Peter 1:8). Far more important than any skill or competency in ministry is the condition of our heart. 'Do you truly **love** me?' A frightening reality in ministry is that we can be so caught up with toning up our leadership muscles that we fail not notice the slow spiritual sclerosis of our hearts. Whilst our ministries grow, our hearts can shrink.

A Question of 'Affections'

Perhaps no one has explored so thoroughly the implications of Jesus question 'Do you truly love me? as the great American theologian and

---

24 Genesis 32:31.

philosopher Jonathan Edwards. Following a remarkable 'great awakening' in his church in Northampton, Massachusetts in 1734-35 Edwards began to document what had occurred, his *Narrative of Surprising Conversions*. But it was only after a second wave of revival blessing five years later that he wrestled with a question that weighed heavy upon him, namely what were the marks of true religion.

It was prompted by two dominant concerns, coming from quite different directions. One was how to defend the genuine godly emotion of the revival against decidedly sceptical colleagues; the other was how to make sense of the fact that mixed with genuine conversions were counterfeit and bogus testimonies. The greatest of his three works on this quest was his *Treatise on the Religious Affections*, published 1746.[25] The 'simple' thesis of the book (382 pages based on the text 1 Peter 1:8 'Whom having not seen, you love'!) is that what characterises true regeneration, above all, is a humble, Spirit-produced overriding affection for God Himself which results in obedient discipleship.

This mark of Christian authenticity is the very thing Jesus was targeting with Peter. It is not so much our Christian knowledge but *our inclination* that matters, the orientation of both will and emotion towards God. Of course, for Edwards, a New England Calvinist, God's love for us must always be prior but still, for him, the fear of God, the love of God and delight in God are the most decisive of all the fruit of conversion. Edwards spent significant time outlining how this differs from seemingly noble signs of conversion, such as gratitude, but which, at the end of the day, can spring from within ourselves rather than being born of God. 'The witness of the Spirit' (Romans 8:16) is not, he argues an inward voice that simply assures us but is a decisive infusion and spreading abroad of the love of God that totally realigns our lives.[26]

The impact of his writings were profound. Outstanding pastors and writers such as Thomas Chalmers, Andrew Fuller and Robert Hall were deeply influenced by the way Edwards held together intellectual rigour with a passionate love for Christ. He modelled and still models the foundational virtue of ministry, a heart softened by the Spirit and filled with love for Christ and his people. All ministry should be sobered with the haunting

---

25 Jonathan Edwards, *The Religious Affections* (Edinburgh: Banner of Truth, Reprint, 1994).
26 Ibid., 165.

indictment of the Ascended Lord to the Ephesian Church, 'You have lost your first love.' As Edwards puts it, 'The more a true saint loves God with a gracious love, the more he desires to love him and the more uneasy he is at his want of love to him.'[27]

What is more, it is this love for Christ that truly shapes us. James K.A Smith, in his book *Desiring the Kingdom* makes a cogent case for this. Human beings, he argues, are more than thinking creatures and believing beings, we are 'fundamentally and primordially lovers'.[28] Rather than the reductionist 'I think therefore I am' the fuller human reality is 'I am what I love'. 'To be human is to love, and it is what we love that defines us.'[29] We are essentially creatures of desire, of affection, and so what distinguishes between us, he notes, is not *whether* we love but *what* we love. It is as we put Christ first and love him above all else that Christ's life becomes transformative for ours. Such (often pre-reflective) desire is what produces the habits, practices and thus virtues of a godly life, 'rituals of ultimate concern' as Smith terms them.[30] Henri Nouwen summarises the demands as well as the joys of recommissioning superbly, 'If there is any focus that the Christian of the future will need, it is the discipline of dwelling in the presence of One who keeps asking us, 'Do you love me? Do you love me? Do you love me?''[31]

Peter the failure tasted the grace of restoration. Only such grace is a solid foundation for ministry. Those who have been forgiven much love much. And sometimes it is those who limp most who others trust most to lead.

---

27 Ibid., 303.

28 James K.A Smith *Desiring the Kingdom: Worship, Worldview and Cultural Formation* (Grand Rapids, Michigan: Baker Academic 2009), 41.

29 Ibid., 51.

30 Ibid., 86.

31 Henri Nouwen, *In the Name of Jesus. Reflections on Christian Leadership* (Darton, Longman and Todd 1989), 28.

Chapter Ten

Self-awareness and Self-deception in Ministry

Lord you know all things, you know that I love you. (John 21:17)

The beach conversation between Jesus and Peter, ending with such a powerful sense of restoration as we have just seen, was nevertheless decidedly uncomfortable. Three times, with slight variation, Jesus pressed the urgent question, 'Simon, son of John do you truly love me?' and, like repeated applications of an antiseptic to a wound, it began to sting. Peter was hurt, dismayed and grieved. All he could do was appeal to Jesus' superior knowledge, 'Lord you know all things, you know that I love you' (21:17). When someone is emotionally bruised it is often difficult to distinguish between a person's true convictions and what are just verbal defence reflexes – and so it is here. Is Peter simply refusing to properly engage with Jesus' question, simply throwing back the responsibility onto his Lord, the one who, after all, 'knows the heart of each person'? (2:25). Or could it just be that Peter has finally come to the conclusion that he can no longer trust his own judgement about himself? He would not be the first or last who, through sudden failure, loses complete confidence in their self-understanding. This was not the time to offer the apostle an on-line Enneagram test!

Self-awareness in Ministry

The ancient aphorism of Socrates 'know thyself' is much easier to agree with than to live out. Daniel Goleman, one of the pioneers of the concept of 'emotional intelligence', recounts a fascinating early research project on a number of young, up-and-coming scientists in the 1950s who were assessed for both their I.Q. and their E.Q. (emotional intelligence). Forty years on their career trajectories were reviewed. It became apparent that their capacity for social and self-awareness was four times more influential in bringing professional success than simply their high I.Q.[1]

'Knowing ourselves' is particularly crucial in pastoral ministry. I have witnessed (and been part of) so many mistakes in pastoral ministry simply because of a lack of self-awareness. I recall seeking to bring reconciliation between a pastor and a somewhat hurt member of his congregation. When I asked the pastor, in the presence of his wounded congregant, if he appreciated the extent of the pain he had caused, the pastor replied 'How can I? I'm not a mind reader.' It wasn't quite the empathetic, bridge-building gesture I had been hoping for! Not being fully aware of our strengths and weaknesses, our broken past and the 'shadow side' of our characters is one of the most common causes of pastoral strife. William H. Willimon, in his book *Character and Calling: Virtues of the Ordained Life*, makes the memorable comment that 'more dangerous for pastoral ministry than *burn-out* is *black-out*, forgetting who we are.'[2] To assess the strength of the apostle Peter's self-awareness is an interesting but impossible-to-answer question. My suspicion is that that more than a few of his gaffs arose from this issue!

There is so much gain once we are aware of our weaknesses and in touch with our emotions. As a Jewish mystic once said, 'The greatest exile is to not know that you are in exile.'[3] It is fundamental to all collaborative ministry. Once we become aware as a pastoral leader that, for example, we are more an 'ear' than a 'mouth' within Christ's Body then we can compensate for our preaching weakness by building a preaching team around us and focusing instead on being the listening, caring pastoral 'ear' we are called and gifted to be. Happy the leader who surrounds his short-comings with *both* a determination to improve in those areas and a freedom to admit the need for help. I guess one of my key 'life verses' is

---

1   Daniel Goleman *Working with Emotional Intelligence* (New York: Bantam Books, 1998), 44-45 quoted in Bob Burns, Tasha D. Chapman, Donald C. Guthrie, *Resilient Ministry* (IVP Books 2013), 103.

2   William H. Willimon, *Character and Calling: Virtues of the Ordained Life* (Nashville: Abingdon Press 2000), 21.

3   Quoted by Jonathan Sachs in *The Persistence of Faith: Reith Lectures 1990* (London: Weidenfeld and Nicolson 1991), 43.

Romans 12:3, 'Do not think of yourselves more highly than you ought, but rather think of yourselves with sober judgment, in accordance with the faith God has distributed to each of you.' This is said in the context of both offering our bodies to God as a living sacrifice and living in the Body of Christ. There is both a vertical and horizontal humility needed.

Soren Kierkegaard and his Conversations by the Sea

There are few who have wrestled with the issue of self-awareness and its vertical and horizontal dimensions more intensely than the Danish philosopher/theologian Soren Kierkegaard (1813–1855). Inspired by his admiration of Socrates and his Lutheran pietism, Kierkegaard gave himself in ten years of remarkable writing to a journey of self-discovery and an exploration of what it is to be truly human. He would pace restlessly up and down the streets of his beloved Copenhagen (and no doubt its beautiful beaches) and ponder the paradoxes and perplexities of the human condition. He was the 'philosopher of the heart'.[4]

His copious writings were deeply Christian, reacting to both the nominalism of the Danish state church and the rational detachment of Hegel's idealism. His overriding concern was personal authenticity - living transparently before God and self, choosing the ethical life (a life of faith) rather than the mere aesthetic life (a life of pleasure). In a letter written in 1835 he wrote, 'One must first learn to know oneself before knowing anything else. Only when the person has inwardly understood himself (sic) and then seen the way forward on his path does his life acquire repose and meaning.'[5]

Kierkegaard's observations were sharp and instructive. Three of his key themes are areas to be explored in practical ways below. First, Kierkegaard was deeply aware of how 'life is to be understood backwards'. He was all too conscious of how his own life had been shaped by difficult relationships. His father had been distant and severe. He had broken off an engagement to a Regine Olsen, an unresolved trauma that haunted him the rest of his life. Both painful experiences left a deeply felt legacy of melancholy and

---

4   This is the title of Clare Carlisle's brilliant biography, *Philosopher of the Heart: The Restless Life of Soren Kierkegaard* (Allen Lane 2019).
5   Letter to P.E. Lind 6th July 1835, quoted in John Lippitt, 'Self-knowledge in Kierkegaard' in Ursula Renz (ed.) *Self-knowledge: a History*, Oxford Philosophical Concepts Series, (Oxford University Press 2017).

anxiety. Second, Kierkegaard became convinced that *alone* we can never fully understand ourselves. Seeking self-knowledge without reference to God, he observed, is like being intoxicated – we become dangerously dizzy, disorientated and deluded. Rather it is only as we place our lives under the gaze of an infinitely different and holy God that we will begin to see soberly – both our sinfulness and our value. The one who has an utterly changeless memory of what we have done is, paradoxically, the one who invites us to experience his changeless forgiveness, rest and grace in Christ.[6] Third, he was acutely aware of how 'life is to be lived forwards'. We don't understand ourselves by standing still, (certainly not for him by speculative theology) but by living obediently, riskily and sacrificially – like Abraham.[7]

It is as we *actualise* ('receive') who we are that we begin to *grasp* who we are. The real possibility of self-delusion can only be avoided by a ruthless and sustained reflection as we move forward in faith. In the end, many would judge Kierkegaard to be far too individualistic and narrowly introspective. Certainly in his quest for self-knowledge the role of the body of Christ is underplayed. Nevertheless his legacy has much to teach us.

Understanding Life Backwards – Unmet Emotional Needs

Simon P. Walker, in the first volume of his trilogy, '*The Undefended Leader: Learning Out of Who you Are*' argues that one of the most determinative factors shaping safe leadership is whether we have understood, taken responsibility for and addressed our own emotional needs, often born out of past experiences.[8] He identifies a deeply unhealthy but common pattern where a leader, through neglecting his or her own emotional needs, finds those needs met in serving others – the approval and appreciation they receive, for example. A dangerous collusion results where 'the followers are used to make up the psychological deficit within the leader.'[9] I have witnessed this many times in colleagues and regularly have seen signs of it within myself. When self-esteem is low there is a temptation to be over-

---

6   Clare Carlisle, op. cit., 227.

7   His famous book *Fear and Trembling* is a remarkable exploration of the story of Abraham sacrificing his son Isaac, an act he saw as both morally problematic and yet exemplary in its obedience.

8   Simon Peter Walker, Vol. 1 of '*The Undefended Leader*', *Leading Out of Who You Are. Discovering the Secret of Undefended Leadership* (Piquant 2007).

9   Ibid., 18.

concerned with feedback; where insecurity lurks there is a tendency to be driven, controlling and competitive and, most ominously, where there is a deficit of personal intimacy it can be sought in surrogate pastoral relationships.

Walker builds on research which has shown, somewhat predictably, that two of the most profound influences on our emotional and social development are our early childhood interactions with our parents and the peer pressure we experienced as adolescents. Influenced by the British psychologist John Bowlby and his work on attachment and loss in childhood,[10] Walker argues that our experience of trust or lack of it has a huge bearing on our present emotional needs. Our response to trust shapes our self-understanding and the emotional ecology of who we are. Based on our different formative experiences Walker goes on to identify four sorts of people, all of whom have distinctive strengths and weaknesses when it comes to adult leadership.[11]

First, he identifies what he terms 'the shaping leadership ego'. These are people who have enjoyed secure upbringings, leading to a positive view of both themselves and their caregivers. They are trusting, unthreatened, optimistic and so are self-assured in shaping reality around them. Such a privileged upbringing allows positive and confident leadership to develop. The lurking 'shadow side', however, is an over-confidence and an inability to receive negative feedback.

Second, Walker identifies the 'defining leadership ego'. In this category are those whose childhood was marked by enjoying praise as a reward for success but a distinct withdrawal of affirmation when things went wrong; the love they experienced was warm but conditional. Such an experience can breed an instinct always to quest for achievement, for defining goals, for relying on inner resources and not trusting others. What can emerge here is a leader who is diligent, hard-working, and high achiever but at the expense of a tendency to control and be driven, an aversion to taking risks and a dread of failure.

The third group Walker describes is the 'adapting leadership ego'. Here the person has struggled with sincere but fragile relationships. Attachment has often been difficult to discern perhaps through caregivers preoccupied

---

10 John Bowlby, *Attachment and Loss* (New York, Basic Books, Vol. 1 1969).
11 Walker, op.cit., Chapters 7-10.

with their own deep struggles. What develops is a low trust in themselves and a pre-occupation with preventing relationships breaking down. As adults it can result in attention-seeking and the need for constant reassurance. Such people as leaders can be warm, accommodating and excellent at consensus-building but are in danger of being overly compliant, anxious and concerned to maintain the peace in a group at any cost.

Finally Walker identifies the 'defending leadership ego', where attachment as a child has not just been fragile but chaotic, unpredictable and unreliable. Such a child grows up with little trust either in themselves or others. As an adult this can transmute into a deep suspicion of others, always assessing whether someone is 'safe' or not. They defend themselves from hurt by a careful discerning of who is for them and who against them.

Clearly life for all of us is more multifaceted and complex than the above. The psychoanalysis is over-simplistic, the photo-fit never that neat. Nevertheless, I find Walker's profiles, much fuller than I have described, shrewd and true to life. I see a reflection of my own image as I gaze down his wells. For each description I also find familiar faces coming to mind. The great value of this sort of self-reflection is that it sharpens our self-awareness and self-understanding and allows us to adjust and know our limits. It is also a salutary reminder of our both our brokenness and the fact that our past does not necessarily and inevitably define us. The transforming grace of Christ can set us free.

The Limits of Self-knowledge

The problem with our self-knowledge, of course, is that it is always limited and fragmentary. There is so much about us emotionally, intellectually, spiritually, subconsciously that we are not aware of and certainly don't understand. Centuries before Kierkegaard, St Augustine (354–430) understood this. He talked of 'an ocean depth' within us, *a grande profundum* of not being able to read fully either the 'abyss of our consciences' or the depth of our hearts. No leader is free of blind spots; to think otherwise is realised eschatology at its worst! Only in glory, when we see Christ face to face, will we 'fully know, even as I am fully known.'[12] In Augustine's famous *Confessions*, written 397–401, more a

---

12 1 Corinthians 13:12.

prayer than an autobiography, he realises his own total dependence on God for self-knowledge. He begins by bemoaning that our lives are much more problematic to read than often we assume. 'For what am I to myself without Thee, but a guide to my own downfall?[13] Later, in Book 10, in his brilliant rhetorical style, Augustine confesses, 'For Thou, Lord, dost judge me because, although 'no man knoweth the things of a man, but the spirit of a man which is in him' yet is there something of man, which not even the spirit of man that is in him itself knoweth.' It leads him to conclude,

'I will confess then what I know of myself, I will confess also what I know not of myself; since what I do know of myself, I know by thy shining light upon me; and what I know not of myself, I know not only until 'my darkness be made as the noonday' (Isaiah 58:10).[14]

For all the intense exploration of his inner life Augustine was very aware of its limits.

Living Life Forwards – Self-deception or Ruthless Honesty in Discipleship and Ministry

Self–deception is when such fragmentary knowledge of self turns to distortion; and this, of course, is when it can become particularly pastorally dangerous. We become not only the deceived but the deceiver. Socrates said 'the worst of all deceptions is self-deception'[15] and more fulsome still was Blaise Pascal's analysis that the greatest threat to the moral life is neither ignorance of the moral law nor moral weakness but self-deception.[16] Such self-deception is when we consciously or unconsciously choose an attractive but illusory narrative about ourselves and then live it out. It is when we invent a morally rosy view of ourselves and begin to believe it. John-Paul Sartre defined self-deception succinctly as 'avoiding using rational standards for evidence whenever it suits our purposes.'[17] It exists, for example, when

---

13 Augustine *The Confessions of St Augustine,* (London: Griffith, Farran, Browne & Co 1886) Book 4: Chapter 1.49.

14 Ibid., Book 10: Chapter 5.185.

15 Bruce Alton, 'The Morality of Self-Deception', *The Annual of the Society of Christian Ethics* 5 1985, 141.

16 Quoted in Joseph Pak, 'Self Deception in Theology', *Themelios*, Vol. 13. Issue 3 1998.

17 Quoted in Gregg A.Ten Elshof, *I told me so. Self-deception and the Christian Life* (Grand Rapids: Eerdmans 2009), 27.

CONVERSATIONS BY THE SEA

we are genuinely convinced of our integrity and our faithfulness but where, somewhere along the line, we have assimilated behaviours and attitudes which, to others, are plainly contradictory. Self-deception is not the same as hypocrisy. The latter is a conscious failure before others to live out our identity and claims whereas self-deception is a conscious or unconscious denial of the reality of our human condition *to ourselves.*

How many times have we encountered denial as we have counselled colleagues about over-familiarity with someone of the opposite sex or, more generally, a cavalier attitude to pastoral boundaries? Yet it can be our mistake too. How often have others seen our emotional rev-counter flickering in the red zone and we just haven't appreciated the dangerous level of our mental and spiritual exhaustion? How often have we sought to protect ourselves by beginning to impute to our critics motives that are not there?

Ian Stackhouse, in his delightful little book *Letters to a Young Pastor,* makes the comment,

> Compartmentalisation, which is the ability to hide yourself from yourself, is probably as rife among the religious as anywhere. What you allow yourself on a Monday when no one is looking, and you feel a bit low, is the very same thing you wouldn't possibly countenance as Sunday approaches.[18]

Gregg Elshof terms the same strategy 'attention management' where avoidance of issues becomes possible by conscious choosing to focus elsewhere.[19]

It is frighteningly easy to adopt such a state of denial and, indeed, I have come to the conclusion that there is something about pastoral ministry which makes self-deception particularly possible. Maybe it is, in part, the simple age-old illusion of assuming that what we preach to others automatically becomes a reality in us. It is a version of James's warning 'Do not merely listen to the Word and deceive yourselves. Do what it says'.[20] That great sermon I preached on costly intercession wasn't actually as totally life-changing for my own feeble prayer life as I thought!

At the most basic level, most pastoral leaders I know pride themselves on being good listeners but many of us patently are not. I have experienced

---

18 Ian Stackhouse, *Letters to a Young Pastor, Reflections on Leadership, Community and the Gospel of Grace* (Eugene, Oregon: Cascade Books 2019), 15.
19 Gregg Elshof, op. cit., 33.
20 James 1:22.

the salutary embarrassment of having a frail, elderly lady literally put her hands to my cheeks, forcibly turn my head round to hers (as I gaze over her shoulder to someone I *really did* need to talk to) and say, 'Andrew I am talking to you!' I have worked with pastors who genuinely see themselves as unreasonably overworked when a careful analysis of a typical week shows otherwise. We routinely define ourselves as 'servant leaders' but the sobering truth is that many of us can be extraordinarily self-seeking, particularly when the pressure is on. We claim, as standard orthodoxy, to be serving the Lord himself and our family as noble top priorities but a careful look at what most occupies our best energies sometimes reveals something different. We perceive ourselves as 'secure people in God' but too many of our dysfunctional moments seems to testify to deep insecurities. We assume we well understand our congregation but learning to 'read the runes' never quite made it on our training curriculum!

Self-deception, as Augustine saw so clearly, is a fundamental dimension of human sin; 'the serpent deceived me' cried Eve 'and I ate.' [21] Jeremiah had famously expressed it, 'The heart is deceitful above all things and beyond cure. Who can understand it?'[22] It arises from disordered desire when we cease to love God and his truth and instead turn inwards, loving ourselves and our own estimation of self.[23]

Self-deception is self-justification, the fruit of human pride. The unattractive reality is that we so often fabricate an inflated view of self that causes us to misread ourselves. Thus we must never avoid the strong ethical dimension in our struggle with understanding our semi-coherent selves. It was the central issue for the super-confident leaders in the clique-ridden Corinthian church. Many of them were 'puffed up', assuming they 'knew it all' (there is none more dangerous than leaders convinced of their unchallengeable omni-competence) and Paul had to write, 'Those who think they know something, do not yet know as they ought to know. But whoever loves God is known by God.' (1 Corinthians 8: 4). 'No more boasting' Paul pleads. 'Do not deceive yourselves. If any of you think you are wise by the standards of this age, you should become 'fools' so that you may become wise.' (1 Corinthians 3:18).

---

21 Genesis 3:13.
22 Jeremiah 17:9.
23 Joseph Pak, op. cit.

The more immediate causes of self-deception can be many. We endlessly procrastinate and assume we are still committed to the task. We become victims of 'group think', becoming pressured into a course of action by a tidal wave of like-mindedness. It can arise through an unconscious avoidance of pain; the mother, for example, who realises all is not well with their teenage child's behaviour but refuses to face it because of the discomfort of admitting possible parental failure. Self-deception is often a product of insecurity. It is sad when, in trying to help someone realise that a particular area of pastoral ministry is not for them, what is encountered is extraordinary resistance – all due to their perception of their identity being totally bound up in that role. Stanley Hauwerwas and David Burrell, in an essay entitled 'Self-deception and Autobiography', point out that it is often when someone has a public role, with perceived expectations, that our vulnerability to self-deception can increase. We can too easily re-conceive questionable actions to fit our honourable social role. [24]

A chilling, admittedly extreme, illustration Hauerwas and Burrell offer is that of the life of Albert Speer, Hitler's Minister of Armaments. Speer was a deeply cultured man, a passionate architect and brilliant logistician who cared little for politics. He managed, it seems, to convince himself that all his involvement in the Third Reich was simply an extension of his architectural passion for order, functional design and noble efficiency. They go on to comment, 'The irony of self-deception is that a cynic is less vulnerable to self-deception than a conscientious person.' [25] When we are not particularly concerned about integrity and our social role we are less tempted to reconfigure in our minds the morality of our actions to fit the narrative. This is precisely why pastoral leaders, with all their sincerity, are *particularly* susceptible to living a self-illusory life.

Growing in Self-awareness and the Antidote to Self-deception

Ewan Kelly begins his superb book on self-understanding in ministry, *Personhood and Presence,* with these words:

---

24 Stanley Hauerwas and David B. Burrell 'Self-deception and Autobiography: Reflections on Speers *Inside the Third Reich*' 1974 Essay) in *The Hauerwas Reader,* ed. by John Berkman and Michael Cartwright (Durham and London: Duke University Press 2001), Chapter 10, 206.
25 Ibid., 206.

The compassionate provision of pastoral or spiritual care does not begin with an assessment of another's needs. On the contrary, it begins with an awareness of who we are as carers and what we bring to a particular encounter.[26]

Self-understanding in ministry is *so* important. Kelly calls self-awareness 'a moral imperative for those entrusted with the care of souls.'[27] How difficult it is to give ourselves freely and openly to others when, deep down, we are unsure of ourselves. How can we confidently seek to read others if we struggle to read ourselves? How disastrous when we are over-sure of ourselves!

I have come to the conclusion that Peter's instinctive retort 'Lord *you know* all things, you know that I love you' (21:17) was actually inspired and insightful, words that have proved to provide enormous hope. The good news is that there is One who knows us through and through. As we learn to listen to him through his Word and his people, he is able to show us ourselves more fully and confidently. It is the eloquent testimony of Psalm 139, 'O Lord you have searched me and you know me.'

Rowan Williams, commenting on St Augustine's *Confessions*, underlines this:

We can read the *Confessions* as how we struggle to be present to ourselves in a full and transparent way yet constantly fail; but also about how this is not a disaster or a tragedy, since we are present to a love which holds together what we cannot unify or sustain by our own resources.'[28]

That perhaps was Peter's growing conviction. True self-knowledge comes as we allow our own story to be placed under the critical gaze of the one true Story; 'a story sufficiently substantive and rich to sustain us in the unavoidable challenges that confront the self'.[29] It is when, like Peter, we allow the gaze of the One who truly loves us unconditionally to penetrate us that we are set free. Such love heals childhood deprivations and past failures. It liberates us from both the fear that inhibits true self-reflection and the pain that leads to self-deception.

---

26 Ewan Kelly, *Personhood and Presence, Self as a Resource for Spiritual and Pastoral Care* (T & T Clark 2012), 1.
27 Ibid., 6.
28 Rowan Williams *On Augustine* (Bloomsbury 2016), 6.
29 Ibid., 207.

The Life and Prayer of *Examen*

There are at least four key practices as disciples and church leaders that we can adopt to nourish self-awareness. The first, famously articulated by the Apostle Paul to the Ephesian elders, is self-vigilance, 'Keep watch over yourselves' (Acts 20:28) and as Paul later wrote, 'Watch your life and doctrine closely' (1 Timothy 4:16). The words of Acts 20:28 became the foundational text for Richard Baxter's classic '*The Reformed Pastor*" (published 1656). He writes,

> Take heed to yourselves, lest you should be void of that saving grace of God which you offer to others, and be strangers to the effectual working of that gospel which you preach; and lest while you proclaim the necessity of a Saviour to the world, your own hearts should neglect Him and you should miss an interest of him and his saving benefits.[30]

For this Puritan scholar the starting point for any true 'watching over ourselves' was Scripture-informed prayerful reflection. We need to grant ourselves regular, unhurried time and space to reflect on our emotional, spiritual and relational selves. It may, for example, involve a daily *prayer of examen*, reflecting on the events of the day just gone. It will certainly involve gazing into the mirror of Scripture. Through the Psalms, the 'anatomy of the soul', we monitor our own emotional health; as we read Proverbs we check whether our moral boundaries are wise and healthy; as we ponder the Gospels we reflect on how close is our walk with Christ; as we study the Epistles we find our doctrine and practice being interrogated. Linked with this is the cultivation of genuinely *reflective* practice through the disciplines of journaling, guided retreats and conversations with a mentor.

In Simon Walker's book referred to earlier, '*Leading out of Who You Are*', he makes the helpful suggestion of looking at our ministries as a theatre with a 'frontstage' and 'backstage.'[31] The 'frontstage' is all the energy and effort we put in to our public persona, our public performance as we chair meetings, lead home groups, preach, speak and serve as a community figure. The 'backstage' is our private lives – our family relationships, our devotional life, our study patterns, our leisure pursuits and our many

---

30 Richard Baxter, *Gildas Salvianus, The Reformed Pastor* (London, James Nisbet and Co. MDCCCLX), 70.

31 Walker op. cit., 23-34.

unseen fears, uncertainties and preoccupations. We live these 'two lives' and, crucially, both are intimately connected. Some leaders give too little attention to their frontstage, never fully grasping the influence they have and the need for care in their presentation. More frequently, many of us are so focussed on the front stage and how we appear to our 'audience' that our backstage becomes neglected. I remember the sadness of walking alongside a pastor who was highly regarded frontstage but whose personal finances and marriage backstage were in such disarray that some sort of breakdown was inevitable. To remain healthy both our front and back stage existence needs a careful 'watching of ourselves'.

Social psychology can aid such self-reflection. In spite of my comments about Peter and the Enneagram, personality tests can be revealing. It really is helpful to know whether we are extrovert or introvert, before taking on that remote Scottish island pastorate, with no ministry team anywhere in sight! Over the years I have been intrigued with how colleagues can really struggle in one context but flourish when transplanted into another. There might be many factors involved but I strongly suspect a personality-type fit is a key part of it. Knowing personality strengths and weaknesses can be crucial in understanding why some aspects a church ministry suit us more than others and gives us insight into why we are tempted to avoid certain duties. It also provides valuable insight into church conflict and often provides something of a neutral language in which to talk about it.

Equally, depth psychology offers important insights.[32] Though we may well have serious questions about both the presuppositions and conclusions of the work of such as Sigmund Freud, Carl Jung and William James, most of us instinctively recognise the reality that our unconscious self is a factor in our conscious behaviour. More than we often like to admit, our dreams, anxieties, imaginations and fantasies can, at times, point to unresolved and often painful issues in our past. They are what Carl Jung termed our 'shadow side'. We may well struggle, as explored earlier with Simon Walker, with repressed anger or low self-esteem from parental lack of affirmation. Our most significant childhood relationships can be shaping our present relationships. We may be haunted by sexual fantasies or irrational fears that, in unguarded moments, still influence our

---

32 Here I am particularly grateful for Ewan Kelly's chapter 'Relational Self' in *Personhood and Presence', op. cit.*, 67ff.

conscious thoughts and actions. Worryingly, such emotional baggage can lead to skewed perspectives in our work of pastoral care. When someone's deep emotional hurt connects with our own past hurt, for example, we are tempted either to avoid explorations which could have been helpful or to react in a disproportionate way. I have witnessed folk rescued from a past of drug and alcohol abuse taking a surprisingly legalistic approach to some moral issue, haunted, I suspect, from their own past inability to maintain boundaries.

Within myself, I have recognised times when my hyper-active pastoral care has been far more about a need-to-be-needed than any selfless compassion for others. As Ewan Kelly observes, despite our best efforts 'the contents of our shadow bubble up and leak out in unintentional and often unexpected ways as we relate to others.'[33] To run away from such personal challenges is dangerous. We need to seek appropriate counsel when issues surface. We live with the prayer that God's Spirit will not only renew our conscious minds but heal unredeemed subterranean darkness. In the meantime, we will be wise to discern when issues of our past can hinder our care (and therefore we need to refer folk on) and when they actually can bring particular clarity and empathy to others. Past struggles can both bind and bless.

Accountable Relationships

A second way of deepening self-awareness is to build intentionally accountability relationships. Scott Peck, the American psychologist, in his bestseller *The Road Less Travelled* puts it well:

> A life of total dedication to the truth also means a life of willingness to be personally challenged. The only way that we can be certain that our map of reality is valid is to expose it to the criticism and challenge of other map makers. Otherwise we live in a closed system.[34]

Accountability in ministry is not a cage to restrict our movements, rather the creation of a loving safety net to allow our calling to be offered with confidence and freedom. One of my deep convictions is that we are only as accountable as the access we grant to other people to enter our lives. We can assemble seemingly impressive accountability structures but, because so

33 Ewan Kelly, ibid., 68.
34 M. Scott Peck, *The Road Less Travelled* (Arrow 1990), 54.

much of pastoral ministry is self-generated and self-supervised, we can all too easily hide uncomfortable realities about our conduct and competence. Sadly, unlike just about all other caring professionals, few have access to regular professional supervision. We must intentionally make possible the scrutiny by others of our life and ministry.

The most obvious way accountability can happen is by cultivating genuinely open relationships with key and safe individuals within the wider church family. 'Group think' which, as we said earlier, can be a cause of self-deception needs to be countered by an intentional engagement with a diversity of viewpoint and yet where all are humbly looking for truth. Small gatherings of leaders from different traditions and perspectives can be exceedingly helpful, particularly where accountability is expected and exercised. This is especially valuable where a group of leaders struggle with the same issue – same-sex attraction, pornography, bullying or divisive members.

I found myself deeply moved by the way R.T. Kendall, in his candid autobiography *Twenty five years at Westminster Chapel*[35] describes the wise way he cultivated and maintained close friendships with a few senior evangelical leaders of different persuasions. He confided in them, often read sermons to them ahead of time, and allowed them to introduce to him leaders from a more charismatic tradition than his own. At a time when breaking free from 'the Martin Lloyd-Jones legacy' proved more than a little torrid, these friends were a ministry life-saver.

Even more important is encouraging accountability across the local church's leadership team. Clearly there will be a difference between the level of accountability appropriate for a full-time stipendiary member of staff and volunteer lay leaders but *mutual* accountability is important. Not least, this is because there is such a thing as abusive accountability where it is more about control, the legitimising of a critical spirit and unreasonable expectations than a prayerful health-check on our walk with God in the service of his people.

At the heart of building healthy accountability is the modelling of non-defensive, open relationships where challenge by others is genuinely welcomed. There is nothing that builds trust like this. It will involve offering

---

35   R.T. Kendall, *In Pursuit of His Glory. My 25 Years at Westminster Chapel* (London: Hodder and Stoughton 2002).

information-rich reports on what we have been doing, a willingness to be vulnerable regarding areas where we know we have been struggling and, most basic of all, a genuine permission-giving to be questioned on our life and ministry. If we never allow others to know what is in our diary, what, for us, Sabbath-practice looks like, what books we have been reading, what pattern our devotional life has been taking and what outside activities we are involved in, then it is hard to see what accountability means.

It is all too common to meet colleagues who say the right thing 'challenge me whenever you like', but whose whole body language, demeanour and busyness deny that they really mean what they say. Just as Stephen Hawking's best-seller *A Short History of Time* used to be the most displayed and least read coffee-table book, so 'accountability' is in danger of becoming the most talked about and least practiced part of ministry.

Appraisals

Third, formal ministry appraisals have a key part to play. 'Accompanied self-appraisals' are popular and safe. Here there is a self-evaluation using a prepared checklist, followed by a discussion of the findings with a colleague. My own view is that these are valuable but never, in and of themselves, fully sufficient. The obvious limitation of self-evaluation is that it too often fails to identify our true blind spots. I am persuaded that it is only our close leadership colleagues, the ones who know us best and see us in action, who can offer a more accurate, if more uncomfortable, evaluation. Paul Beasley-Murray, in a helpful reflection 'Annual Reviews are to be Welcomed' suggests a healthy format could consist of two representative lay leaders from within the church, along with an external ministerial facilitator (e.g. a hospital chaplain.)[36] He comments refreshingly, 'I have found that, without exception, my annual reviews were amazingly positive experiences – so much so that I came to look forward to the annual review.'[37] My experience has been similar.

Self-understanding in Creative Ways

Finally, it seems to me that there are much more creative (and indeed enjoyable!) ways for self-exploration. One such is to take time out and

36 Paul Beasley Murray, *Fifty Lessons in Ministry: Reflections on Fifty Years of Ministry* (Darton, Longman and Todd 2020), 148.
37 Ibid., 149.

shadow a respected ministry colleague, observing how they fulfil familiar pastoral tasks. It happens, of course, with student placements, assistantships and curacies but sadly rarely goes beyond that. We have much to learn from the medical profession where medical electives, team learning, and inter-disciplinary case conferences are the norm. Similarly I have found that one of the many healthy spin-offs of global church partnerships has been to discover that personal weaknesses can become prominent through living in a different culture. To see my Romanian translator falter and wince at my ridiculously complex sentence structures was a somewhat painful insight into why folk at home struggle with my sermons! To witness the liberty of African worship (deacons dancing around the communion table) does tend to explain why my 'wooden' body language doesn't help communicate the new wine of the Kingdom!

At the conclusion of my first pastorate in Newcastle upon Tyne, where I had been for 13 years, I invited the church leadership as a parting shot (slightly to their surprise) to review my ministry. Their insights were particularly valuable because, of course, they were free of any self-interest by the church. Their report had an enormous influence on me for good. One of their insights that particularly jolted me was that of all the key changes that had occurred over those years, few had been initiated by me! But what they kindly went on to say was that I had been good at spotting fruitful proposals (when and by whoever offered) and backing them. It liberated me to see with new clarity that leadership is not always about being the out-there-in-front-visionary but can be about being the less-prominent *enabler*. It also reminded me that self-awareness is not primarily about bracing ourselves to discover yet another personal fault but is about celebrating our strengths and our passions.

When Peter exclaimed, 'Lord you know all things, you know that I love you' (21:17) it had sober realism, as we have explored. But it also had the accent of something so positive, 'You know that I love you'. This is indeed self-disclosure made and shaped in the supreme safety of divine grace. I'm sure Jesus smiled. Re-commissioning was now safe.

Chapter Eleven

The Fisherman who Became a Shepherd

> Jesus said, 'Feed my lambs', 'Take care of my sheep',
> 'Feed my sheep'. (John 21:15-17)

Simon Peter, first called 'to fish for people' (Luke 5:10, though interestingly this is not a theme of John's Gospel), is now recommissioned by the Risen Lord to lead, teach and care as a shepherd. His worn nets were to be replaced with a shepherd's crook. This new calling, however, marks not so much a radical change of direction of ministry but the taking on of greater and fuller responsibility. The Gospel net is still to be cast, wider and wider in fact, as Gentiles are included, but to Peter is now also being given the privilege of shepherding. The re-commissioning of Peter has the clearest of echoes of John 10; it is a call to follow in the steps of the Good Shepherd.

In this re-commissioning what is particularly striking is how Jesus deliberately brings together the importance of both *feeding* and *caring* for God's people. The primary way we love God's flock (and it is *His* flock – '*my* sheep', '*my* lambs') is by offering them God's Word; and the only effective way we can offer that Word is by doing so with a deep tenderness in our hearts. I love the words of Gregory the Great in his *Pastoral Rule*, 'The seed of the word springeth easily when the kindness of the preacher watereth it in the breast of the hearer.'[1] The intertwining of pastoral kindness and preaching is not always present but is potent when it is so. Richard John Neuhaus, an American Lutheran pastor and social activist was, for a number of years, privileged to work

---

1   Quoted in C. Cockworth and R. Brown, *Being a Priest Today: Exploring Priestly Identity* (Norwich: Canterbury Press 2002), 93.

alongside Martin Luther King Jn. He recalls one of Martin Luther King's favourite sayings 'Whom you would change you must first love'. It was a truth, comments Neuhaus, that King not only 'powerfully declared – but embodied.'[2]

The Reformed designation of ministry as 'Ministry of Word and Sacrament' is not the whole story (and hardly a New Testament designation).[3] It is, according to Jesus here, the gospel ministry of Word and Care. It is not insignificant that in the church offices of Ephesians 4:11 there seems to be a deliberate grammatical link between shepherds **and** teachers. It is speaking the truth – in love (Ephesians 4:15). Peter clearly took this dual commissioning seriously. Luke's portrayal of him in Acts is of an apostle noted both for his courageous preaching of repentance and his tender care, represented in the healing of Aeneas and Tabitha (Acts 9: 32-42). A similar combination can be found in Peter's letters where there is an equal emphasis on both 'craving pure spiritual milk' (1Peter 2:2) and 'loving one another deeply from the heart' (1 Peter 1:22).

Starting Points

It is true that in the New Testament there are many images of ministry. Arguably however, the image of 'shepherd' is central and foundational. Thomas Oden views 'shepherding' as the 'pivotal analogy' and the 'central paradigm', an image that enhances, enriches and extends the meaning of other images.[4] I share his conviction that whatever our leadership shape and style there is an irreducible minimum of 'core competencies' captured here in the pastoral image offered by Jesus to Peter. It is the ability to both feed and to care, two roles inextricably bound together by Jesus.

Theologically, this bringing together of preaching/teaching and pastoral care is the recognition that the God who speaks is the God who cares; the God who reveals himself in Scripture is the One who does so with healing in his wings. God never speaks idly, he always speaks with loving, creative and redemptive purpose. Thus the God of Israel, addressing his broken, exiled people speaks *tenderly* to Jerusalem, 'Comfort, comfort, my people' (Isaiah 40:1). For those of us called to the high privilege of expounding

2   Richard John Neuhaus, *Freedom for Ministry* (Grand Rapids: Eerdmans 1979), 16.
3   See the trenchant criticism in E.E. Ellis, *Pauline Theology, Ministry and Society* (Grand Rapids, Eerdmans; Exeter: Paternoster 1989), 121.
4   Thomas C. Oden, *Pastoral Theology: Essentials of Ministry* (Bravo Ltd 1997), 52.

God's Word there comes the equally high calling to do so with genuine compassion and grace in our hearts. How easy it is to speak out of personal frustration or out of a sense of 'having to say the right thing'. Again and again I find myself moved by the apostle Paul who, so keen to 'defend and confirm the Gospel' (Philippians 1:7), unfailingly does so with the 'longing and affection of Christ Jesus' (Philippians 1:8). Our hearers instinctively know whether our words are born out of genuine concern for them or whether they are offered because it is simply our Sunday duty, or worse, because we have some churchly axe to grind.

Pastoral care and preaching involves the dynamic of the 'one' and the 'many'; we sit alongside the 'one' and we preach to the gathered 'many'. Unless we genuinely see the *dignity* of the 'one', (rather than the 'one' as a 'pastoral problem' or 'a pawn in our church programme') then we have no credibility in preaching to the 'many'. Donald MacKinnon, the Cambridge academic and Anglo-Catholic, in a very insightful comment, contrasts Christ with Caiaphas. The Good Shepherd leaves the ninety-nine to search for the 'one'; the false shepherd, Caiaphas, counsels that it is expedient that 'one should die for the good of the nation'.[5] Far too often in pastoral ministry we have 'used' people for seemingly honourable ends, and thus followed Caiaphas not Christ.

Equally foundational to the holding together of 'feeding' and 'caring for the flock' is a consideration of *why* we are called to do any of what we do. Our ultimate purpose under God is moral and spiritual *transformation*; our spiritual feeding and caring are united in the one aim of 'presenting everyone mature in Christ' (Colossians 1:28). The church is God's primary construction site for Christ-likeness. Thus our preaching is not primarily to impart biblical knowledge and our pastoral care is not simply to allow people to feel loved (though both these things are important). Rather, both are divine agents of the transforming Spirit. True Christian conversion, as an on-going process, has many inter-related dimensions: a renewal of the mind, a re-orientation of our affections and will, a healing of relationships and a change of our ultimate goals. All this happens through *both* the ministry of the Word and the loving modelling of that Word in the power of the Spirit. The classic example is the young church in Thessalonica

---

5   Donald M. MacKinnon, *The Stripping of the Altars. The Gore Memorial Lecture* (Collins, Fontana Library 1969), 20.

where the Gospel came through Paul 'not simply with words, but also with power, with the Holy spirit and deep conviction' (1 Thessalonians 1:4-5) and yet equally the apostle calls them to imitate him (the highest form of pastoral care) and to model it to others. 'We loved you so much that we were delighted to share with you not only the gospel of God but our lives as well, because you had become so dear to us. (1 Thessalonians 2:8) We need not just 'text books' but 'text people'.[6]

Preaching as Pastoral Care

The ministry of God's Word in preaching, teaching, group study and personal discipleship is fundamental to all ministry; it is absolutely central for nurturing healthy churches. It is so striking, for example, how the paralysis of the returned exiles regarding the rebuilding of the Temple was dramatically overcome through the prophetic preaching of Haggai and Zechariah (Ezra 6:14). Such was the close relationship between biblical preaching and spiritual and numerical growth in the early church that Luke repeatedly uses the shorthand, 'And the Word of the Lord spread.'[7]

The words of 2 Timothy 4:2 capture well the overall emphasis and ethos of the New Testament, 'Preach the Word; be prepared in season and out of season, correct, rebuke and encourage – with great patience and careful instruction'. I, for one, have never encountered a vibrant, growing, outward-focussed church where the ministry of God's Word was not central. And I have never encountered a fruitful pastor who has not given his or her full attention to prayer and the ministry of the Word. (Acts 6:4). Peter's personal legacy, following his recommissioning on the beach, is impressive. Justin Martyr (AD 100–165) comments that Mark's Gospel was largely based on the preaching ministry, 'the memoirs', of Peter. That surely represents an exceedingly rich ministry. Martin Hengel, the German New Testament scholar, goes as far as to conclude that *in relation to the Gospels* 'one could even say, concerning the apostolic witness, that Peter is – without having left us with a single sentence that he himself wrote – the teacher of us all.'[8] His book is entitled *Saint Peter: The Underestimated Apostle*.

---

6   Attributed to the Jewish writer, Abraham Hershel.
7   Acts 6:7; 12:24;13:49;19:20.
8   Martin Hengel, *Saint Peter: The Underestimated Apostle* (Grand Rapids: Eerdmans 2001), 89. His work characterises Peter and Paul as often 'competitors' in a way that, ironically, underestimates Peter's humility.

Preaching is an exacting and costly business. It involves life-long learning. There are no short cuts to a careful wrestling with the biblical text, to a prayerful listening to the Spirit and to an insightful application for the congregation's growth in grace. More than that, truly life-changing preaching arises not just from many hours in the study but from a life given over to personal discipleship. Good preaching will flow naturally as we walk close to Christ each day. Preaching is nurtured and shaped as we allow ourselves to be 'marinated' in his Word[9] *for our own benefit*, as we develop habits of theological and general reading, as we become attentive watchmen to the changing cultural landscape around us and as we pray over the needs of God's people. Such consistent, attractive and well-prepared preaching will have a Spirit-given authority and life about it. Eugene Peterson, with characteristic verve, warns,

> Too often the Living Word made flesh is desiccated into propositional corpses and then sorted into exegetical specimens in bottles of formaldehyde.'[10]

Rather, God's redemptive story will come alive as Scripture is expounded with deep respect for its integrity, richness, diversity, authority and purpose. People will be drawn in, there will develop a healthy expectancy and, best of all, a learning culture will be nurtured.

So much could be written on preaching (and has been written!) but my limited focus here is to argue that our best preaching is when it is pastorally applied and our best pastoral work is actually done from the pulpit. If this is at all true, then the oft heard comment 'he/she is not a good preacher but a great pastor' is deeply flawed. We may have a greater gifting in one area rather than the other but woe betide the pastor who neglects to work hard at both and particularly the area where there is least gifting. This, I would argue, holds true, at least to some extent, even when we have the privilege of a staff team carrying different areas of expertise. We are called not only to 'rightly handle God's Word' but to rightly handle God's people.

For a number of years I adopted the habit of going down to the church building on a Saturday evening and spending time praying for the congregation. I would deliberately sit in various seats around the church

9   Christopher Cockworth and Rosalind Brown, op. cit., 83.
10   Eugene Peterson, *As Kingfishers Catch Fire. A Conversation on the Ways of God Formed by the Words of God* (Hodder 2018), 72.

and think of the person who would normally occupy that place. I would imagine them and pray for them – those who never quite smile, those who seem so keen, those who are clearly carrying heavy burdens, those who occasionally fall asleep! I would pray that as we worshipped and as I preached the next morning they would truly hear the shepherd's voice and encounter his love.

Growing as a Pastoral Preacher

What is it in our preaching that can hold together what the Risen Lord held together for Peter - both feeding and caring? I offer five reflections. First, I would advocate the practice of allowing the whole church leadership (or a preaching team) to give input into what themes should be tackled over the course of a year. All God's Word is inspired and profitable but we do need to discern what *particular* part of the counsel of God is important for this *particular* congregation at this *particular* season. For that to be discovered it is important, it seems to me, to listen carefully to the views of others. Too often we preach what *we* are interested in or what *we* have been recently been studying. A true servant-pastor preaches on what is most needed, however exacting or personally uncomfortable that may be. I remember my reluctance when the elders encouraged me to preach on the Book of Revelation but it proved to be one of the most pastorally helpful, uniting and inspiring series of that year.

Second, preaching pastorally is to preach the Good News. It is to preach Christ. We don't preach our problems but preach the One who is our Saviour and Good Shepherd in the midst of all that would pull us down. We lift people to God's grace as we preach what God has done in Christ and only then draw out the implications for our living. As P.T. Forsyth put it,

> To be effective, our preaching must be sacramental. It must be an act prolonging the great Act, mediating it and conveying it. It's energy and authority is that of the great Act.[11]

We bless people with God's promises and remind people that he only commands what he promises. We call people again and again to their true identity as those who live in Christ where every spiritual blessing is found. No book of the Bible was written in a pastoral vacuum and we preach

---

11 P.T. Forsyth, *Positive Preaching and the Modern Mind* (London: Independent Press, 1964), 57.

all God's Word with confidence and expectancy. Though there must be room for the moral challenge and the prophetic 'hard word', the staple diet of biblical ministry is *encouragement*. It is about a whole congregation looking to the full, objective drama of God's salvation with the earnest prayer that it will make sense of and transform our decidedly messy lives. Pastoral preaching elicits faith, offers hope, empowers people with God's love and fuels the imagination with what *is* possible under God. We take baptism and the Lords supper with great seriousness as visual and communal declarations of that same Word.

Third, preaching pastorally means a willingness to be vulnerable. This is not about colourful disclosures of personal failure but about preaching with genuine humility and openness. It is about recognising there is truth in the post-modern critique of homiletics as 'discourses of power'. The words of Jesus to Peter are telling, 'But I have prayed for you, Simon, that your faith may not fail. And when you have turned back, strengthen your brothers.' (Luke 22:32). Simon Peter's ministry of 'strengthening' flowed out of all he had been through. Preaching with vulnerability is about appropriately owning of our struggles and scars in order to build effective 'empathetic bridges'[12] with the congregation. Without such a sense of empathy our words may touch minds but certainly will not move hearts and re-direct affections. It is about having thoughtful respect for how bruised some are in our congregation; about being honest when we don't quite know how a text should be interpreted.

There are attention-grabbing illustrations we will need to lay to one side since we know they will distract and even disturb some. We will be vigilant not only with gender-inclusive language but with gender-inclusive content; the kind of stories we use and quotes we offer. There are caveats to be offered in our interpretation of a text not because of lack of courage but because of integrity. There *is* a genuine speaking of 'us' and not 'you'. I suggest that the *tone* of our preaching communicates far more powerfully, for good or ill, than our most memorable sermon outline. 'All preaching is communal' writes Richard John Neuhaus, 'its tone tempered by the relationship between pastor and people'.[13] Equally – and this is often missed – to be willing to be vulnerable is also to preach courageously,

---

12 A term used in Ewan Kelly, *Personhood and Presence. Self as a Resource for Spiritual and Pastoral Care* (T&T Clark 2013), 95.
13 Richard John Neuhaus, op. cit., 159.

prophetically. I have felt far more vulnerable confronting than confessing! 'Speaking the truth in love' is never comfortable. There is the perennial temptation to preach 'peace, peace' when there is no peace. Pulpits can indeed be 'cowards' castles'.[14] Preaching on Jesus' words to the rich in comfortable suburbia is no fun; neither is preaching on the necessity of heartfelt reconciliation to a deeply divided and obstructive congregation.

Fourth, preaching with pastoral effect will involve using others. However gifted or insightful we may think we are, there are some for whom other voices will have more effect. To preach on 'evangelism in the workplace' when the office environment is a very distant memory or to preach on 'depression' when our lives have been relatively trouble-free may be entirely appropriate as we faithfully expound Scripture, but our voice may well not be the most credible or insightful. I wince as I recall my encounter with a middle-aged single woman after I had preached on the 'privileges and pressures of singleness'! I got what I deserved! Within thirty seconds of the benediction, she was in my face. 'What did I possible know?' she said with red-faced frustration. Even when I (tamely) told her that I had indeed deliberately given my sermon to a single woman to read ahead of time, she was less than impressed! Involving others in preaching, in offering testimony or in simply illustrating a point, can be pastorally invaluable. As Barbara Brown Taylor well puts it,

> It was part of God's genius to incorporate us as one body, so that our ears have other ears, other eyes, minds, hearts and voices to help us interpret what we have heard. Together we hear our calls, and together we can answer them, if only we will listen to the still small voice that continues to speak to us in the language of our lives.[15]

Fifth, part of the value of good pastoral preaching is that it will create a context where sensitive pastoral conversations can more easily happen. There are some things easier to address in public than in private. I have found over the years that the great temptations of life – money, sex and power – are easier to tackle from the pulpit than in the home. To talk winsomely about Jesus warnings to the rich as you sunbathe with a member

---

14 Michael J. Quicke. *360-Degree Leadership. Preaching to Transform Congregations* (Grand Rapids, Michigan: Baker Books 2006), 39.
15 Barbara Brown Taylor, *The Preaching Life. Living out your Vocation* (Norwich: Canterbury Press 1993), 25.

of the congregation next to his swimming pool needs considerable skill! By naming sensitive issues in the pulpit, be it pride, pornography or personal debt, we are indicating they are not no-go areas. We are giving permission for these subject to be talked about. One of the signs of good preaching is that people open up in new ways. This can happen in a 'ministry time' after a service or, more often, in the privacy of a home.

Pastoral Care as 'Preaching in Private' – Commending Biblical Truth in Conversations of Love

Pastoral care is also fundamental to ministry. Augustine of Hippo famously described the cure of souls as 'preaching in private'. To our ears this sounds remarkably like an alarming absence of listening and the worst form of confrontational biblical counselling. But his intent was simply to underline that the linkage Jesus makes here between 'caring for sheep' and 'feeding lambs' are co-dependent ministries. Our best pastoral care is to encourage people to seek God's wisdom for their lives found in his Word. If person-centred pastoral care is uncoupled from biblical engagement then it ceases to be *Christian* pastoral care. To read Scripture as part of a pastoral visit must surely be the norm. No conversation we will ever have will concern a matter that falls outside the limits of God's redemptive plan. Eugene Person in an insightful essay, 'Teach us to care and not to care' (quoting a line from T.S Eliot's poem 'Ash Wednesday') warns us of how, because all human beings are basically self-centred, we can all too easily allow pastoral care to collude with selfishness and self-pity. He writes,

> The wound must not be bandaged over as fast as possible; it is there to be a listening post, a chance to exit the small confines of a self-defined works and enter the spaciousness of a God-defined world.[16]

When Jesus re-commissioned Peter with these words, 'Feed my lambs', 'Take care of my sheep', 'Feed my sheep' (John 21:15-17) there are clearly echoes, as we have said, of his discourse on the Good Shepherd (John 10). The content of that teaching must shape our understanding of the pastoral care advocated here in Chapter 21. At the heart of both (John 10 and John 21) is the recognition that the quality of love being advocated is the love of

---

16 E.H. Peterson, *Subversive Spirituality* (Grand Rapids: Eerdmans; Vancouver: Regent College Publishing 1994), 160.

someone who is 'willing to lay down his life for the sheep' (10:11). Pastoral care is deeply costly work. It requires time and sacrifice to get to know folk, to know not just names (10:3) but to win trust. Only then will folk listen to our voice, 'they will never follow a stranger' (10:5).

It is an all-too-common experience that, after a few years in pastoral ministry, such are the calls on time to be present at endless (very worthy) functions that spending quality time with our own people can rapidly disappear. There are *always* more urgent things to do than routine pastoral visits. We can allow ourselves to become so caught up in busyness that *to loiter* with pastoral intent becomes a lost art. When people begin to approach us with the words, 'I know you are far too busy to listen to my small issues but . . .' we realise our calling as shepherds is in serious danger. For sure, pastoral care will never be the sole remit of one person. It is essential to build, train and resource a pastoral team, be it an eldership or others (1 Peter 5:1-2) and even more important to cultivate a culture of caring 'for one another' (Romans 12:13). But that said, pastors lead more effectively by what they do more than by what they say. Some of my most moving moments in ministry have been in homes, by a hospital bed, in a local café, walking along a beach, having Jesus-like conversations by the sea.

I want to commend three dimensions of biblically-rooted pastoral care. First, at the heart of all pastoral care is *attentiveness*; and attentiveness comes not only as we listen carefully to what is being said but as we listen to the Spirit of Truth. As people share their joys and pains we prayerfully offer them to God. Pastoral conversations are always three-way. It is not a question of us crassly thinking 'what bible passage can I conclude this conversation with?' but the much more demanding matter of being in step with the Spirit for that person.

Second, it constantly surprises me how in the course of a few visits some of the most stretching theological issues 'innocently' come up. I well remember in the course of just one afternoon, whilst visiting 'ordinary folk,' being invited to comment on the difference between 'heaven' and the 'new heavens and new earth,' being asked about how atonement works for contemporary Judaism and having to field some uncomfortable questions about suffering! Pastoral conversations are deeply challenging; biblical and theological alertness is vital.

Third, pastoral work is as sacramental as preaching. It is as we listen, talk and pray with Scripture as our guide that God's presence so often becomes real. I am sometimes haunted by C.S. Lewis' famous words in his *Grief Observed*, 'I need Christ, not something that resembles him'.[17] It is as we allow his Spirit and Word to shape our thinking and speaking that Christ himself graciously draws alongside.

Pastoral Leadership

Jesus dual commission to 'Feed my lambs' and 'Take care of my sheep' both imply a fundamental call to leadership. The role of preacher and carer must never be played off against the role of leader; we lead as we preach and we lead as we care. The Good Shepherd 'goes on ahead of them, and his sheep follow' (10:8). It is, in fact, precisely the genius of the Middle Eastern pastoral image that it holds together the calling of a rugged leader with that of an attentive carer and provider. As Alistair V. Campbell describes it, the Eastern shepherd in the Judean desert was more like a Wild West cowboy than a settled farmer; it was a physically exacting, hazardous and somewhat despised occupation.[18] The idea that it is impossible to be a strong, effective leader and, at the same time, a gentle carer is false and dangerous. There can be no doubt that central to Peter's recommissioning was a call to lead.

The more I've mused on it over the years (and largely in an urban setting) the more comfortable and helped I have become with the pastoral image. For all its strangeness, it does indeed combine elements of the call to leadership that no other image quite achieves. For a start, the Eastern shepherd's overriding aim is to guide the flock, in the midst of dusty, scorched, semi-arid terrain, to nourishing pasture and refreshing water holes. Our aim is to lead people to the only One who promises 'life and life to the full' (10:10) – a promise central to the Good Shepherd discourse. Our aim is to lead people to the nourishing, saving, life-giving God, through Christ.

Equally important to note is the central concern of the eastern shepherd for the *whole flock*. Pastoral leadership involves the emotionally demanding, time-consuming and skilled art of facilitating corporate decision-making that allows clear, united and enthusiastic journeys to be made. Dictatorial pastors are deeply divisive and dangerous, precisely because they have

17 C.S. Lewis, *A Grief Observed* (London: Faber and Faber 1961), 51.
18 Alistair V. Campbell, *Rediscovering Pastoral Care* (London: Darton, Longman and Todd 1981), 27.

completely lost sight of this rather basic feature of shepherding. Although it can be fatal to go at the pace of the slowest, I fear that pastoral fallouts are sometimes as much a result of the impatience of the shepherd as the stubbornness of the sheep. Observing closely how a shepherd patiently and carefully rounds up, whistles to, guards and leads *the whole flock* is, in my view, a salutary exercise. They go after the one sheep that is lost.

I have spent many hours visiting potentially out-of-sorts church members before a crucial church meeting, not to coerce them into agreeing with my view but to listen to theirs. I have discovered that the people we dignify with our careful listening are the people who often become surprisingly open to being led in totally new, and even risky, directions. Admittedly this is not always the case. But sometimes colleagues confide that it is impossible for them to lead as there are just too many 'difficult people', forgetting that leadership means precisely an ability to bring change and progress where there is dysfunction. True, occasionally we are called to be a Jeremiah and prophesy to a sheer stubbornness that only awaits judgment. But largely, by God's grace, our calling is to preach and care with the quiet confidence that God's Spirit can re-direct the most difficult of flocks.

For this to happen pastoral leadership depends utterly on a careful nurturing of trust. The Good Shepherd 'goes on ahead of them, and his sheep follow *because they know his voice*' (10:8). The Good Shepherd Discourse is all about moving from being a stranger to being the trusted shepherd who knows us by name (10:3). Trust grows in the soil of careful listening and non-coercive management. For trust to truly flourish there is no substitute for spending time with individuals and ministry groups, for faithful preaching and care, for modelling discipleship and creating safe places for disagreement. Trust is absolutely fundamental to the body of Christ and, when lost, has devastating effects. Like a carefully crafted piece of pottery trust takes many hours to be formed but can be shattered in a single, thoughtless moment of ecclesial infidelity. Too often I have witnessed gifted colleagues who have had to step down due to an erosion of congregation trust.

Finally, an inevitable part of an eastern shepherd's role is to take risks. He characteristically leads from the front, rather than drives from behind. The terrain is often treacherous and the mountain passes dangerous. There is no true pastoral leadership without risk-taking. We take risks by raising highly sensitive but potential life-changing issues with individuals, we take risks by encouraging our leadership to set goals for which the needed resources are not immediately obvious; we take risks by taking on a church where problems abound. It is all too easy to cloak what is simply a lack of faith in the Good Shepherd with talk of 'wise caution' and 'seeking consensus.' My sense is that when, after listening prayer and consultation, we stretch a congregation to new ventures in mission, ('I have other sheep that are not of this fold' (10:16), to new staff appointments for the sake of the gospel, to new patterns of worship, to fresh ways of being a learning community, then God has a habit of graciously providing the resources. The Good Shepherd took the ultimate leadership risk and laid down his life for the sheep. We are called to 'follow him' (21:19). For Peter, the fisherman-cum-shepherd, leadership cost him his life too (21:18).

Living Under the Over-Shepherd

Standing on the beach that day, being restored by Christ and listening to his fresh commission, Peter was very aware of who was the True Shepherd. Jesus had come to Galilee looking for him 'the lost sheep'. Later Peter writes about Jesus as 'the Shepherd and Overseer of your souls'[19] and deliberately invites his fellow elders to see themselves as shepherds under the 'Chief Shepherd'.[20] There is only one Pastor and Leader that matters. Happy the leader who lives each day with the freedom and adventure of letting Jesus do the leading as they declare God's Word and care for God's flock.

---

19 1 Peter 2:25.
20 1 Peter 5:4.

Chapter Twelve

Leading When not in Control[1]

When you are old you will stretch out your hands,
and someone else will dress you and lead you
where you do not want to go.' (John 21:18)

In the beach conversation between the Risen Lord and Peter,
Jesus not only took Peter back to his recent failure and not only re-
commissioned him but cast his gaze much further forward. Jesus
chose to map out how it would all end. Peter, after a life-time of
following Jesus, would glorify God through suffering and death
(21:19). The prophetic words of Jesus are introduced with great
seriousness, 'I tell you the truth' (lit. 'truly, truly I say to you')
characteristic words of intensity, last used by Jesus when predicting
Peter's betrayal (13:38).

As we observed in Chapter Nine there was, ironically, something
deeply assuring about this – Peter would make the finishing line well!
But in another sense, how hard these solemn words must have been
for Peter to hear. A time was coming when the apostle, the ever-
energetic, strong-minded activist, would be profoundly restricted.
His ability to shape his own life would be removed, someone will
'lead you where you do not want to go'. His dignity to make simple
choices would be denied, 'someone else will dress you'; and, it seems,
martyrdom by crucifixion was being predicted, 'you will stretch out
your hands.' The likely image is of a condemned man carrying his
cross-beam (*patibulum*) with outstretched arms and being led out to
the place of execution. Tradition has it that Peter died as an old man

---

1   I am grateful to Revd Lynn Green, General Secretary of the Baptist Union of
Great Britain, for suggesting a chapter on this theme.

by crucifixion in Rome.[2] It was Eusebius of Caesarea in his 4th century *Ecclesiastical History* who added the famous detail that the apostle was crucified upside down, which he, in turn, attributes to Origen c.184–253.[3]

This prediction by Jesus involved four stark contrasts.[4] First there is the contrast between when Peter was young and when he will be old. This is followed by the contrast between Peter in normal life, self-contained, in control, confident, 'dressing himself', and Peter in extreme circumstances, weak, dependent, limited, with someone 'having to dress him'. Third is the comparison between Peter travelling freely and Peter being forcibly led. Finally there is the ultimate contrast between the apostle choosing to do as he pleased and being taken to where he did not wish to go. Together it adds up to a powerful image of a once dynamic leader being reduced to so much less.

Times When We are not in Control

There are moments in leadership when it becomes very clear that our desire to shape things is not going to be easy. We are no longer in control – and how tough that can feel! We fear it will lead to others managing us. Often a loss of control is due to circumstances overtaking us. I remember the frustration of breaking my leg through a cycling accident just as a new academic year was about to begin in St Andrews. A whole new cohort of students needed to be welcomed into the church and all I could contribute was to rest at home with my leg in the air! For some, being forced by prolonged illness to let go and rely on others ('others will dress you') becomes literal and deeply painful. The sense of powerlessness and often self-induced guilt is hard to bear.

At a global level, the upheaval caused by Covid-19 pandemic raised many issues about leadership when not in control. It involved decision-making very much shaped by the agenda of the national government. The demand for constant reviewing, for learning new technology, for coping with a new set of pastoral issues was exhausting, precisely because of a

---

2   See R.E. Brown, *The Gospel According to John*, X11-XX1. Anchor Bible (Geoffrey Chapman, 1972), 1108. where he quotes 1 Clement and Tertullian as the first we know of who mention Peters martyrdom.
3   Ibid., 1108.
4   This is noted by S.B. Marrow, *John 21: An Essay in Johannine Ecclesiology,* (Rome: Gregorian University 1968) quoted by R.E. Brown, 1107.

sense of not quite having a handle on things For those particularly reliant on their physical presence for their pastoral work, new skills and strategies had to be quickly adopted. Irrespective of the pandemic, for millions there is the constant reality of persecution and religious restrictions. Negotiating transformative leadership when fear and reprisals are a daily threat requires great courage and care.

However, it is not just adverse circumstances that sometimes create a context in which we need to learn to lead when not in control. It may be demanded by the very nature of the organisation we serve. For example, there are times we sense a need to shape things and yet we are not in a position of authority to do so; the gifted associate pastor watching on as her senior colleague fails to read the church well; the youth leader struggling to implement change whilst his management group offers little support. The challenge becomes how to offer direction and guidance without undermining the leadership of others.

A Reality Check

The great blessing, hidden in the frustration of restrictive circumstances, is that it becomes a powerful reminder that we are never in control! All our days and all our service are in the hands of a Sovereign God who works as he pleases and indeed specialises in using our weaknesses to confound us and display his power instead. Jesus' parable of the seed that germinated and grew 'all by itself' whilst the farmer slept is a humbling reminder of who is in charge.[5] No doubt it was originally aimed by Jesus at those, such as the Zealots and Pharisees, who sought to bring in God's Kingdom through their own violent or religious means. 'No,' says Jesus, 'there is a mystery to the Kingdom; it is all about God's coming'. How many of us have witnessed, to our delight and puzzlement, the church actually growing in times of prolonged illness or difficult circumstances! So often it has been as we have had to be cared for that we have discovered new insights in how to care for others. Frequently in times of being severely limited we have discovered a new freedom in trusting God. Henri Nouwen tells of the time when he made the radical decision to move from his prestigious teaching post at Harvard to the life of being a member of a L'Arche community serving those with severe learning difficulties:

5   Mark 4:26-29.

After twenty years of being free to go where I wanted and to discuss what I chose, the small, hidden life with people whose broken minds and bodies demand a strict daily routine in which words are the least requirement does not immediately appear as the solution for spiritual burnout. And yet, my new life at L'Arche is offering me new words to use in speaking about Christian leadership in the future because I have found there all the challenges that we are facing as ministers of God's Word.[6]

Embracing Vulnerability

There is something about those very periods in leadership where we feel most cast aside that opens up for us new vistas of God's grace and love. Like Peter, we feel we are being 'lead where we do not wish to go', only to discover it is a place of surprising fruitfulness. It is significant that these strong predictive words of Jesus to Peter come immediately after his appointment as a shepherd of God's people and immediately before Jesus's fresh call for Peter to follow him. Safe leadership and true discipleship both flow out of the humility of first being willing to be led. People can sense the authenticity of ministry which springs from an experience of having had to be totally dependent on God and others. John Hull's moving book, *Notes on Blindness. A Journey through the Dark*, is the record of the first few years of his life as an academic after becoming totally blind at the age of 45. His wife, Marilyn, comments on how, in his total dependence on others, he became, ironically, a person many relied on. She recollects,

> When you were with John you felt his whole attention was focussed upon you, what D.H. Lawrence described as 'a man in his wholeness, wholly attending.' People often confided in him readily, and were changed because of their meeting. He listened intently, partly because, without being able to see body language, he had to work harder at listening just to hear. And he was never distracted by the delicious tray of nibbles being carried past or the annoying pile of clutter in the corner.[7]

Jesus knew that vulnerability was important to mission and ministry. He deliberately, it seems, sent out his disciples and other mission teams

6   Henri J.M. Nouwen, *In the Name of Jesus. Reflections on Christian Leadership* (Darton, Longman and Todd 1989), 11.
7   John M. Hull, *Notes on Blindness. A Journey Through the Dark* (London, Profile Books, Wellcome Collection, 2017 edition), 200.

without material resources, 'no bag for the journey or extra tunic or sandals or a staff'[8] so they would need to depend on others. It is as we rely on God and others, as we receive hospitality and allow others to open doors for us, that new vistas of ministry appear. The very humility required in order to receive causes our credibility to grow. Jesus modelled such vulnerability himself. He allowed others to serve him, allowed his own emotions to be seen and, most poignantly, allowed others to lead him where he did not want to go, all the way to a Roman crucifixion. It was a chosen vulnerability.

Far too often we like to be in control, 'to hide behind a shell of professionalism'[9] and to be seen as the care providers. Like Peter, we exclaim. 'You shall never wash my feet!' (13:8). I heard the story from a colleague of a working class estate church which he had formerly pastored, faithful for so many years in serving their community, one day being badly damaged by fire. The local youth of the estate who had previously been seen as a 'target' for mission (and a constant thorn in the flesh of the congregation) suddenly offered to help restore 'their church'! The grateful receipt of such an offer led to a whole new level of relationship and opportunities for the Gospel.[10]

In Paul's First Letter to the Thessalonians the apostle sketches out some moving images of pastoral ministry. In chapter 2 he famously describes his ministry as 'a mother caring for her little children and as a father 'encouraging, comforting and urging'.[11] But there is another potential image too. 'We could have asserted our authority', he writes, 'but we were like young children among you.'[12] It is a striking reference to their vulnerability, to their chosen powerlessness. Leading-when-not-in-control exposes us to particular vulnerabilities. There is the possibility of being taken for granted, of having unreasonable expectations placed on us, of

---

8 Matthew 10: 9-10.

9 Vanessa Herrick and Ivan Mann, *Jesus Wept. Reflections on Vulnerability in Leadership* (Darton, Longman and Todd 1998), 6.

10 Portrack Baptist Church, Stockton, a story told by Roy Searle of the Northumbria Community.

11 1 Thessalonians 2:7,11.

12 1 Thessalonians 2:7a. This is often translated as 'being gentle' and linked to the image of the caring mother. But the best manuscript evidence is of the variant word translated 'babes'.

being misunderstood because we are not in a place to explain ourselves. We are vulnerable to the temptation of criticising those above us or at least of publically disassociating from decisions we do not like, rather than be loyal to the team of which we are part.

Faithful to What *is* in our Control

Faithfulness is the foundational virtue of leadership, the commitment to serving God and his people irrespective of the cost. The real test of godly fidelity is remaining steady and energised irrespective of status, opportunity or authority. We simply serve with diligence wherever God chooses to place us. Faithful leadership in a team setting requires a clear commitment to loyalty – to supporting our senior colleagues, to guarding their reputations as much as ours, to sharing concerns with them before anyone else. Joseph is the outstanding Old Testament example of all this. Whether serving as a slave in Potiphar's house or acting as an unpaid prison chaplain or being the all-powerful national foodbank logician, Joseph was utterly consistent in his trustworthiness.

Perhaps his New Testament equivalent is the 'other Joseph', nicknamed Barnabas. Through his leadership a young colleague Paul was drawn in to the church plant at Antioch and later allowed to take the lead in subsequent missionary work.[13] Yet Barnabas, no longer in full control, remained the faithful encourager, teacher and missionary colleague. His overriding concern was to help others; his life marked by a delightful lack of self-regard. Of equal note is Timothy, of whom Paul wrote, 'I have no one else like him, who takes a genuine interest in your welfare.'[14] Timothy modelled faithfulness, 'the brothers of Lystra and Iconium spoke well of him.'[15] Every time we read of him he seems to have has been sent on yet another pastoral assignment by Paul – Thessalonica, Ephesus, Corinth, Jerusalem, back to Ephesus – yet there is never a hint of complaint or a disloyal word.

The Art of Leading from Behind

There are ways to lead when not an overall leader which neither ignore appropriate submission nor involve any sort of unhealthy subversion. All

---

13 It is often pointed out that in Acts the early references to 'Barnabas and Saul' (e.g. Acts 13:2) are soon replaced by 'Paul and Barnabas' (e.g. Acts 13:42).
14 Philippians 2:20.
15 Acts 16:2.

on a leadership team of any worth are able to contribute to both the overall vision and the day to day governance of a church. The skill is offering what we feel appropriate in a humble, non-threatening way. A simple way is to request an item on a leadership agenda. I have found writing vision papers particularly useful. These can be offered openly and dispassionately and if they have theological and pastoral credibility are invariably welcomed on the table. They allow colleagues to reflect on ideas ahead of time. The key is to offer things creatively and supportively without being precious about ownership. If a different vision is finally adopted, so be it.

Most important is the commitment to pray. Intercession both frees us from our need to be in control and puts the leadership where it truly belongs – in God's hands. Prayer is 'humbling ourselves under the mighty hand of God'; it is 'casting all our anxieties on Him'[16] Prayer nourishes contentment, not resentment; it increases sensitivity and decreases our need always to be heard, for there is One who has heard. Prayerful communal discernment is a delightfully liberating thing. Our calling is not to prove ourselves with our impressive leadership ideas, rather it is to enjoy the corporate journey of discovering the mind of Christ. Peter discovered this. He was very clear in his writing about both our calling to 'be shepherds' and our accountability to, and dependence on, the 'Chief Shepherd.'[17]

'Someone will Lead you Where you do not Want to Go' – the Cost of Ministry

In whatever ways the sobering words of Jesus to Peter would play out as he got older, Jesus overall prophetic message was very simple - Peter's following of Jesus would be costly. Indeed for him it would involve martyrdom. There is no discipleship without a dying to self and, if leadership is discipleship writ large – 'exemplary discipleship' (see Chapter 2), then there is certainly no leadership without serious cost. There are places we would rather not go and things we would rather not do. For all our careful guarding of boundaries in all ministry there is a cost of time and personal freedom and a significant drain on emotional, mental and spiritual energy.

16 1 Peter 5:6-7.
17 1 Peter 5:2-4.

Certainly a balance is needed when we come to talk about the cost of Christian leadership. On the one hand, leaders can sometimes overplay their 'hard lot', being more than a little insensitive to the enormous daily struggles that followers of Jesus face in difficult work places, holding down highly responsible jobs, encountering alienation and hostility. 'Hard done by' leaders are not an attractive breed to encounter! On the other hand, however, I do think that there are some subtle and almost unique pressures Christian leaders have to face, never quite understood until personally encountered.

First, there are complex *emotional* costs to ministry. There is, for example, a sort of leadership loneliness that is difficult to describe but very real. For sure, all biblical leadership is meant to be corporate and supportive colleagues should be the norm. But there are times when the weight of responsibility for tough decisions is ultimately left to just one. There are times when pastoral confidences, hard to carry, have to remain unshared. There are times when criticisms received feel very personal; times where I really have not wanted to open my emails!

Another stress is the having to say 'no' to legitimate pastoral requests in order to guard time for family and personal wellbeing. Boundary keeping is easy to agree to but often uncomfortable to maintain. It is an issue for all caring professionals but one that can be particularly prominent when home life and work life are often so intertwined. Another emotional cost, too rarely commented on, is that when mental illness affects a leader it can become deeply complex. I have often witnessed how, when a colleague is struggling with depression for example, there is potential for a high degree of misunderstanding and the pressure to handle this well whilst being so ill is very demanding. Mark Meynell, in his moving reflections on life and ministry with depression, talks about the tricky business of when to wear, and not to wear, a 'mask' (this before the pandemic!). At times sharing our vulnerabilities is pastorally inappropriate and we simply soldier on with a dutiful mask. But there comes a time for integrity's sake when transparency about our true struggles in needed, not least to invite support.[18]

Perhaps the greatest cost of all emotionally is when those you love in the family of God choose not just to criticize but to leave. I have seen the most stable and secure of leaders almost unravel when a dissenting group refuse to be reconciled. Jonathan Edwards (1703–1758) after twenty three

---

18 Mark Meynell, *When Darkness Seems My Closest Friend. Reflections on Life and Ministry with Depression* (London: Inter Varsity Press 2018), 5.

years as pastor of a church in Northampton, Massachusetts, where a great spiritual awakening had been witnessed, was unceremoniously voted out over Edwards' opposition to the unconverted receiving communion. In his farewell sermon on July 1st 1750, a model of graciousness, he admitted,

> The contentious which have been among you since I first became your pastor have been one of the greatest burdens I have laboured under in the course of my ministry – not only the contentions you have had with me, but with those you have had with one another.[19]

Second there are clearly *mental* and intellectual sacrifices which come in many guises. There is a need for constant alertness, often unacknowledged but potentially very draining. It can come in the form of what I term 'filling-in-the gaps' ministry. It is that sense of duty which makes us aware of those gaps which, when all the best delegation in the world has been achieved, still remain. It is the writing of that letter of thanks that no one has thought of, the offering of a meal to the speaker booked at the last minute, the chairing of that meeting where someone has failed to turn up, the quiet word of assurance when someone has been forgotten in a vote of thanks. At a more prominent level, the need in our preaching and teaching to be fresh and relevant is deeply demanding intellectually. Carving out time for serious study and wide reading involves making difficult choices at times.

Most of all, the *spiritual* cost of ministry can be huge. There is a spiritual weariness that comes when good people refuse to even entertain simple and godly change. The constant disappointment of encountering people's lack of commitment can make us cynical and angry and spoil our walk with God. The sheer relentlessness of pastoral duties can leave us spiritually wrung out. Above all the simple, prayerful concern to see a church truly flourish is a burden we are called to carry. When the apostle Paul reviewed the hardships of his missionary journeys, after an astonishing catalogue of trials and setbacks, he concludes,

> Besides everything else, I face daily the pressure of my concern for all the churches. Who is weak and I do not feel weak? Who is led into sin and I do not inwardly burn.[20]

---

19 Quoted in Iain H. Murray, *Jonathan Edwards, A New Biography* (Edinburgh: Banner of Truth Trust 1987), 328.
20 2 Corinthians 11:28-29.

In other words what was most spiritually taxing of all for the apostle was not his own suffering but his 'identification with the weak and his indignation over those who lead others into sin.'[21] Loving others to this depth and passion *is* exhausting! John Calvin uses these words of Paul to remind us that underlying all the spiritual challenges to be faced is a spiritual battle that is real and tough. He comments soberly,

> From Paul's words here we may infer that nobody can have a heartfelt concern for the churches without being burdened by many difficulties; for the government of the Church is not a pleasant occupation which we can undertake with joy and delight . . . it is a hard and bitter warfare, in which Satan again and again stirs up for us as much trouble as he can and leaves no stone unturned to annoy us.[22]

It's All Worth it!

Jesus prophetic words to Peter, 'Someone else will dress you and lead you where you do not want to go' came just after his commissioning to care for God's flock. Between that commissioning and his ultimate martyrdom there were to be many joys and many hardships. But what is very clear is that for Peter there was never any doubt that it was all worth it! I often think, for example, when reading Peter's First Epistle that his simple aim was to explain to his readers *why* it was all worth it. It is worth it supremely because Jesus is worth it, the one who fills us with 'an inexpressible and glorious joy'![23] It is worth it because of the greatness of the salvation that is ours, the inheritance waiting for us, the privilege of being built into a new Temple and ultimately the glory that goes to God himself.[24] And if our ultimate goal really is to glorify God then it doesn't matter *at all* if I am 'leading when not in control', or not!

---

21 Scott J. Haffemann, *The NIV Application Commentary on 2 Corinthians* (Grand Rapids: Zondervan 2000), 441.

22 *Calvin's New Testament Commentaries. The Second Epistle of Paul to the Corinthians and the Epistles to Timothy, Titus and Philemon*, tr. T.A Smail (Eerdmans 1964), 153.

23 1 Peter 1:8.

24 1 Peter 1:9, 1:4, 2:5, 4:11.

Chapter Thirteen

Comparisons, Competition and Cul-de-sacs

When Peter saw him, he asked 'Lord, what about him? (John 21:21)

Jesus and Peter were not alone as they walked along the beach deep in conversation. The Beloved Disciple was following close by, no doubt anxious not to miss a moment of this resurrection encounter. At first, it seems, Peter didn't hear the footsteps behind them, preoccupied as he was with what had just been told him. Peter's own life, like that of his Master, would end with a loss of freedom and dignity, with suffering and martyrdom. Following Jesus was to cost him everything. But then Peter senses someone following. He spins round, sees the Beloved Disciple a few yards behind and, impulsive as ever, blurts out 'So what about him?' (The original is singularly stark, literally, 'Lord and this man, what?) Were Jesus words becoming too personal and Peter wanted to deflect attention? Or was it rather a gesture of warm inclusion – a longing that the immense privilege of martyrdom would also be bestowed on his close colleague? After all, the Beloved Disciple had been so close to Jesus at the farewell supper. Was the question simply asked out of pure curiosity? Or did it reveal, as some have suggested, a hint of rivalry? We will never know. But one way or another Peter was doing what we all do so often and so instinctively – make comparisons.

Jesus answer is 'unexpectedly sharp in tone.'[1] 'If I want him to remain alive until I return, what is that to you?' And then, repeating what he had said to Peter just a few moments before, 'You must follow me' – with

---

1   G. Beasley Murray, *John, The Word Biblical Commentary* (Waco Texas: Word Books 1987), 410.

an emphatic 'you' (John 21:22). His first responsibility was his own life. He needed to mind his own business. His eyes must be on Jesus, on no one else.

Defining Ourselves by Others

There is something deep within us that seeks to define ourselves by constantly looking over our shoulder at others. Our self-esteem is so often pegged to how we judge ourselves in relation to others. We walk around with mental score cards and appraisal sheets. We worry over our lot compared to others. We fret, wondering whether the praise our friend has just received is coming our way too. From the days of playground comparisons when the label on our clothes mattered, to the Facebook posts of our present friends, compare.com becomes a way of life. I read the alumni news of my university cohort and wonder where I have gone wrong!

Some social psychologists see the constant temptation to define our identity by comparisons as an almost innate human drive.[2] Leon Festinger (1919-1989) the American social psychologist most famous for his concept of 'cognitive dissonance' is one. In an influential paper he wrote in 1954, 'A theory of social comparison processes'[3] he argues that we particularly tend to evaluate ourselves with those of similar abilities and circumstances to our own. Novice chess players, he says, tend not to compare themselves with chess masters!

Festinger went on to describe how, as a result of comparison, we tend to do what we can to minimise perceived discrepancies. We either alter our estimation of ourselves or others or work hard to match their ability. We tend to make 'downward social comparisons', (evaluating ourselves in relation to those performing worse than ourselves) in order to make us feel better and make 'upward social comparisons' in order to motivate us to better things. In a more recent study a group of dieters were found to post pictures of thinner people on their refrigerators to inspire them![4]

---

2   Interestingly John Calvin agrees! 'For it is almost innate in us to examine the lives of others rather than our own, and in them to grasp at empty excuses'. *Calvin's New Testament Commentaries The Gospel According to John 11-21* (tr. T.H.L Parker, Grand Rapids: Eerdmans, reprinted 1979), 224.

3   Festinger L. 'A theory of social comparison processes', *Human Relations* (1954), 7, 117-140.

4   Collins R.L. (1995) 'For better or worse: The impact of upward social comparisons on self-evaluations'. *Psychology Bulletin*, 119 (1) 51-69.

When the ability to decrease the discrepancy with those we are comparing ourselves becomes problematic then negative and even hostile attitudes can set in.

None of this is too surprising. But the unredeemable inevitability of our desire to compare ourselves to others does need challenging. It was why Jesus was stern in his rebuke of Peter. He saw it as a dark cul-de-sac. It is in following Jesus and not in fretting over the fate of others that liberation comes. Whilst it is certainly true that we are inherently social beings and that relationships around us matter hugely and help shape our identity we are not ultimately *constituted* by *human* relations. Our worth comes from a loving Creator and Redeemer who made us in his image. The only one with whom we are to relate for identity is Jesus Christ, the one who is the perfect image of God.[5] This frees us from the constant need for human comparison. How so often we fail to enjoy such freedom.

There is much recent research on how, when people seek to evaluate themselves on the basis of comparison with others, psychological ill-health often follows. In a recent survey (2017) 60% of those using social media reported that it had impacted their self-esteem in a negative way.[6] Even more is this the case among young people. Combining a need for affirmation with a curiosity about how peers are doing, their Instagram and Facebook feeds become fertile ground for massive self-doubt.

Competition and 'Zero Sum' Mentality

One particularly unattractive snare of social comparison is its propensity to turn allies into competitors. When this happens the ugly face of jealousy, envy, suspicion, lack of empathy and even hostility can begin to take a grip. The sibling rivalry that so marks the book of Genesis comes back in a new form to haunt us. At worst, self-worth becomes correlated to the number of people beaten.

This tragically taps in to the competitive spirit that is all-pervasive in our society. It is the zero sum game; 'I flourish means you diminish', we are either 'winners' or 'losers'. It is rhetoric that extends all the way from

---

5   2 Corinthians 10:12. Here Paul warns of having ourselves as our only standard. Speaking of his detractors he comments, 'When they measure themselves by themselves and compare themselves with themselves, they are not wise.'
6   https://www.hufffpost.com/entry/social-medias-impact-on-self-esteem_b_58ad0 38e4b0d818c4f0a4e4

the superpowers to the insecure car salesman. The fun and playfulness of competitive sport is one thing; jostling for power, space and significance at the expense of others is quite another. Such a pervasive mind-set deserves careful and urgent Christian challenge. Life in God's Kingdom is utterly non-competitive. The same God who nourishes me, nourishes all. The same Lord Jesus who offers me grace offers it to every other sinner.

Indeed, even more fundamental, the very world God brought into being was a creation marked by inter-dependence and non-competitive harmony[7] and, though we now struggle in our sin and self-centredness, through Christ there is an even fuller eschatological harmony that awaits us. The church now, as a sign of that coming new creation, is called to model this.

The Spirit of the Age to come binds me now to others in a life of inter-dependence and mutual enrichment. It would be a strange winning football team where the goal scorer, in a post-match interview, implied that his brilliance meant the defensive players had been weak. The church is the body of Christ where 'if one part suffers, every part suffers with it; if one part is honoured, every part rejoices with it.'[8] Henri Nouwen expresses it well,

> Through union with God we are lifted out of our competitiveness with each other into the divine wholeness. By sharing in the wholeness of the one in whom no competition exists, we can enter into new, compassionate relationships with each other.[9]

Competitiveness – a Dark Place in Ministry

Whilst all in leadership would affirm that a self-seeking, competitive spirit is utterly alien to the values of God's Kingdom, sadly, at the same time, few of us would deny that a well-disguised but real rivalry has at times dogged our steps. David Bebbington, in his history of nineteenth century evangelicalism, comments, 'Church against chapel was probably

---

7 The whole issue of the inherent competitiveness of evolutionary natural selection needs careful thought. Conceding its possibility as a way God may have created does not lead to a view of humanity as essentially in competition. Humanity is to steward the creation, not be a victim of it.

8 1 Corinthians 14: 26.

9 H.J.M. Nouwen, Donald P. McNeill and Douglas A. Morrison, *Compassion. A Reflection on the Christian Life* (London: Darton, Longman and Todd 2008) 19.

the sharpest social division of all in Victorian England and Wales.'[10] He recounts the story of a Simon Richardson, an American Methodist circuit rider who was utterly delighted and untroubled when all the episcopal families except one joined his own church in St Mary's Florida![11]

Such a competitive spirit is perhaps more hidden today but still abounds. I recall walking back to our chalets after a Spring Harvest evening celebration with that evening's female speaker. She confessed to being more than a little troubled by the display of male competitive egos on the platform that night. I recall too with a wry smile a time when our denominational year book made a printing error and recorded sixty conversions and baptisms for our local church rather than six! It led to a colleague in a much larger church apprehending me as I walked down the street and then looking visibly relieved (rather than dismayed) when I declared the truth!

But the reality is more painful than amusing. My own awareness of being threatened by the brilliant website of a neighbouring church and the eloquent podcast of a friend makes me realise the darkness in my own heart. Even more so when I quietly celebrate the demise of a gifted leader. 'What about him, Lord?' I ask, as we face yet another tension in the church and my colleagues down the road seemingly enjoy untroubled progress. I have found myself overly pained when good folk with good grace have left to attend a neighbouring good church. They have not for a moment been lost to God's church so why exactly am I so threatened? I find myself shocked by my own emotional cul-de-sacs, shabby spirituality and theological poverty.

Calling and Contentment

Jesus words to Peter, 'What is that to you? You follow me' are both liberating and life-giving. A competitive spirit is crucified, as is our whole ego, by our union with Christ in his death. It is crucified by a knowledge of the depth of Christ's cruciform love *for me,* by an assurance that every spiritual blessing is mine in Christ and by the conviction that his gifting and calling *of me* is unique. The outstanding model here is John the Baptist. When John was informed that the crowds were now flocking to Jesus for

---

10 David W. Bebbington, *The Dominance of Evangelicalism. The Age of Spurgeon and Moody* (IVP 2005), 60.
11 Ibid., 61.

baptism and teaching and no longer to him there was not a hint of being threatened. He was utterly secure and content in his God-given assignment. 'A man can receive only what is given him from heaven' (3:27). He was clear that Jesus was not his rival. John was merely the 'best man' to the long awaited bridegroom and for that he was full of joy. 'That joy is mine and it is now complete. He must become greater; I must become less' (3:29-30). It is a secure person indeed who rejoices over his own redundancy caused by another's appointment. Such security and contentment in discipleship and ministry can be found as we too look away to Christ. John Calvin uses the image of warfare to spell out the inappropriateness of comparisons:

> Since there are different kinds of Christian warfare, let everyone learn to keep his own position and not ask like non-combatant spectators about this or that person. For our heavenly leader urges on each of us, and we ought to be so intent on his command as to forget everything else.[12]

The contemporary image of the London Marathon comes to my mind. It is a competitive race for sure with world class marathon runners but accompanied by the weak, the wild and the wacky - all with their own calling to support their own charities and their only desire to just complete the course. The unique race of the believer in a competitive world is to run towards the prize which is Christ.[13] He is our only motive and our only goal. But within that race we all have our own pace and place, our own God-given calling and gifting. We cheer each other on as we run. We wave and laugh as the wheel chair participants race by. We share smiles with runners from countless ethnic backgrounds. It is non-competitive togetherness, a solidarity of sharing our vulnerabilities and strengths. We allow kingdom values to forge a counter-cultural partnership between ambition and contentment.

Peter Morden, in his book on discipleship, speaks about the need for 'militant contentment'. He gets this unusual couplet of words from a blog post by Pete Grieg of the 24/7 prayer movement. Pete Grieg was using the phrase to encourage strongly counter-cultural gestures on Black Friday, 'the day we could defy greed with a little gratitude – with militant

12 Calvin, op. cit., 224.
13 1 Corinthians 9:24.

contentment'.[14] Such serious and counter-cultural contentment is an urgently needed practice in the evangelical world of ministry as well as in our protests over rampant consumerism.

To Will the Good of the Other: Five Practices for Unthreatened Collaboration

Thomas Aquinas' famous definition of love 'to will the good of the other' points the way forward. To love is not essentially an emotion, it is an intentional choosing always to protect, trust, hope and persevere.[15] For me, five 'comparison–busting practices' have been of huge benefit.

The first is a **commitment to pray regularly** for neighbouring churches and colleagues, particularly those I am tempted to view as rivals. To bring such into God's love and light is to see my fears for what they are. 'To will the good of the other' is most authentically expressed as we sincerely intercede for the other. It is as we take time to lift up to God those we find difficult or are secretly jealous of that we begin to discover a deep solidarity with them both in shared struggles and shared goals. As Bonhoeffer puts it,

> Intercession is the most promising way to reach our neighbours, and corporate prayer, offered in the name of Christ, the purest form of fellowship.[16]

Listening in prayer to our Heavenly Manager give a 'team talk' can be far more uncomfortable than a bad day at Old Trafford! One time, being part of a 24/7 united church prayer event, I sat in front of a circle of candles and prayed for God's blessing on all the churches in the town. In the silence I had a real sense of God speaking to my heart about what my head knew all too well: 'As much-loved parts of the One Body of Christ I will bless each local church, differently but equally'. It was a simple but releasing rebuke.

Second, it is as we **intentionally gather** with other local colleagues from other traditions and backgrounds that we grow in love and appreciation of one another. This is of huge importance. We live in a culture where so many just skim read, scan an article and surf the net. Similarly we can all

14 Pete Grieg 'Black Friday Blues' quoted in Peter Morden, *The Message of Discipleship* (London: Inter-Varsity Press 2018), 178.
15 Corinthians 13:7.
16 D. Bonhoeffer, *The Cost of Discipleship* (Revised and unabridged English Edition, London: SCM Press 1959), 88.

too easily 'skim read' colleagues and badly misjudge. Only as we listen to each other, pray with and for each other, study and debate together, plan together do we discover that 'diversity-in-unity' is far more attractive than 'co-existence-with-competition'. In Rupert Shortt's biography of former Archbishop Rowan Williams he quotes a bishop who was deeply impressed with how Williams modelled this:

> Rowan assumes he knows what liberals think, that he represents their view, so doesn't feel he needs to surround himself with them. Some time ago, I went to a day conference at Lambeth on the future of the Church. No one to the theological Left of me was present. Almost all the rest were Evangelicals and other traditionalists.[17]

Third, the real test comes when we learn genuinely **to rejoice when others experience blessing.** Robert Murray McCheyne's (1813-1843) fruitful ministry at St Peter's Dundee is well known. Less well known is the story of how he invited a younger colleague, William Chalmers Burns, to oversee the church whilst he went to Israel in 1839. Whilst away the church experienced an extraordinary revival! The outpouring of the Spirit began first in July 1839 in Kilsyth when Burns went to preach and then spread to St Peters itself in August. On August 8th 1839 Burns records:

> Suddenly the power of God seemed to descend and all were bathed in tears. The next evening there was a prayer meeting in the church. There was much melting of heart and an intense desire after the beloved of the Father . . . No sooner was the vestry door opened to admit those who might feel anxious to converse, than a vast number pressed in with awful eagerness.

In the following months over 700 people 'conversed' with a minister about their need of Christ. What is so striking in all this is that when, a few months later, Murray McCheyne returned to his church he wasn't at all threatened by the success of his junior colleague. He was simply overcome with joy! He wrote:

> When God sent me away from you about 18 months ago, I think I could number in my mind more than 60 souls who I trusted has visibly passed from death unto life during the time I had been among you. Now I do

---

17 Rupert Short, *Rowan's Rule. The Biography of the Archbishop* (Hodder and Stoughton 2008), 9.

trust I would number many more – aye twice as many more – I trust there is not a family in this church who have not some friend or relative really born again.[18]

Would that such a non-threatened attitude be true of us all!

Fourth, I have discovered that when **we share mission together**, realising that our common goal is sharing Christ and our common enemy are the forces of darkness, all comparisons become laughable. I heard recently of no less than eighty church leaders gathering in a town near London to pray specifically over the issue of the rise of knife crime. It was a powerful occasion. For many years, in a number of different settings, an undoubted highlight of the year for me has been to walk alongside members from many different Christian traditions carrying a cross on Good Friday and meeting in the open air at sunrise on Easter morning. To stand under the cross and to celebrate an empty tomb puts everything in perspective.

Finally I have found that to choose **to bless others in specific ways** has huge benefit for my own soul. This may involve simply joining another congregation on a Sunday off. It may involve sending a card of encouragement. It may involve inviting a colleague to preach. Such modest gestures are not to be belittled – they embody a powerful message of affirmation.

'What is That to You? You Must Follow Me'

Peter and the Beloved Disciple, both crucial to the founding of the Christian community, would eventually be led in quite separate directions as they faithfully followed their Lord. Peter would become the leading spokesman, preacher and missionary to the Jews. Tradition has it he would end his days in Rome and die a martyr's death as Jesus predicted. The Beloved Disciple (assuming it was John) would become the pastor of Ephesus and the faithful witness whose writings would be so influential. He would die at an old age, we are not sure where. Both kept their eyes on Christ alone; the idea of comparison and competition being utter folly. Without their distinctive contributions we would all be incalculably poorer.

---

18 David Robertson, *Awakening: The Life and Ministry of Robert Murray McCheyne* (Authentic Media 2004), 110-114.

Chapter Fourteen

Follow Me: Returning to our First Call

You must follow me.   (John 21:19)

John Chapter 21 ends with two striking themes, themes that have
been central to, and interwoven throughout the whole of John's Gospel.
The first is the renewed call of Jesus (repeated twice) for Peter to 'follow
him', arguably the two most important words in the Gospels (21:19,
22). The word disciple (*mathetes*) occurs in John's Gospel more often
than in the first three gospels (it occurs seventy-eight times)[1] and has
been described as 'the primary category in John.'[2]

The second theme, expressed by the Beloved Disciple, is the
importance of faithful witness, 'This is the disciple who testifies
to these things and who wrote them down' (21:24). It is a witness
affirmed by the wider community, 'We know that his testimony is
true,' (21:24b).[3] This theme too pervades the whole of John's Gospel.
Indeed, the Gospel has been likened to a courtroom scene, reflecting
the cosmic courtroom scenes of the Old Testament. Throughout the
narrative witnesses are called to give evidence regarding the claims of
Jesus of Nazareth.[4] Interestingly, both of these themes were introduced

---

1   The term '*mathetes*' occurs seventy-three times in Matthew, forty-six times in
Mark and thirty-seven times in Luke. R.M. Chennattu, *Johannine Discipleship as
a Covenant Relationship* (Peabody: Hendrickson 2006), 2.
2   R.E. Brown, *The Community of the Beloved Disciple; The Life, Loves, Hates of
an Individual Church in New Testament Times* (New York: Paulist 1979), 84.
3   C.K. Barrett, 'The 'we' is to be taken with full seriousness; there exists an
apostolic Church capable of verifying and affirming the apostolic witness.' *The
Gospel According to St John* (London: SPCK 1955), 489.
4   See Andrew Lincoln, *Truth on Trial: the Lawsuit Motif in the Fourth Gospel*
(Peabody: Hendrickson 2000).

in John Chapter 1, with John the Baptist *witnessing* to two of his own disciples about Jesus, disciples who then *followed* Jesus.[5] Thus, with these two themes now also ending the Gospel there is a classic 'bookends' feel to the whole. Put another way, Jesus is now inviting his disciples to return to how it all began. It is an invitation to return to their first call.

We need to do the same. There is something healthy about re-visiting how it all began for us. Have we 'forsaken our first love'? Do we need to repent, as the church of Ephesus needed to, and 'do the things you did at first?'[6] Radical disciples and radical leaders, by definition, need to keep returning to their roots. Rekha Chennattu, an Indian biblical scholar, has argued that the discipleship material in John's Gospel echoes the Old Testament idea of a covenant renewal. Just as the covenant between Yahweh and Israel was not static but 'a vocation that calls for on-going choices and decisions . . . so too discipleship is as a *journey* made with Jesus . . . the evangelist presents discipleship as a process of becoming, a process of growth.'[7]

Though her overall argument may not be altogether convincing, there is a real sense of covenant renewal as Jesus calls Peter back to how it all began three years before. Forgiveness, restoration and recommissioning are all part of this most basic of callings, 'follow me'. Eugene Peterson in his *Subversive Spirituality* puts it like this,

> We do not progress in the Christian life by becoming more competent, more knowledgeable, more virtuous or more energetic. We do not advance in the Christian life by acquiring more expertise. It is by returning each day and many times each day to Square One . . . to a place of adoring and listening.[8]

Peterson goes on to quote the testimony of Karl Barth when he said that we are constantly 'being thrown back on the start and always opening up afresh.'[9] There can be nothing more fundamental to Christian living and Christian ministry than being both a faithful follower of Jesus and a faithful witness to Jesus.

---

5   John 1:35-37.
6   Revelation 2:4-5.
7   R. Chennattu, op cit., 42.
8   Eugene Peterson, *Subversive Spirituality* (Grand Rapids: Eerdmans; Vancouver: Regent College Publishing 1997), 30.
9   Ibid., 30, from Karl Barth, *Church Dogmatics* 1/1 (Edinburgh: T&T Clark 1936), 15.

A few years ago I returned to the village of Ulrome near Hornsea on the East Coast of Yorkshire with my elderly father. It was there (as mentioned in the Introduction) where, at a Christian boy's camp, my father had helped me find faith in Christ. It was the place of my call to a lifetime of discipleship. To return to that place was moving. Whilst making this trip down memory lane we went to inspect the cliff edge, famous for its rapid erosion. We were shocked with how many hundreds of yards had been eroded since those camp days. (The forty miles stretch of beach from Flamborough Head in the north to Spurn Head in the south is the fastest eroding coastline in Europe.) Whole caravan sites and farmer's fields were no longer there. The Second World War defence concrete slabs where we would lay our clothes to swim were now so far out they were hardly visible.

I have reflected on that image. How much erosion rather than growth has occurred in my life over the many years of ministry? Have years of service been denuding or transforming? Have the many knocks and bruises of leadership detracted or enhanced my journey to be more like Christ? It is salutary to return to our first call.

Being Faithful Followers

Throughout this book there has been a constant emphasis that Christian ministry is fundamentally 'exemplary discipleship'. Our primary calling is simply 'to be' – to be a consistent, faithful, passionate follower of Jesus. I sense in my own life a constant need to keep rediscovering the simplicity of this. Without a daily sense of the magnetic majesty and grace of Jesus of Nazareth, without a daily experience of his love and cleansing, my service for him remains a task, not an 'overflowing'. Our primary calling, in the words of Simon Walker, is surprisingly 'close at home.' 'It is', he writes, 'to grow up. It is to learn, through the experiences we are given, who we are – what it means to be courageous, what it is to serve, what it is to be loved and to love, what it is to be real, what it is to be fully human.'[10] Leadership is always secondary to all this. Unless we are listening to and obeying the Lord Jesus, unless we are growing in our humanity and Christ-like maturity, then we are in no position to call others to follow our lead. The words of Paul, 'Follow my example, as I follow the example of Christ'[11]

10 Simon P. Walker, *The Undefended Leader Vol. 1. Leading Out of Who We Are* (Piquant 2007), 154.
11 1 Corinthians 11:1.

are as challenging as they are bold. People want from us authenticity, consistency, humility and integrity.

This involves at least three key aspects, all of which already have been explored but need to be underlined. First it involves living close to Jesus on a daily basis. The core vocation of the first disciples was simply 'to be with him.'[12] How that looked in practice for a married man like Peter can only be imagined – but at every available opportunity Peter and the others would be travelling, eating, relaxing, discussing and ministering with Jesus – and, in it all, being apprenticed by him. It would involve an attentive listening to Jesus and a conscious imitating of him. All too easily and all too often we seek to enjoy the *benefits* of Christ (his forgiveness, his new life, his protection) without the willingness to follow the *person* of Christ – with all the *obedience* that entails. Dallas Willard, in his classic *The Divine Conspiracy* says,

> The narrow gate is not, as so often assumed, doctrinal correctness. The narrow gate is obedience – and the confidence in Jesus necessary to it . . . The broad way, by contrast, is simply doing whatever I want to do.[13]

Second, being a faithful follower (before being an effective leader) demands a wholehearted commitment to the ongoing transformation of our lives by Christ. We readily teach the lofty truth of 'being transformed into his likeness with ever increasing glory, which comes from the Lord, who is the Spirit'[14] – but often fail to model it. At the end of a long stint in a particular ministry can people not only see the difference we have made but see the difference Christ has made *in us*? I have a friend in the Scottish Borders of whom a non-Christian commented (not knowing how biblical he was!) 'Whenever I meet him he smells of Jesus!'[15] It reminds me of the wonderful Jewish instruction in the Mishnah for disciples of a rabbi, 'Be dusty with the dust of your rabbi.'[16] We are to live so close to Jesus that we share something

---

12 Mark 3:14.
13 Dallas Willard, *The Divine Conspiracy. Rediscovering Our Hidden Life in God* (William Collins 1998), 302.
14 2 Corinthians 3:18.
15 2 Corinthians 2:15.
16 As quoted in Peter Morden where he also discusses the debated authenticity of this rabbinic saying. *The Bible Speaks Today. The Message of Discipleship* (Inter-Varsity Press 2018), 4.

of his very aroma . . . and dust! I have always found deeply suggestive the comment made by Luke about Peter and John in the early church after they had been arrested, 'They (the religious authorities) took note that these men had been with Jesus.'[17] As A.W. Tozer warned, it is possible to adopt the view that 'the *gift* element in the gospel is held to be its exclusive content and the *shift* element is accordingly ignored.'[18] The 'shift' from the old self to the new, by the power of the Spirit, must be our constant prayer.

For those of us in 'fulltime' Christian leadership the idea of 'whole-life' discipleship needs to be particularly monitored. The call to be Christ-like in a hostile, secular workplace is tough but the challenge is clear. When life revolves much more around the church community the temptations are more subtle but no less real and fierce. The ease with which it is possible, under the guise of Christian service, to become self-centred, over-familiar with holy things, ill-disciplined in our mental habits, manipulative in our relationships and ungenerous towards those closest to us is frightening. Whole-life discipleship is not just about allowing Christ to be Lord over the varied terrains of my typical week but Lord over every contour of my complex, flawed personality.

Central to this is surely a growth in our humility, perhaps the most basic and 'earthy' of virtues ('humility' and 'humus' are from the same root.)[19] Michael Ramsay, a former Archbishop Canterbury, writes:

> There is only one kind of person who makes God known and realised by other people, and that is the person who is humble because he knows God and knows God because he is humble . . . May it be said one day of you, not necessarily that you talked about God cleverly, but that you made God real to people . . . only humility can do that.[20]

This and all dimensions of holiness grow, in turn, out of a willingness not only to know the power of Christ's resurrection but to experience a 'sharing in his sufferings, becoming like him in his death.'[21] Martin Hengel, the celebrated New Testament scholar, defines discipleship in this searching

---

17 Acts 4:13.
18 A.W. Tozer *The Divine Conquest* (London: Marshall, Morgan and Scott, 1950) 35.
19 Stephen Cherry, *Barefoot Disciple. Walking the Way of Passionate Humility* (Continuum 2011), 39.
20 Michael Ramsey, *The Christian Priest Today,* 78, quoted in Stephen Cherry ibid., 38.
21 Philippians 3:10-11.

way: 'an unconditional sharing of the master's destiny, which does not stop even at deprivation and suffering in the train of the master, and is possible only on the basis of complete trust on the part of the person who follows; he has placed his destiny and his future in his master's hands.'[22] For leaders this may take many forms (as discussed in Ch.12) but essentially it is the cross-shaped selflessness of ordinary, everyday service to others. There is no discipleship without cross-bearing and certainly no authentic leadership. Only a few weeks before this beach scene Peter and the other disciples had heard Jesus say, 'I tell you the truth, unless a grain of wheat falls into the ground and dies, it remains only a single seed. But if it dies it produces many seeds.'[23] Significantly Jesus call to Peter to 'follow me!' comes immediately after Jesus prediction of Peter's martyrdom (21:19). Not all perseverance in ministry produces attractive holiness (there is nothing less winsome than a cynical Christian leader) but there is no holiness without costly perseverance.

Third, being a faithful follower is a life full of joy in the Holy Spirit. Post Pentecost this was to be the experience of Peter and the other apostles. Later in life Peter would write about being 'filled with an inexpressible and glorious joy.'[24] Faithful following of Jesus is never at the expense of fullness of life, it is rather the gateway to it. The sheer joyful privilege of following Jesus should be the overwhelming hallmark of all Christian leadership. It is also the basis for freedom in ministry. Only when our primary vocation is crystal clear – to delight in Christ and to please him – are we liberated from both the burden of obligation and the temptation to serve in order to please others.

A Faithful Witness

John 21 and the whole Gospel of John ends with the focus moving from Peter 'the faithful follower' to the Beloved Disciple 'the faithful witness'. Richard Bauckham argues there are seven key witnesses throughout the narrative of John's Gospel: John the Baptist (e.g.1.7), Jesus himself (e.g.3:11), the Samaritan woman (4:39), God the Father (5:32) Jesus' works

---

22 M. Hengel, *The Charismatic Leader and his Follower* (1968; ET T&T Clark, 1981), 72 quoted in Derek Tidball, *The Bible Speaks Today. The Message of the Cross* (Inter Varsity Press 2001), 289.
23 John 12:24.
24 1 Peter 1:8.

(5:36), the Scriptures (5:39) and the crowd who testify about Jesus raising Lazarus from the dead (12.17). Looking to the future, the Gospel claims there are now essentially only two: the Holy Spirit (15:26) and the disciples (15:27) - one of whom is the Beloved Disciple. Indeed the testimony of the Beloved Disciple is absolutely vital for he was the eye witness at key moments (19:35) and, crucially, the one who records it all, allowing the seven witnesses to continue to be heard (21:24).[25] Earlier in John 21 it is the same disciple who is portrayed as the key witness. After the miraculous catch of fish and a Stranger speaks from the beach it is the Beloved Disciple who first proclaims, 'It is the Lord!'

Over the years I have often found leadership and pastoral ministry a struggle. What a relief to know that all that the Lord expects of me is faithfully to follow him and bear witness to him. Far more important than the eloquence of my sermons or the creativity of my leadership is the integrity of my witness. Along with the Beloved disciple, John the Baptist is the other great example of witness in John's Gospel. Indeed, as Richard Bauckham observes, this is emphasised through an impressive *inclusio*. 'The Beloved Disciple's present-tense testifying (*is* testifying) in 21:24 is matched by John the Baptist's present tense testifying (he *testifies*) in 1:15.'[26] I particularly love the comment of the crowds to Jesus in John 10:41 when he retreated to John the Baptist's former stomping ground, 'Though John never performed a miraculous sign, all that John said about this man was true.' What a remarkable obituary! Signs and wonders are no match to simply and plainly speaking the truth about Jesus!

What does this faithful witness look like? Faithful witness has been likened to a Marco Polo returning with news of newly discovered marvels in the Eastern world. We cannot prove what we have discovered but we can tell of 'a new world' with passion, reason and excitement.[27] More prosaically, it looks like being a finger that points to Jesus. It is well known that Karl Barth had on his desk a reproduction of Matthias Grunewald's celebrated painting '*Crucifixion*' (completed 1515) with John the Baptist to

---

25 Richard Bauckham 'The Fourth Gospel as the Testimony of the Beloved Disciple' in *The Gospel of John and Christian Theology*, eds. Richard Bauckham and Carl Mosser, (Grand Rapids: Eerdmans 2008), 123.
26 Ibid., 129.
27 James Wm. McClendon, Jr., *Witness. Systematic Theology*. Vol. 3 (Nashville: Abingdon Press 2000), 309.

the left of the cross pointing to the crucified Lord. The finger of John the Baptist is enlarged. A lamb is at his feet. Faded words in the background read in Latin, *Illum oportet crescere, me autem minui*. ('He must increase, but I must decrease'). For Barth it perfectly summed up the crucial task of theology (and all ministry), pointing beyond ourselves to the person of Christ. There is great freedom in this realisation; the simplicity of bearing testimony Sunday by Sunday, weekday by weekday, to the One full of grace and truth. All in the congregation are *His* disciples, never ours.

This faithful witness involves taking with great seriousness (as with the Beloved Disciple) the apostolic witness. The church is the 'creature of the Word' (Luther) and without the regular and faithful opening up of that written Word then God's people will neither be nourished nor renewed. It involves us personally making priority for God's Word to grip us, shape us and saturate us. Sinclair Ferguson tells of a widow he knew who said of her husband that he devoured Scripture like a novel 'and wore out his Bible in the last year of his life.'[28] George Beasley Murray, at the end of his commentary on John's Gospel reflects on the aside offered in that a rumour had spread (that the Beloved disciple would not die) due to a misunderstanding of Jesus words to Peter, 'If I want him to remain alive until I return what is that to you' (21:23). He comments on the implied warning, namely 'to carefully listen to what the Lord actually said, and not to be content with second hand repetitions of his words and opinions about it.'[29] Quite so. Would that all our preaching and teaching were a result of a real encounter with the text and the Spirit and not internet 'rumours'! I have found it liberating, when people have disagreed with me, to invite them, with me, to search the Scriptures. The focus of authority immediately changes. Sometimes, in the light of the witness of Scripture, I have to have had to admit to being in the wrong.

To be a faithful witness is to live as an 'open book'. The flipside of whole-life discipleship is whole-life witness. The way we relate to our family, the way we conduct ourselves in the gym, the way we spend our money and time, the concern we have for issues of injustice and inequality invariably offers a more winsome witness than our best sermon. In particular, the

---

28 Sinclair Ferguson, *Some Pastors and Teachers* (Edinburgh: Banner of Truth 2017), 754.

29 George R. Beasley-Murray, *Word Bible Commentary, John* (Waco, Texas: Word Books 1987), 418.

way we endure hardship, criticism and suffering is a powerful witness. I'm struck by the comment of the American theologian, James Wm McClendon Jr., when he comments that for many early Baptists their most powerful written witness was not to be found in polished published writing (as with the scholarly Reformers) 'but from the preserved criminal records of much of Europe and from surviving tracts, some old hand-written chronicles, and a few early songbooks.'[30] 'Witness' and 'martyr' spring from the same root word; it was their suffering which spoke and still speaks powerfully.

Finally, to be a faithful witness is to be full of the wisdom that comes from an attentive listening to Christ 'in whom are hidden all the treasures of wisdom and knowledge.'[31] This is surely what the Beloved Disciple was seeking to express when he ends his Gospel with his famous, almost exasperated, words:

> Jesus did many other things as well. If every one of them were written down, I suppose that even the whole world would not have room for the books that would be written (21:25).

It signifies the unfathomable mystery, wonder and wisdom of Christ. Edwin Hoskins quotes a delightful contemporary Jewish parallel that highlights this emphasis on the never-ending riches of wisdom. It is from Rabbi Johanan b.Zakkai (first century AD):

> If all heaven were a parchment, and all the trees produced pens, and all the waters were ink, they would not suffice to inscribe the wisdom I have received from my teachers: and yet from the wisdom of the wise I have enjoyed only so much as the water a fly which plunges into the sea can remove.[32]

Capturing, by the Spirit, just something of this inexhaustible wisdom is what we desperately need in our preaching and pastoral care, in our leadership discernment and mission approach; the wisdom to help people re-imagine the world through a biblical lens. It is wisdom to be truly human. King Solomon's request is surely the desire of all godly leaders, 'Give me wisdom and knowledge, that I may lead this people, for who is

---

30 Op. cit., 346.
31 Colossians 2:3.
32 Quoted in Sir Edward Hoskyns, edited by Francis Noel Davey, *The Fourth Gospel* (New and Revised Edition, London: Faber and Faber 1947), 561.

able to govern this great people of yours?'[33] Sadly, too often highly gifted leaders trip up through lack of praying this particular prayer. Yet part of our faithful witness is to a humility, to the mystery of our faith and to a recognition that, this side of glory, at best we only see in part; 'fly size' wisdom compared to the majestic being of the Triune all-wise God!

The Divine Invitation: Fruitfulness, Fellowship and Following

I have attempted, using the resurrection narrative of John 21, to identify and reflect on fourteen evocative images relevant to Christian discipleship, mission and ministry. As I conclude, these images can perhaps be gathered together under three dominant themes; three gracious invitations from the hand of God himself. The first is an invitation to a fullness of life, a fruitfulness like no other. As we have seen, the theme is introduced in the Prologue, 'From the fullness of his grace we have all received one blessing after another' (1:16) and finds its climax here in the Epilogue with, what has been called, 'an excess ending'[34]; an excess of fish, of welcome, of questions and of love. The second is an invitation to fellowship with the living Lord. The Gospel opens with an invitation from Jesus 'come and see' (where I am staying/ abiding) (1:39) and closes with the invitation, 'Come and have breakfast' (21:12). It is the call to a lifetime of abiding in God's love in Christ. The third is the invitation to a life-time vocation of following Jesus which is the beginning and the end of the matter.

William Temple ends his devotional commentary on John with this image.

> So the Gospel ends with a little group standing apart from the company of the disciples. It consists of three: the Lord of love; the disciple in whom self would be offered; and the disciple in whom self would be forgotten.[35]

May we not stand apart from them but imitate them as we enjoy the divine invitation and continue the conversations by the sea.

---

33 2 Chronicles 1:10.

34 B.R Gavanta, 'The Archive of Excess: John 21 and the Problem of Narrative Closure' in John R.A. Culpepper and C.C. Black, *Exploring the Gospel of John*, (Louisville, Westminster John Knox Press 1996), 241-249.

35 William Temple, *Readings in John's Gospel* (London: Macmillan and Co. 1955), 410.

Appendix: John Chapter 21
– an integral epilogue

Although there is no manuscript evidence that the Gospel was ever circulated without Chapter 21 the majority of contemporary Johannine scholars view the chapter as a later addition to the Gospel. It is seen as an 'appendix', shaped by an editor/redactor sometime after the main body of the Gospel was written. It was added for the particular reason of explaining to the early church the eventual trajectory of the two great apostles Peter and John.

The evidence, they argue, is very clear. Many of the key themes of the Gospel seem to find their triumphant conclusion in Chapter 20 and thus John 20:30-31 has all the feel of the Gospel coming to an appropriate climax. In the famous words of the French scholar Loisy, 'L'évangile est fini, très bien fini!'[1]

The Crucified One is now the Risen Lord who points to his ascension, who offers peace, breathes out his Spirit and commissions his disciples for mission. The chapter ends with the highest Christological claim of the whole Gospel. Thomas exclaims, 'My Lord and my God!' followed by a fitting final beatitude for those who, unlike Thomas, are able to believe without seeing. Added to this, these scholars point to both specific details and linguistic features that suddenly emerge in chapter 21 suggesting a fresh hand is now at work.[2] All this seems to leave John 21 as an authoritative but later 'supplement'.

However, more recently, such eminent New Testament scholars as Paul Minear and Richard Bauckham have seriously challenged this consensus. They view the material of Chapter 21 as building naturally on what has gone before, particularly the dominant Johannine theme

---

1   Quoted in C.K Barrett, *Essays on John* (London: SPCK 1982), 159.
2   R.E. Brown, *The Gospel According to John* (Garden City, Doubleday 1966) 1.xx1v: '[Chapter 21] differs from the rest of the Gospel in small stylistic details that betray difference of authorship'.

of 'witness' and the follow-through from Peter's denials. They see how Chapter 21 develops important themes regarding mission, pastoral leadership and apostolic authority all typical of how the Synoptic Gospels end. For Minear the key observation is that the last two verses of chapter 20 are to be read *not* as a conclusion to the whole Gospel but rather as a fitting conclusion to this particular chapter.[3] The words 'These things are written that you might believe that Jesus is the Christ' (20:31) follow on naturally from Thomas's confession of faith. Equally, he argues, the words of 20:30 'Jesus did many other signs in the presence of his disciples' are not so much a reference to all the previous signs in the Gospel but to the momentous signs of chapter 20 where true believing was now possible. The events of John 20 fulfil the words of John 2:18-22, 'After he was raised from the dead, his disciples recalled what he had said. Then they believed the Scripture and the words that Jesus had spoken.'

So what then is the significance of Chapter 21? Minear sees it not so much as offering further evidence of the resurrection as providing an 'edifying end'[4] to the story of both Peter and John. Jesus had said to Peter, for example, 'Where I am going you cannot follow now, but you will follow later' (13:36) and sees that fulfilled with Jesus's final words to Peter 'Follow me' (21:19). Even more important for the readers of the Gospel was a comment on the future of the Beloved disciple, the one who had such access to Jesus and was the witness (and author) of such key events (19:35).

Richard Bauckham finds this line of argument convincing and adds further weight to it. He sees that, rather than the second conclusion to the Gospel being repetitive and redundant, there is something deliberate about a two-stage conclusion (20:30-31 and 21:25). It allows a 'fencing off' of Chapter 21 from the main narrative of the Gospel, indicating it is a distinct epilogue and yet indicating it is still part of the whole.[5] He further notes that both conclusions consist of 43 words, both have parallel features, and together they aim to create a growing climax.[6] Thus, in the first

---

3   Paul S. Minear, 'The Original Function of John 21', *Journal of Biblical Literature* 102/1 (1983) 87.

4   Ibid., 91.

5   Richard Bauckham, *Jesus and the Eyewitnesses. The Gospels as Eyewitness Testimony* (Grand Rapids: William B Eerdmans, 2006) 364.

6   Ibid., 364.

conclusion at the end of Chapter 20 *all* the disciples are seen as witnesses, 'Jesus performed many other signs in the presence of his disciples' (20:30); whilst in the second conclusion at the end of Chapter 21 one key witness is highlighted, 'This is the disciple who testifies to these things and who wrote them down.' (21:24). Bauckham identifies this 'Beloved disciple' with the unnamed disciple accompanying Andrew in John 1 (John 1:35). He uses this to argues for an important *inclusio* – the crucial eye witness who was there both at the beginning and at the end – and whose identity is withheld until the last minute so that his credentials (the witness to the whole gospel narrative) are now clear.[7]

In the light of all this, the approach adopted in this study has been to see John 21 as integral to the whole Gospel. As such the final chapter can be seen as having both intriguing and suggestive 'flash backs' to earlier gospel stories, and also a distinct, forward-looking emphasis. Just as the Prologue reaches as far back as creation (1:1-18) so this Epilogue reaches forward to celebrate the new creation heralded by the resurrection of the Son of God, pointing even to the Second Coming (21:23). Thus the drama of this final chapter sets out symbolically the future mission and ministry of the church.[8] The interaction of the risen Christ with Peter and the Beloved Disciple offers numerous hints as to what this can look like.

---

7   Ibid., 368.
8   Ibid., 367.

Bibliography

Anderson, Ray S., *The Soul of Ministry: Forming Leaders for God's People*. Louisville, Kentucky: Westminster, John Knox Press 1997.

Augustine, *The Confessions of St,Augustine*, Book 4.

Barrett, C.K., *The Gospel According to St John*. London: SPCK 1955.
    – *Essays on John*. London SPCK 1982

Barton, Ruth Haley, *Pursuing God's Will together. A Discernment Practice for Leadership Groups*. IVP 2012.

Bartholomew C and Thorsten Moritz T., *Christ and Consumerism. A critical Analysis of the Spirit of our Age*. Paternoster Press 2000.

Barth, Karl, *Church Dogmatics* 1/2. Edinburgh: T and T Clark 1936.

Bauckham, Richard, 'The Beloved Disciple as Ideal Author', *Journal for the Study of the New Testament* 49, 1993.
    – 'The 153 Fish and the Unity of the Fourth Gospel', *Neot* 36 2002.
    – *Jesus and the Eye Witnesses. The Gospels as Eyewitness Testimony*. Grand Rapids: Eerdmans 2006.
    – *The Gospel of John and Christian Theology*, ed. Bauckham, R. and Mosser, C. Grand Rapids, Michigan, Cambridge UK: Eerdmans, 2008.

Baxter, Richard, *Gildas Salvianus. The Reformed Pastor*. London, James Nisbet and Co. MDCCCLX.

Beasley-Murray, George R., *Word Bible Commentary John*. Waco, Texas: Word Books 1987.

Beasley-Murray, Paul, *Fifty Lessons in Ministry: Reflections on Fifty Years of Ministry*. Darton, Longman and Todd 2020.

Bebbington, David W., *The Dominance of Evangelicalism. The Age of Spurgeon and Moody*. IVP 2005.

Berger, Peter., *A Rumour of Angels: Modern Society and the Re-discovery of the Supernatural*. Garden City, N.Y: Doubleday & Co. 1969.

Berkman, John and Cartwright, Michael S. (eds.), *The Hauerwas Reader*. Durham and London: Duke University Press 2001.

Blaine Jn. Bradford B., *Peter in the Gospel of John. The Making of an Authentic Disciple*. Atlanta, Society of Biblical Literature 2007.

Bochmuehl, Markus, *Simon Peter in Scripture and Memory*. Baker Academic 2012.

Bond Helen K and Hurtado Larry W. (eds.), *Peter in Early Christianity*. Grand Rapids, Michigan, Cambridge UK: Eerdmans 2015.

Bonhoeffer D., *The Cost of Discipleship*. Revised and unabridged English Edition, London: SCM Press 1959.

Bowlby, John., *Attachment and Loss,* New York: Basic Books, Vol 1. 1969.

Brown, R.E., *The Gospel According to John*. The Anchor Bible, London, Dublin, Melbourne: Geoffrey Chapman 1971.
    – *The Community of the Beloved Disciple; The Life, Loves, Hates of an Individual Church in New Testament Times*. New York: Paulist 1979.

Bruce, Steve, *British Gods: Religion in Modern Britain*. Oxford: Oxford University Press 2020.

Brueggemann, Walter, *Virus as a Summons to Faith. Biblical Reflections in a time of Loss, Grief and Uncertainty*, Paternoster 2020.

Burns, B., Chapman T.D. and Guthrie D.C., *Resilient Ministry. What Pastors told us about Surviving and Thriving*. Illinois: IVP Books 2013.

Buxton, Graham, *Dancing in the Dark. The Privilege of Participating in the Ministry of Christ*. Paternoster Press 2001.

Calvin, J., *Calvin's New Testament Commentaries. The Second Epistle of Paul to the Corinthians and the Epistles to Timothy, Titus and Philemon*, tr. T.A. Smail, Eerdmans 1964.

Campbell, Alistair V., *Rediscovering Pastoral Care*. London: Darton, Longman and Todd 1981.

Carlisle, Clare, *Philosopher of the Heart: The Restless Life of Soren Kierkegaard*. Allen Lane 2019.

Chennattu, Rekha, *Johannine Discipleship as a Covenant Relationship*. Michigan: Baker Academic 2005.

Cherry, Stephen. *Barefoot Discipleship: Walking the Way of Passionate Humility*. Continuum 2011.

Clarke, Andrew D.A., *Pauline Theology of Church Leadership*, Bloomsbury: T&T Clark 2013.

Clarke, N., 'The Ministry. A Review and An Assessment' in *The Baptist Quarterly* Vol. XX1V Oct 1971 No. 4 p.150.

Cockworth C. and Brown R., *Being a Priest Today: Exploring Priestly Identity*. Norwich: Canterbury Press, 2002.

Cullmann, Oscar, *Peter: Disciple, Apostle, Martyr*. trans. Filson, F.V. London: SCM 1953.
    – *Unity through Diversity*. Philadelphia: Fortress Press 1987.

Currie Thomas W.111, *The Joy of Ministry*. Louisville, London: Westminster John Knox Press 2008.

Dodd C.H., *Interpretation of the Fourth Gospel*. Cambridge University Press 1968.

Delattre, Ronald Andre, *Beauty and Sensibility in the Thought of Jonathan Edwards. An Essay in Aesthetics and Theological Ethics*. Wipf & Stock Publishers, Eugene Oregon 2006 (previously published Yale University Press 1968).

Drane, J., *Cultural Change and Biblical Faith*. Paternoster Press 2000.

Ecclestone, Alan, *The Scaffolding of the Spirit: Reflections on the Gospel of John,* Darton, Longman and Todd 1987.

Edwards, Jonathan, The *Works of Jonathan Edwards*. Gen. Ed. John E. Smith. New Haven: Yale University Press 1977–2009.
  – *The Religious Affections*. Edinburgh: Banner of Truth, Reprint, 1994.

Elshof, Gregg A.Ten, *I told me so. Self-deception and the Christian Life*. Grand Rapids: Eerdmans 2009.

Escott, Harry, *P.T Forsyth and the Cure of Souls. An Anthology*. George Allen and Unwin 1948.

Eswine, Zach, *Sensing Jesus. Life and Ministry as a Human Being*. Wheaton, Illinois, Crossway 2013.

Fiddes, Paul S., *Participating in God. A Pastoral Doctrine of the Church*. Darton, Longman and Todd 2000.

Ferguson, Sinclair B., *Some Pastors and Teachers. Reflecting a Biblical Vision of what Every Minister is Called to Be*. The Banner of Truth Trust 2017.

Ford, David F. *The Drama of Living. Becoming Wise in the Spirit*. Norwich: Canterbury Press 2014.
  – *The Gospel of John. A Theological Commentary*. Grand Rapids: Baker Academic 2021.

Forsyth, P.T., *The Church and the Sacraments* 1917. London: Independent Press 1964.
  – *Positive Preaching and the Modern Mind*. London: Independent Press, 1964.
  – *The Cure of Souls*. Grand Rapids: Eerdmans, 1971.

Foster, Richard, *Celebration of Discipline*. London: Hodder and Stoughton 1984.
  – *Streams of Living Water: Celebrating the Great Traditions of Christin Faith*. Trowbridge: Eagle Publishing, 1999.

Foucault, M. *Discipline and Punish. The Birth of the Prison*. Penguin Books, ET 1977.

Francis L. J. and Richter P., *Gone for Good? Church-leaving and Returning in the 21st Century*. Peterborough: Epworth Press 2007.

Fraser, Liam J., *Mission in Contemporary Scotland*. St Andrew Press 2021.

Goodliff, P.W., *Shaped for Service. Ministry Formation and Virtue Ethics*. Eugene, Oregon: Pickwick Publications 2017.

Gorman, Michael J., *Abide and Go. Missional Theosis in the Gospel of John.* The Didsbury Lectures 2016, Eugene, Oregon: Cascade Books 2018.

Green, Michael, *Evangelism in the Early Church.* London: Hodder and Stoughton, 1970.

Greene Mark. *Fruitfulness on the Frontline. Making a Difference Where You Are.* IVP 2014.

Gregory the Great, *The Book of Pastoral Rule*, Trans. George E. Demacopoulos, New York: St Vladimir's Seminary Press 2007.

Greggs, Tom, *Dogmatic Ecclesiology. The Priestly Catholicity of the Church,* Volume One. Grand Rapids: Baker Academic 2019.

Gunton, Colin E, *The One, The Three and the Many. God, Creation and the Culture of Modernity. The 1992 Bampton Lectures.* Cambridge University Press, 1993.

Hengel, Martin, *Saint Peter: The Underestimated Apostle.* Grand Rapids: Eerdmans 2001.
  – *The Johannine Question.* London: SCM Press; Philadelphia: Trinity Press International 1989.

Hafemann, Scott J., *2 Corinthians, The NIV Application Commentary.* Grand Rapids: Zondervan 2000.

Hansen, David, *The Art of Pastoring. Ministry Without all the Answers.* IVP 1994.

Herrick, Vanessa and Mann, Ivan, *Jesus Wept. Reflections on Vulnerability in Leadership.* Darton, Longman and Todd 1998.

Hoskyns, Edwyn, ed. Noel Davey. *The Fourth Gospel.* London: Faber and Faber 1947.

Hudson, Neil, *Imagine Church. Releasing Whole Life Disciples.* IVP 2012.

Hughes P.C. and Patterson, B., *Mastering the Pastoral Role.* Portland, Oregon: Multnomah 1991.

Hull, John M., *Notes on Blindness. A Journey through the Dark.* London, Profile Books, Wellcome Collection, 2017 edition.

Hunter, James Davison, *To Change the World. The Irony, Tragedy and Possibility of Christianity in the late Modern World.* Oxford University Press 2010.

Hurtado, L.W., 'You've got to "Accentuate the Positive". Thinking about Difference Biblically', *Scottish Bulletin of Evangelical Theology* Vol. 30. No. 1, Spring 2012.

Kearsley Roy, *Church, Community and Power.* Ashgate 2008.

Kelly, Ewan, *Personhood and Presence, Self as a Resource for Spiritual and Pastoral Care.* T&T Clark 2012.

Kendall, R.T., *In Pursuit of His Glory. My 25 Years at Westminster Chapel.* London: Hodder and Stoughton 2002.

Koyama, Kosuke, *The Three Mile an Hour God.* SCM Press 1979.

Langberg, Diane, *Redeeming Power. Understanding Authority and Abuse in the Church.* Grand Rapids: Brazos Press 2020.

Lee, D.A., *The Ministry of Women in the New Testament. Reclaiming the Biblical Vision for Church Leadership.* Baker Academic 2021.

Lewis, C.S., *A Grief Observed.* London: Faber and Faber 1961.

Lindars, B. and Smalley, S.S., *Christ and the Spirit in the New Testament.* Cambridge University Press 1973.

Lincoln, Andrew, *Truth on Trial: the Lawsuit Motif in the Fourth Gospel.* Peabody: Hendrickson 2000.

Loughlin, G., *Telling God's Story, Bible, Church and Narrative Theology.* Cambridge University Press 1996.

MacDonald, Gordon., *Rebuilding your Broken World.* Godalming, Surrey: Highland Books, 1988, updated edition 2004 with Epilogue.

MacIntyre Alasdair, *After Virtue, a study in moral theory.* Duckworth, 2nd edn. 1985.

Maclaine, Shirley, *Going Within.* London: Bantam 1990.

Manson, T.W., *The Church's Ministry* London: Hodder and Stoughton 1948.

Martyn, J.L., *The Gospel of John in Christian History: Essays for Interpreters.* New York: Paulist 1978.

May R., *Power and Innocence, a Search for the Sources of Violence.* New York: Norton 1998.

McClendon, James Wm. Jr., *Witness. Systematic Theology. Volume 3.* Nashville: Abingdon Press, 2000.

Meynell, Mark. *When Darkness seems My Closest Friend. Reflections on life and ministry with depression.* London: Inter Varsity Press, 2018.

Minear, Paul S., 'The Original Function of John 21', *Journal of Biblical Literature* 102/1 1983.

Moltmann, Jurgen, *The Church in the Power of the Spirit.* SCM Press 1975.

Morden, Peter, *The Message of Discipleship.* London: Inter-Varsity Press 2018.

Morris, Danny E. and Olson, Charles M., *Discerning God's Will Together. A Spiritual Practice for the Church.* Nashville: Upper Room Books 1997.

Munzinger, Andre., *Discerning the Spirits. Theological and Ethical Hermeneutics in Paul.* Soc. for N.T. Studies Monograph Series 140, Cambridge University Press 2007.

Murray, D., *The Madness of Crowds. Gender, Race and Identity.* London: Bloomsbury Continuum 2019.

Murray, Iain H., *Jonathan Edwards, A New Biograph.* Edinburgh: Banner of Truth 1987.

Neill, Stephen, *On the Ministry.* London: SCM Press 1952.

Newbigin, Lesslie, *Foolishness to the Greeks. The Gospel and Western Culture.* SPCK 1986.
   – *Proper Confidence: Faith, Doubt and Certainty in Christian Discipleship.* Grand Rapids: Eerdmans 1995.

Neuhaus, Richard John, *Freedom for Ministry*. Grand Rapids: Eerdmans 1979.

Newcome, James, *Facing Disappointment. The Challenge for Church Leaders*. Grove Booklet, Ridley Hall, Cambridge 2016.

Nouwen, Henri J.M., *The way of the Heart. Desert Spirituality and Contemporary Ministry*. London: Darton, Longman and Todd 1981.
- *In the Name of Jesus. Reflections on Christian Leadership*. Darton, Longman and Todd, 1989.

Nouwen, Henri, McNeill, D.P. and Morrison, D.A., *Compassion. A Reflection on the Christian Life*. London: Darton, Longman and Todd 2008.

Oakey, Lisa and Humphreys, Justin, *Escaping the Maze of Spiritual Abuse. Creating Health Church Cultures*. SPCK, Thirty One: Eight 2019.

Oden, Thomas C., *Pastoral Theology: Essentials of Ministry*. Bravo Ltd 1997.

Peck, M. Scott, *The Different Drum*, London: Rider 1987.
- *The Road Less Travelled*. Arrow, 1990.

Percy Martyn with Markham, Ian.S., Percy, Emma and Po, Francesca (eds.) *The Study of Ministry: A comprehensive Survey of Theory and Best Practice*. SPCK 2019.

Peterson, Eugene H., *Life at its Best*. Grand Rapids, Michigan: Zondervan 1993.
- *Working the Angles. The Shape of Pastoral Integrity*. Grand Rapids: Eerdmans,1987.
- *Subversive Spirituality*. Grand Rapids: Eerdmans; Vancouver: Regent College Publishing 1994
- *As Kingfishers Catch Fire. A Conversation on the Ways of God Formed by the Word of God*. Hodder 2017.

Peterson, M., *At Personal Risk. Boundary Violations in Professional-Client Relationships*. New York, London: W.W. Norton 1992.

Purves, A., *Reconstructing Pastoral Theology: A Christological Foundation*. Louisville, London: Westminster John Knox Press 2004.

Quast, Kevin, *Peter and the Beloved Disciple. Figures for a Community in Crisis*. Journal for the Study of New Testament Supplement Series 32, Sheffield, JSOT Press 1989.

Quicke, Michael J., *360-Degree Leadership. Preaching to Transform Congregations*. Grand Rapids, Michigan: Baker Books 2006.

Roberts, P., *The Impulse Society: What's Wrong with Getting What we Want?* Bloomsbury 2014.

Robertson, David, *Awakening: The Life and Ministry of Robert Murray McCheyne*. Authentic Media 2004.

Root, Andrew, *The Relational Pastor. Sharing Christ by Sharing Ourselves*. IVP 2013.

Roxburgh, Alan J. and Romanuk, Fred, *The Missional Leader. Equipping your Church to Reach a Changed world*. Jossey Bass 2006.

Sacks, J., *The Persistence of Faith*, Reith Lectures 1990. London: Weidenfeld and Nicolson 1991.

Smart, Dominic, *When We get it Wrong. Peter, Christ and our Path through Failure*. Paternoster Lifestyle 2001.

Smith, James K.A., *Who's Afraid of Postmodernism?* Grand Rapids: Baker Academic 2006.
– *Desiring the Kingdom: Worship, Worldview and Cultural Formation*. Grand Rapids, Michigan: Baker Academic 2009.

Stackhouse, Ian., *The Gospel Driven Church. Retrieving Classical Ministry for Contemporary Revivalism*. Paternoster 2004.
– *Letters to a Young Pastor, Reflections on Leadership, Community and the Gospel of Grace*. Eugene, Oregon: Cascade Books 2019.

Strathern, Paul, *The Essential Foucault*. Virgin Books 2002.

Taylor, Barbara Brown, *The Preaching Life. Living out your Vocation*. Norwich: Canterbury Press 1993.

Temple, William, *Readings in John's Gospel*. London: Macmillan and Co. 1955.

Thompson, M., *The God of the Gospel of John*. Grand Rapids: Eerdmans 2001.

Took, Patricia M., *'It shall not be so among you'. Power and Love in the Community of Christ*. Hertford Baptist Association Booklet; Signposts for a New Century 2000.

Torrance T.F., *Atonement, The Person and Work of Christ*. Ed. Robert T. Walker Paternoster, IVP Academic 2009.

Tozer, A.W., *The Divine Conquest*. London: Marshall, Morgan and Scott 1950.

Volf, Miroslav, *After Our Likeness. The Church as the Image of the Trinity*. Grand Rapids, Michigan, Cambridge UK: Eerdmans 1998.
– *Exclusion and Embrace: A Theological Exploration of Identity, Otherness and Reconciliation*. Nashville: Abingdon Press, 1996.

Walker, Simon P., *The Undefended Leader*, Vol. 1. *Leading with Nothing to Lose*. Piquant 2007.

Watson, D., *I Believe in Evangelism*. London: Hodder and Stoughton 1976.
– *I Believe in the Church*. London, Hodder and Stoughton, 1978.
– *Discipleship*. London: Hodder and Stoughton, 1981.
– *You are my God; An Autobiography*. London: Hodder and Stoughton, 1983.

Watkin, Christopher, *Michel Foucault*. Great Thinkers Series. P&R Publishing, New Jersey 2018.

Webster, J., *Word and Church: Essays in Christian Dogmatics*. London: T&T Clark 2006.

Weston, Paul, *Lesslie Newbigin: Missionary Theologian. A Reader*. SPCK 2006.

White, James Emery, *Meet Generation Z. Understanding and Reaching the New Post-Christian World*. Grand Rapids: Baker Books 2017.

Willard, Dallas, *The Divine Conspiracy. Rediscovering Our Hidden Life in God*. William Collins 1998.

Williams, Rowan, *On Augustine*. Bloomsbury 2016.
  – *Being Disciples*. SPCK, 2016.
  – *Christ the Heart of Creation*. Bloomsbury Continuum, 2018.

Willimon, William H., *Character and Calling: Virtues of the Ordained Life*. Nashville: Abingdon Press 2000

Wright D.F. (ed.), *Spirit of Truth and Power Studies in Christian Doctrine and Experience*. Rutherford House 2007.